Shipwrecks

Evan McHugh has been a keen sailor and collector of maritime stories for many years. His previous books include travel guides to Sydney, *The Rot Stuff* and *Pint-Sized Ireland*. He writes a weekly column, 'Dry Rot', in *The Australian*'s 'Weekend Magazine' and has written for television and radio. He is married, lives in Sydney and currently owns an Endeavour 24.

Evan McHugh

Shipwrecks

Australia's Greatest
Maritime Disasters

VIKING
an imprint of
PENGUIN BOOKS

To all those whose voyages remain unfinished

Viking

Published by the Penguin Group
Penguin Books Australia Ltd
250 Camberwell Road, Camberwell, Victoria 3124, Australia
Penguin Books Ltd
80 Strand, London WC2R 0RL, England
Penguin Putnam Inc.
375 Hudson Street, New York, New York 10014, USA
Penguin Books, a division of Pearson Canada
10 Alcorn Avenue, Toronto, Ontario, Canada M4V 3B2
Penguin Books (NZ) Ltd
Cnr Rosedale and Airborne Roads, Albany, Auckland, New Zealand
Penguin Books (South Africa) (Pty) Ltd
24 Sturdee Avenue, Rosebank, Johannesburg 2196, South Africa
Penguin Books India (P) Ltd
11, Community Centre, Panchsheel Park, New Delhi 110 017, India

First published by Penguin Books Australia Ltd 2003

3 5 7 9 10 8 6 4 2

Design by John Canty, Penguin Design Studio
Cover images: AAP (top) and Mitchell Library, State Library of New South Wales
Typeset in 10/16 pt Centennial Light by Post Pre-press Group, Brisbane, Queensland
Printed and bound in Australia by McPherson's Printing Group,
Maryborough, Victoria

National Library of Australia
Cataloguing-in-Publication data:
McHugh, Evan.
Shipwrecks: Australia's greatest maritime disasters.

Bibliography.
Includes index.
ISBN 0 670 04019 3.

1. Shipwrecks – Australia. I. Title.

910.4520994

www.penguin.com.au

CONTENTS

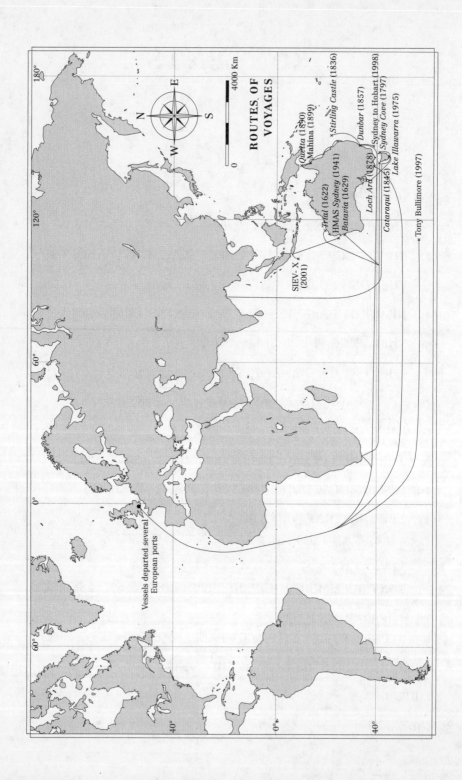

ROUTES OF
VOYAGES

N

W ⊕ E

S

0 [■■■■] 4000 Km

SIEV-X ✕
(2001)

Trial (1622)
HMAS *Sydney* (1941)
Batavia (1629)

Quetta (1890)
Mahina (1899)

✕ *Stirling Castle* (1836)

Dunbar (1857)
Sydney to Hobart (1998)
Sydney Cove (1797)
Lake Illawarra (1975)
Loch Ard (1878)
Cataraqui (1845)

✕ Tony Bullimore (1997)

Vessels departed several
European ports

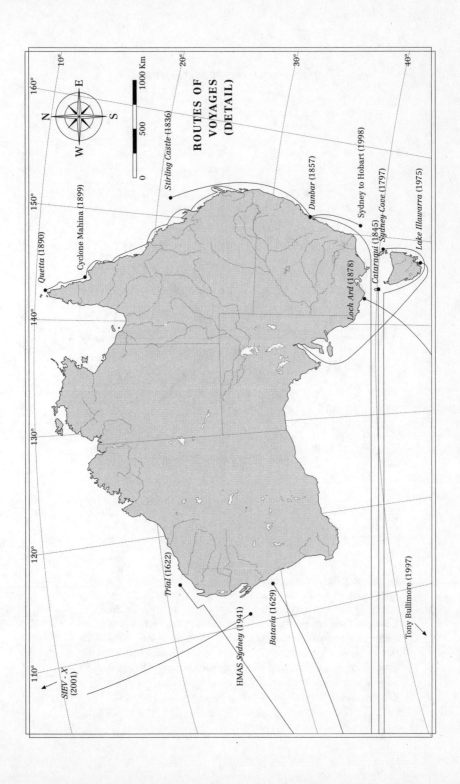

ROUTES OF
VOYAGES
(DETAIL)

N
W · E
S

0   500   1000 Km

10°
20°
30°
40°

160°
150°
140°
130°
120°
110°

Stirling Castle (1836)

Dunbar (1857)

Sydney to Hobart (1998)

Sydney Cove (1797)

Cataraqui (1845)

Lake Illawarra (1975)

Loch Ard (1878)

Quetta (1890)

Cyclone Mahina (1899)

Trial (1622)

Batavia (1629)

HMAS Sydney (1941)

Tony Bullimore (1997)

SIEV - X
(2001)

THE POINTS OF THE COMPASS

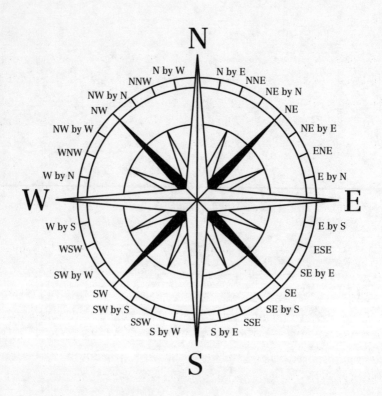

In the early days of navigation 32 points of the compass were used to set courses for helmsmen to steer by. Obviously N, S, E and W stand for the four cardinal points of the compass: North, South, East and West, respectively. The compass points in between were comprised of combinations of the four cardinal points. Thus, ENE is read as east-north-east. NE by E is read as north-east by east. In modern times, with more accurate navigation instruments, vessels usually steer courses that are given in degrees where 0 degrees is north, 90 degrees east, 180 south and 270 west.

INTRODUCTION

On a lonely island off the coast of Western Australia a small group of people begins to fashion makeshift weapons with which to defend themselves from their fellow shipwreck survivors. On a small beach in Victoria a young man who has just struggled out of the freezing waters of the Southern Ocean hears a woman's cry in the darkness and wades back into the sea to rescue her. And off the New South Wales coast, a policeman looks from his helicopter to the raging ocean below, then gives the thumbs up to be winched down into the maelstrom.

The story of Australia's shipwrecks, spanning Australia's history from 1622 to the present day, is studded with famous tales of disaster, treachery and despair. Vessels litter all our coasts (over 5000 at the most conservative estimate), decaying monuments to countless lives tragically cut short. In many ways it is a bitter legacy, and there appears to be little good in the destruction of a fine vessel and the many lives it carried. Yet many shipwrecks tell a surprisingly different story. The abrupt end to a ship's voyage, the centuries that pass with the sea folded over the wreck, the accounts of the survivors that wait quietly in archives around the world, create one of the most vivid doorways into the past. They allow us to see incredibly clearly into our history, and not surprisingly, understand far more about who we are, and how we came to be here.

A wreck like the *Trial* in 1622, for example, occurred at the very beginning of Australian history and shows how the European voyagers were groping blindly as they gradually mapped the world, in particular the Great South Land that was to become known as Australia. The tale of her perfidious captain only underlines how the unscrupulous could prey on the ignorance of their lords and masters back home.

The *Batavia* shows that even knowing where the dangers were wasn't enough; careful navigation was to become fundamental to a safe voyage to our shores. *Batavia* and the other Dutch wrecks of the Western Australian coast have all yielded fabulous treasure; what's far more valuable is the information they've provided about life on board the Dutch merchantmen, and the incredibly fine detail of technologies and techniques that have often been forgotten over the centuries. Perhaps the most potent example is the reconstruction of the *Batavia*, which benefited from the knowledge gained from the salvaged timbers of the original. *Batavia* and her associated wrecks also raise fascinating questions about who really were the first European settlers in Australia.

The *Sydney Cove* underlines the importance of a 'well-found' ship for the incredible distances involved in the voyage to Australia. The average leaky boat simply was not up to such a journey, as her crew eventually discovered in a huge storm off the coast of Tasmania. *Sydney Cove* has also yielded fascinating insights into what happened at the moment of first contact between Europeans and indigenous Australians.

The same is true of the *Stirling Castle,* with the subsequent terrible experiences for her crew, including the skipper's wife, Eliza Fraser. The tale of the rescue of the survivors is one of the great stories of Australia's maritime history, but what is just as remarkable is the chain of events that the wreck triggered. On the one hand, it gave ammunition to the forces that wanted to exterminate Australia's indigenous population, while on the other it made the need to establish better relations more urgent. The resolution is closely linked to the establishment of the State of Queensland.

For anyone who can trace their Australian heritage to the early emigrant ships, the tale of the *Cataraqui* is harrowing to read. It makes us realise that many of us are here because our forebears were the lucky ones, those who survived the hazards of the voyage to Australia's shores. It also highlights the conflicting demands of nation-building, especially for countries in their infancy. In this case, it made all the more urgent the need for costly lighthouses at the hazardous entrance to Bass Strait.

In a remarkable coincidence, only twenty years after the *Stirling Castle* was lost, the New South Wales Parliament was debating a request to give Queensland statehood on the day after Sydney's worst shipwreck, the *Dunbar.* Again, the cause was in part due to lighthouses but, in an amazing twist, it wasn't the lack of one that resulted in the *Dunbar*'s loss. It was the decision on the placement of the Macquarie Lighthouse, made at the very beginning of European settlement in Sydney Cove, decades before, that led to the graceful clipper's demise.

It was the loss of one of the most beautiful sailing ships of all – the *Loch Ard* – that provided a true story of romance to rival that of Hollywood's *Titanic.* It didn't have a 'Hollywood ending' and nor did the romantic age of sail. Instead, the *Loch Ard* eloquently illustrates the slow decline of the clippers, as they struggled against the speed and manoeuvrability of steamships.

The wreck of the *Quetta* demonstrates how the steamships didn't have it all their own way. Using her manoeuvrability to negotiate the Torres Strait on her way to London, she discovered why James Cook wrote just one word to describe the reefs, shoals and channels of the Great Barrier Reef: 'Labyrinth'. And like Sydney in the wake of the *Dunbar* disaster, so too Queenslanders felt the impact of having so many of their prominent citizens taken by the sea without warning.

Of all Australia's professions, fishing remains one of the most dangerous pursuits. Yet the loss of life barely rates a mention in the media. Perhaps the ever-present dangers make the seemingly inevitable fatalities seem unremarkable. However, that hardly explains the lack of interest after one of Australia's worst maritime disasters, when an entire pearling fleet was wiped out by Cyclone Mahina. The catastrophe was remote from the major centres of the country, and so were its victims. Yet the disaster was keenly felt in the fishing community of Thursday Island, at the tip of Cape York. It may have lost a fifth of its population, almost all of them the bread-winners for the families left behind.

The loss of HMAS *Sydney* was a totally different story. Sunk with barely a trace near the beginning of World War II, it was front-page news, although the lack of survivors was matched by a lack of infor-mation about what happened. Controversy about what might have occurred has raged ever since, sometimes descending into bitter exchanges and cruel hoaxes. And the search for answers by the fam-ilies of those lost continues over half a century later.

The people of Tasmania well know how much impact a shipwreck can have, after their capital city, Hobart, was cut in half by the *Lake Illawarra*'s collision with the Tasman Bridge. There were immediate transport problems, but yet again, there was a twist. For many, it meant they got jobs with one of the State's largest employers: a ferry-building company that owed its existence to the disaster.

In recent years, when the yachts of Thierry Dubois and Tony Bullimore were capsized near Antarctica, the subsequent rescue effort was not only another of the great maritime stories of all time; it showed us what we could achieve. The Air Force and Navy's can-do attitude revealed a side of Australia some of us may have doubted. It remains one of the longest-range rescues ever attempted.

From the longest rescue to the biggest, only a year later the 1998 Sydney to Hobart put Australia's search-and-rescue resources to the ultimate test. Six sailors lost their lives in the race, but the tragedy was matched by a remarkable triumph. Many more would have died but for another aspect that permeates the tales of Australia's shipwrecks –

sheer courage. Time and time again in the stories that make up this volume, individuals or small groups of people have defied the odds or risked their lives in order to survive or save others.

The span of time from Wiebbe Hayes and his soldiers fighting the *Batavia*'s mutineers on the Abrolhos to the rescue workers in the air over the yachts of the Sydney to Hobart is 369 years. Yet the men and women involved are cut from the same cloth. Their stories, and those of others who put their lives on the line, are one of the inspiring elements that recur throughout the tragedies of shipwreck. There are, of course, many others.

The narratives in this volume for the most part follow a straight-forward chronological format. However, anyone who has researched an interesting shipwreck will attest that most accounts are anything but straightforward or chronological – incidents are out of order, there is disagreement from one account to another about when they occurred, and accounts will even contradict themselves. In order to maintain narrative momentum, and not become enmeshed in dis-cussions of conflicting viewpoints, I've tended to reach my own conclusion about the likely sequence of events and get on with the story. As such, the narratives should not be taken as definitive (indeed you should be very suspicious of anyone who suggests theirs is). Rather, they are one of the possible logical sequences of events.

On the same point, in some cases a small degree of narrative licence has been taken with some quoted speech. For example, if a contemporary account has said 'the captain ordered the masts to be cut away', I've turned it into 'Cut away the masts,' the cap-tain said. In some chapters some quoted text has also been edited for clarity.

There is also much more to most of these stories than space has allowed me to include. This is particularly the case where what has been discovered about a wreck, rather than providing answers, has simply raised more questions about events. There are numerous books on individual wrecks that fill in more of the picture, so, for those interested to discover more, the selected bibliography lists excellent, strongly recommended sources.

Many of those sources and, in some cases, their authors made it possible for me to write *Shipwrecks*. Other excellent sources include the Vaughn Evans Library of the Australian Maritime Museum, the Mitchell Library, John Oxley Library and the State Archives of New South Wales. The resources of these libraries are first rate and the professionalism and ready assistance of their staffs are gratefully acknowledged. Much of the storytelling in this book relies heavily on the accounts of eyewitnesses and unnamed reporters. Many of them have long since passed away, yet the feedback and generous assistance of survivors and rescuers involved in the 1998 Sydney to Hobart, in particular, have been both extremely helpful and reassured me that those who have not been able to give permission for their voices to be included would also have been as generous and supportive.

Readers should note that the maps in this book have been prepared based on historical records and should be considered indicative only. Maps should not be relied upon in attempting to locate any wreck.

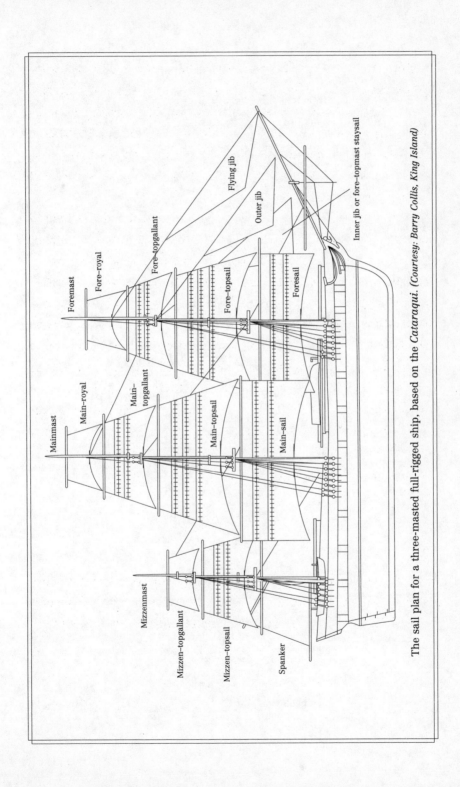

The sail plan for a three-masted full-rigged ship, based on the *Cataraqui*. *(Courtesy: Barry Collis, King Island)*

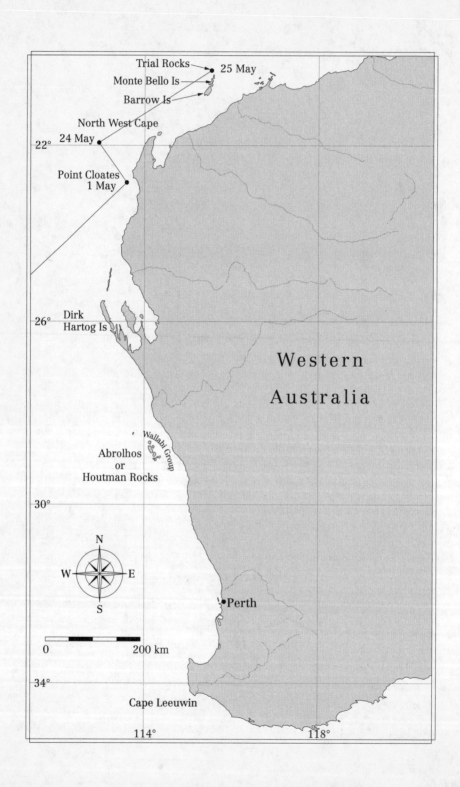

Trial Rocks
25 May
Monte Bello Is
Barrow Is
North West Cape
22° 24 May
Point Cloates
1 May

Dirk
26° Hartog Is

Western

Australia

Wallabi Group
Abrolhos
or
Houtman Rocks

30°

N

W   E

S

Perth

0   200 km

34°

Cape Leeuwin

114°   118°

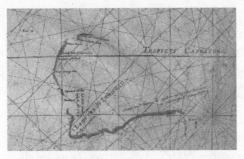

Detail of Dutch East Indies map, circa 1633
*(Mitchell Library, State Library
of New South Wales)*

1. CHINESE WHISPERS:
TRIAL, 1622

The written history of the island continent of Australia begins with the sea, with ships and shipwrecks. In 1606, the crew of the tiny Dutch sailing vessel *Duyfken* (*Little Dove*), Willem Jansz master, became the first Europeans to set eyes on the Australian coast. They partially mapped and described the west coast of Cape York, though they thought it was part of New Guinea. At the time, the Dutch were already busy voyaging to Batavia, in the Dutch East Indies (now Jakarta, Indonesia), for the spice trade, but in so doing they were starting to discover the shape of the north and western coasts of the Great South Land.

Under the circumstances, the first shipwreck in Australian waters should have been Dutch, but that dubious honour actually goes to the English, in 1622. Not that it was realised, or at least admitted, at the time. It was to take 350 years, considerable confusion, several more shipwrecks that may have been caused by the confusion, and some remarkable detective work to get to the truth of Australia's first shipwreck, of the merchant vessel *Trial*, John Brookes master.

Brookes was the second choice for the job. On 20 July 1621, some months prior to the *Trial*'s departure from England, the Court of Committees of the company that owned her, the English East India Company (EEIC, formed in 1600), received a letter explaining that their preferred man, Mr Newport, 'who had formerly been named to the Company to go Master of the *Trial* cannot yet resolve whether to undertake the charge . . . until he have first satisfied his wife, which he would do forthwith and then give his answer.'

It seems Mrs Newport couldn't be satisfied, and who could blame her? The return voyage to the East Indies would see her husband gone for two years at least. Had she seen any of the maps of the oceans he planned to voyage, she would have noted illustrations of the potential calamities that might befall him. The fertile imaginations of the mapmakers filled the empty spaces between continents with enormous creatures spouting water or wrapping tentacles around hapless ships, and still others that were temptingly half woman, half fish. Mrs Newport may also have persisted in the belief that the earth was flat and that her husband would sail off the edge into the abyss of space, despite the fact that by 1621 the world had been circumnavigated numerous times.

Indeed, while the EEIC was looking for a skipper, the Roman Catholic Church still treated the idea of a spherical earth revolving around the sun as heresy. Not even great scientists of the time, like Galileo Galilei, were immune. In 1612 he'd used the heretical model (devised by the astronomer Copernicus) to devise a method for calculating longitude on land. It was a major step forward in the development of navigation, but only a year later the Church began secretly collecting evidence against him, at the instigation of the powerful counter-Reformation Cardinal,

Robert Bellarmine. In 1633, Galileo's continued support for the Copernican system led to his trial by the Inquisition. He was shown the instruments of torture on two occasions, forced to recant, and finished his days under house arrest.

The EEIC, Mrs Newport notwithstanding, had a less blinkered view of the world, where they were expanding with a zeal motivated by the immense profits to be enjoyed through the spice trade. At the time, the Protestant English and Dutch were allies against the Catholic states – an alliance that extended to trade. On 23 July 1621, the EEIC received letters from a fleet of the Dutch United East India Company (the *Nederlandse Verenigde Oost-Indische Compagnie* or VOC, formed in 1602). The vessels were returning from the Indies and, on the basis of their advice, the EEIC determined what cargo the *Trial* would carry to Batavia: sheathing nails, hunt horns, cartridges and sheet lead.

The EEIC had already found a crew for the *Trial*, which was being paid wages while waiting to sail. By 10 August 1621, they'd also found their skipper. 'Mr Brookes, Master of the *Trial* being now ready to go down to Plymouth desired allowance for the carrying down of himself and four servants. The Court ordered he should have £13.'

The *Trial* set sail from Plymouth on 4 September with a crew of 143 'good men.' None of them, including Brookes, had done the trip to the Indies, so at the Cape of Good Hope, where the *Trial* met the returning East Indiaman *Charles*, under the command of Captain Bickle, Brookes asked if any of Bickle's crew would join him for the voyage to Batavia. Bickle was happy for any of his mates to do so, but there were no volunteers.

After replenishing her supplies, the *Trial* left the Cape on 19 March 1622. She now followed the sailing instructions for the so-called 'Brouwer Route' pioneered by the Dutch, though Brookes based his course on the journal of the first English ship to use it, in 1620, under the command of Captain Humphrey Fitzherbert.

Up until 1611, ships heading for the Indies had followed the route
pioneered by the Portuguese Vasco da Gama in 1497 and 1498. After
rounding the Cape of Good Hope, ships turned north and followed
the east coast of Africa. Once they were through the Mozambique
Channel, they turned north-east to pass north of the island of Madagascar and head for the Indies. In the 16th century, after the Catholic
Portuguese turned against the Protestant Dutch, VOC ships avoided
the Mozambique Channel and the Portuguese base on the African
coast. They sailed up the east coast of Madagascar, then north-east
and on to the Indies.

Both routes had problems. Heading up the African coast, the prevailing wind and current worked against the ships the whole way.
When ships got to the equatorial regions, where they remained as
they headed east, the winds became light and ships often drifted in
crippling heat, their provisions rotting and disease taking a terrible
toll on their crews. To add to the difficulties, the central Indian Ocean
was littered with shoals, reefs and small islands which presented
a constant shipping hazard.

In 1610, one of the VOC's directors in the Indies (later its Governor-
General), Hendrik Brouwer, suggested a different route to his
masters – the seventeen VOC directors known as the *Heren XVII*. He'd
noticed that strong westerlies prevailed south of the Cape of Good
Hope, so he suggested that ships first sail south from the Cape, then
catch the westerlies and head east in the cooler climate until they
were due south of Java, then head north.

The *Heren XVII* responded by sending Brouwer to attempt the route.
From the Cape, it took Brouwer only six months to reach the Indies,
compared to over a year on the old route, and the crew arrived in
much better health. Not for the last time in the history of ocean navigation, the preferred route between two points was found to be
anything but a straight line.

It wasn't long before the Brouwer Route was adopted (1616),

although it underwent continual refinement in the ensuing years. The most significant change was to take account of the large landmass that ships met if they sailed too far east. The first to do so was the *Eendracht*, Dirk Hartog master, which reached Cape Inscription on 25 October 1616. Hartog left a pewter plate inscribed with details of his visit nailed to a post. (This plate now hangs in the Rijksmuseum in Amsterdam, though a replica dish made eighty years later by the explorer Willem de Vlamingh, which includes details of de Vlamingh's visit, is in the Western Australian Maritime Museum.) It was only the second time a Dutchman had set eyes on this land. Hartog's landmass, meanwhile, became known as Eendrachtsland, *'t Zuyd Landt* (the South Land) or *'t Grote Zuyd Landt* (the Great South Land).

The *Duyfken*'s Willem Jansz, now on board the *Mauritius*, also wrote to the VOC that: 'On the 31st July 1618 we discovered an island and landed on the same . . . its northern extremity is in 22 degrees south latitude.' In fact, the island was the mainland near present-day North West Cape.

Commander Frederick de Houtman also sighted the coast, in 1619, when he came upon a shoal now known as the Houtman Abrolhos in latitude 28 degrees south. Abrolhos was a corruption of the Portuguese *abri vossos olhos* or 'spiked obstructions.' To Spanish navigators it sounded like *abre ojos* or 'open your eyes' and the term came to be a common warning of low rocks and danger. While posing a potential problem for the Brouwer Route, Houtman wrote to his masters suggesting it could be avoided with some modifications and careful navigation.

It appears Houtman's suggestions weren't adopted by the EEIC in time for Brookes' voyage in the *Trial*. Instead he took the original route, heading south to latitude 39 degrees, then east for some 7000 kilometres. He then started heading north for Batavia. On 1 May he was 22 degrees south of the equator when he saw land. In a letter to the EEIC of 25 August 1622, Brookes explained where he believed himself to be: 'Which land had been formerly seen by the Dutch and is said in the cards north-east by north and south-east by south from the Sunda Strait. This island is 18 leagues [90 kilometres] long and we were all very joyful at the sight thereof.' He is referring to the 'island' seen by Willem Jansz in the *Mauritius*.

Then he adds that: 'We found by our judgement and by Captain Fitzherbert's journal that he went 10 leagues [50 kilometres] to the southwards of this island . . . steered north-east by east and fell with the east end of Java.'

Brookes was wrong on this point. The 'island' seen by the Dutch was actually part of the mainland, so Fitzherbert couldn't have sailed to the south of it on a north-easterly course – he'd have hit land. Even if he had been able to do so, Fitzherbert wouldn't have reached the east end of Java. Timor or New Guinea would have been more likely.

Nevertheless Brookes maintained that, following Fitzherbert's instructions, he continued north-east. Unfortunately, at this point in the voyage the ever-reliable south-east trade wind failed him. From 5 May to 24 May, he had a wind blowing into his face from the north-east, the direction he wanted to go. This was remarkably bad luck, considering that in May you can expect the trades to be blowing from the south-east up to 80 per cent of the time. About the only thing that can overshadow them is a sea breeze caused by the coastal effect of a large landmass.

Finally, on 24 May, 'the great island with his three small islands at the eastern end bearing south-east 20 leagues [100 kilometres] from us, the wind veering to the south-east and fair weather, we steered north-east thinking to fall with the western part of Java.'

The vessel maintained its course all that day and through the next. But then, as Brookes explained to the EEIC:

The 25ᵗʰ day, at 11 o'clock at night, fair weather and smooth the ship struck. I ran to the poop and hove the lead and found but three fathoms

[5.5 metres] of water. Sixty men being upon the deck, five of them would not believe that she struck. I cried to them to bear up and tack to the westwards. They did their best, but the rock being sharp the ship was presently full of water.

For the most part these rocks lie two fathoms under water, [so that] it struck my men in amazement when I said the ship struck and they could see neither breach, land, rocks, change of water nor sign of danger. The ship sitting a good while after [that], I hove the lead while I brought my sails a-backstays when she struck [again]. The wind began suddenly to freshen and blow. I struck round my sails and got out my skiff and bid [the crew] to sound about the ship. They found sharp sunken rocks a half a cable-length astern. These rocks were steep too, so I made all the way I could to get out my long boat and by two o'clock I had gotten her out and hanged her in the tackles on the side.

Seeing the ship full of water and the wind to increase, [I] made all the means I could to save my life and as many of my company as I could. The boat put off at four in the morning and half an hour after the fore part of the ship fell in pieces! Ten men were saved in the skiff and 36 in the long boat.

Out of the crew of 139 (4 are believed to have died during the voyage), 93 were left aboard the rapidly disintegrating *Trial*. They knew they were going to die, far from their homeland without a shred of hope that a vessel might appear out of the empty vastness of the ocean to pluck them to safety.

As the waters rose and waves swept the decks, men started being washed overboard. For those who couldn't swim, the end came quickly. For about ninety seconds, a drowning person will hold their breath, fighting the urge to breathe underwater while still struggling to regain the surface. If they don't get a breath, the carbon dioxide in their blood increases. The brain senses this and knowing that carbon-dioxide build-up is fatal, it will force the body to breathe, water or no water, even against the victim's will. When that happens, water floods the upper reaches of the respiratory system. In 10 per cent of drownings, it gets no further. In such cases anything that touches the vocal cords triggers an instant reaction, a contraction of the throat that effectively stops the water getting any further. Consequently, nine of the *Trial*'s crew probably drowned without any water reaching their lungs.

For the remaining eighty crewmen, the water entering their lungs would have ended any oxygen uptake. In either case, without oxygen and with the carbon dioxide continuing to accumulate, a veil of unconsciousness would have descended, and the last moments before death would have been passed in oblivion.

Those crew who could swim lasted longer, but they were eventually overcome by exhaustion or taken by sharks. Those clinging to floating wreckage survived longer still. Others fought to keep hold of the last remnants of the vessel remaining above water. And when that was gone, they grabbed at each other or anything that remained afloat to keep their heads above water. Some were pushed under by their terrified crewmates, who would follow them under only moments later. Eventually, drowning, exhaustion, exposure, dehydration and the creatures of the sea claimed them all.

The crew who made it to the boats fared better. Brookes was in the skiff with a small supply of water and bread. The longboat had a barrelful of water and several that were empty, plus a small amount of wine and bread, but it wasn't enough for its larger number of survivors. Fortunately, daylight revealed some islands nearby.

According to Brookes, the longboat, 'Stood back for the great island, which is seven leagues [35 kilometres] to the south-eastward of the place where the ship was cast away. The boat found a little low island.' There the longboat replenished its supply of water.

'These rocks and islands with their latitude, longitude, variations, courses and distances I have given two drafts to your worship's president [in the East Indies] which his worship intends to send you by

the first conveyance,' Brookes explained. Meanwhile, having continued on his course, 'I fell in with the eastern end of Java the 8th
day of June, 1622; at Bantam the 21 ditto and at Jaccatra [Batavia]
the 25th of the same month.'

According to Brookes' account of the disaster, he had expected to
strike Java at its western end, but instead found himself at the eastern end. This he explained by writing of his approach to the 'island'
seen by the Dutch that 'this iland lieth false in his longitude 200
leagues [1000 kilometres].'

So he originally estimated his position to be 2000 kilometres west
of North West Cape. Then he dismissed the reckoning he achieved
through logs, magnetic variations and the like and decided that the
island formerly seen by the Dutch was 1000 kilometres further east,
but still 1000 kilometres west of the Cape. More significantly, by his
new reckoning, the Trial Rocks, as they became known, lay due
south of the Sunda Strait, right across the route of ships following
the Brouwer Route to Batavia.

Indeed, Brookes was of the opinion that the Brouwer Route was
fundamentally flawed. He wrote to his masters that

not any ship should pass 37 degrees and so run 1000 leagues [5000
kilometres] in that parallel and thence to steer right for the Sunda
Straits. Let any man presume that when he finds 10 degrees variation,
having run 1300 leagues [6500 kilometres] being in the latitude of 18
or 19 [degrees south, the distance needing to be sailed east being
longer the further one gets from the South Pole], the Sunda Straits will
bear of him north-north-east. The current sets strong to the eastward
always. In that course experience of variation is the greatest help to
any man.

Brookes added that the Dutch had gone off the Brouwer Route
as well, after their ships the *Wapen van Hoorn*, *Amsterdam* and

Dordrecht had got into difficulties going as far south as 42 degrees. 'This remote passidge ye Dutch general doth not like,' he wrote.

The EEIC Governor in the Indies backed up Brookes' opinion in a letter, dated 27 August 1622, to head office:

> Whereas formerly we are of the opinion that Captain Fitzherbert's journal of his voyage from England was the surest course to get a speedy passage from the Cape to this place, do now we recant from our said opinion and refer it unto your worships to set a more [appropriate] course for your ships to follow.
>
> The Dutch intend also to write their masters at home to send no more of their ships too southerly a course, for some of their ships have now lately escaped very narrowly upon the south main continent, which you may please to take notions of, and reform your sea cards [maps and sailing instructions], according to the draught which we sent you previously from Mr Brookes.

The Dutch did indeed write to their head office, but stopped short of abandoning the faster Brouwer Route. A letter of 6 September 1622 from the Dutch Governor-General in the Indies explained:

> On the 5th of July there arrived here a skiff with ten men forming part of the crew of an English ship, named the *Trial*, and on the 8th her boat with 36 men. They state they have lost and abandoned their ship with 97 [sic] men and the cargo she had taken in, on certain rocks situated in latitude 20 degrees 10 minutes south, in the longitude of the western end of Java. These rocks are near a number of broken islands, lying very wide and broad . . . lying 30 mijlen [220 kilometres] north-north-east of a certain island which in our charts is laid down in 22 degrees south latitude.

After outlining the difficulties experienced by Dutch ships, the Governor-General concluded:

Whereas it is necessary that ships, in order to hasten their arrival, should run on an eastward course for about 1000 mijlen [7400 kilometres] from the Cape between 40 and 30 degrees southern latitude, it is equally necessary that great caution should be used and the best measures taken in order to avoid such accidents as befell the English ship *Trial*. They say that they met with this accident through following the course of our ships; that they intend to dissuade their countrymen from imitating their example, and that their masters are sure to take other measures accordingly.

So the Dutch weren't going to let a few rocks get in the way of their profits.

With the benefit of hindsight, it is easy to see some curious anomalies in Brookes' story. For example, if he'd really headed north-east from North West Cape, he'd have ended up east of Timor. And a quick look at a modern map of the Indian Ocean at 22 degrees south of the Sunda Strait reveals that it's one of the deepest bodies of water in the world, without a shoal, rock or island to be seen.

However, in 1622 no-one looking at a map of the Indian Ocean while sitting in an office in London, Amsterdam or even Batavia knew that. The maps were drawn up by playing a version of the child's game of Chinese Whispers, with the whispers coming from the other side of the world and taking up to two years to arrive. Across the top of the map, India, Java and Sumatra were clearly marked. Down the left side was Africa. But in the middle and down the right it was all murky water and squid cloud. The few disconnected reefs, capes and coasts were based as much on rumour as fact. So when Brookes said he'd been wrecked, the mapmakers simply marked the rocks where he said they were. His letter giving all the details was filed and forgotten. Then the Chinese Whispers continued.

The earliest known map showing Trial Rocks is Hessel Gerritsz's chart of 1627. They are also in the charts published by the Blaeu family between 1635 and 1664. A map in Sir Robert Dudley's sea atlas of 1646, the first published entirely on the Mercator projection, shows the Trials in much more detail, suggesting Dudley had seen Brookes' charts of the Rocks. If he did, he was fortunate. All subsequent searches for the charts have turned up nothing.

Efforts were also made to confirm the position provided, and even drafted, by John Brookes. In September 1622, an expedition from Batavia was briefed, but it never set out. Then in 1636 Commandeur Gerrit Tomaszoon Pool passed the supposed location and found nothing. In 1688, William Dampier aboard the pirate ship *Cygnet* sought them without success, as did the frigate *Jane* in 1705. Then, in 1718 or 1719, a Dutch ship reported finding the Trials, but placed them 600 kilometres further east of the position given by Brookes.

Some mapmakers took notice of the report and moved the Trial Rocks to a new position, only 400 kilometres from the coast of Australia. Samuel Dunn's *New Directory of the East Indies* did so in 1780, as did the British Hydrographic Office in 1782.

Adding to the confusion, in 1777, the *Fredensborg Castle*, Martin Foss master, reported seeing the Trials, and even gave a description. But in 1787, the EEIC's hydrographer, Alexander Dalrymple, expressed doubts because the new position of the Rocks was wrong. However he noted that 'which Rocks take the name from one of our East India ships that was lost thereupon, called the *Tryal*. (Note: this event is said to have happened in 1622, but I can find no traces of this ship's journal.)' After 165 years, the company could not find its own files. And in the same year as Dalrymple's report, the *Vansittart*, Captain Wilson master, visited the position given by the *Fredensborg Castle* and found nothing.

Part of the problem was that finding longitude at sea was an uncertain business until the invention of the chronometer, by John Harrison, in 1761. Until then, finding longitude was largely the result of guestimation, and a ship finding Trial Rocks might actually be hundreds of kilometres from where it believed itself to be. Or else the ship that didn't find the Rocks when it visited the reported position could be off course.

Armed with a chronometer, Matthew Flinders searched for the Trials during his circumnavigation of Australia in 1802 and 1803, aboard the leaky survey ship, HMS *Investigator*. After the voyage, Flinders produced the first detailed map of Australia's coast. On it the route of his voyage is shown, including the point where he sailed 1000 kilometres away from the Western Australian coast, into the Indian Ocean. Then, at 22 degrees due south of the Sunda Strait, he zigzags all over the ocean searching for the Trials. He didn't find a thing. Meanwhile, the West Australian coastline at 22 degrees south is completely blank, like a missing piece of a jigsaw puzzle.

After Flinders' search, the British Admiralty's Hydrographic Office finally stated that the Trial Rocks simply didn't exist, although some mapmakers continued to mark them on their charts. And the fact remained that the *Trial* had hit something, somewhere, and over ninety people had died. Then, in 1818, the English brig *Greyhound* came upon a shoal near latitude 20 degrees south, on the section of coast Flinders had left blank. The shoal became known as Ritchie's Reef, after the *Greyhound*'s captain, and it was nowhere near the supposed position of Trial Rocks. But Captain Ritchie and a colleague who was also on board, Captain Campbell, had their suspicions.

The British Admiralty sent Lieutenant Phillip Parker King to the location. On 30 October 1820, King made a careful survey of the rocks, shoals and islands and compared them with all the available writings and maps of the Trials, including those of the Dutch. His conclusion: 'There remains no doubt in my mind but that Barrow

Island in 20 degrees 40 minutes south, 115 degrees 27 minutes east
and Trimouille Island and the numerous reefs around them, are the
identical Tryal Rocks.'

Case closed? Not quite. Everything seemed to make sense, particularly since two centuries of Chinese Whispers meant no-one knew
the exact details of the original story – the storyteller, John Brookes,
had passed away long ago and his original letter had long since been
lost in the EEIC's files. Yet just enough of the story survived for questions to remain. If this was where the *Trial* was wrecked, was this
the first shipwreck in Australian waters, seven years before the
supposed first wreck, *Batavia* in 1629? Who had been the first
Englishmen to see and set foot on Australia: William Dampier in
1688, when he'd gone ashore at Cape Leveque, north of Broome, or
John Brookes' ill-fated crew in 1622?

The questions went unanswered until 1934 when a researcher
named Ida Lee, intrigued by the story behind Trial Rocks, went looking through the EEIC records in the India Office. She must have
looked harder than EEIC hydrographer Dalrymple in 1787 for there,
where it had been gathering dust for 312 years, was the letter from
Brookes explaining the loss of the *Trial*. The game of Chinese Whispers was over.

With Brookes' account and the benefit of accurate charts of the
Australian coast, Lee was able to follow the course of the *Trial*
exactly. First, there was the land Brookes had sighted on 1 May in
latitude 22 degrees south which 'had formerly been seen by the
Dutch . . . this island is 18 leagues long and we were all very joyful
at the sight thereof.' Lee identified it as 'doubtless the point of the
Australian mainland to the southward of North West Cape, in lat 22
degrees 42 minutes S., known as Point Cloates. Owing to the trend
of the coast here and the elbow in its outline, seamen on sighting it
were unable to distinguish its true form or extent. Brookes, like the
Dutch captains who first saw it, believed that it was an island.'

Lee makes no comment on the fact that Brookes' belief that Fitzherbert had sailed 10 leagues south of this 'island' heading north-east was therefore impossible. However, she does note that 'in the accounts of Fitzherbert's voyage, there is no mention that he sighted any land in this locality.'

Brookes' description of 'the great iland with his 3 small islands at the Easter end' matches the tip of North West Cape, which has three islands on its eastern side. From there Brookes heads 100 kilometres north-west in the contrary winds, then gets the wind shift he wants to help him head north-east for 'the western end of Java.' Even taken literally, this information would see the ship pass dangerously close to Ritchie's Reef. With just a small allowance for error, he'd have struck there. Ritchie's Reef was starting to look like the true Trial Rocks. All the pieces were fitting neatly into place.

Yet one question remains: why doesn't Brookes' plot of the wreck's position and his subsequent claim that he headed to the north-east make sense? That's where Lee hit the jackpot. For in the EEIC files, she didn't find one letter regarding the loss of the *Trial*, she found two. The other one was unsigned but appears to have been written by a man named Thomas Bright, the *Trial*'s factor (or shipping agent), who ended up on board the longboat.

In an article based on her research, Lee included those parts of the second letter that confirmed the *Trial* as the first English ship to see Australia and the Monte Bellos as the scene of the wreck. It also made it clear that Ritchie's Reef was the true Trial Rocks. But Bright had plenty more to say – especially about Brookes. However, those details had to wait another forty years before a publication by marine-archaeologist Jeremy Green brought them to light.

Recruited from England in 1971 to run the Western Australian Museum's marine-archaeology program, Green's first project was an investigation of the *Trial*. His first paper on the vessel, published in 1977, included more from Bright's letter:

May the 25ᵗʰ, about ten o'clock at night, fair weather and little wind, the ship *Tryall*, by carelessness for want of looking out, struck upon the rocks. Before any breach was discovered [she] billidged her hold full of water in an instant . . . [Brookes'] crew and fellow and consorts providing provisions and saving his things, bearing Mr Jackson and myself with fair words, promising us faithfully to take us along, but like a Judas, [while I was] turning my back into [the] great cabin [Brookes] lowered himself privately into the skiff only with nine men and his boy. [He] stood for the Straits of Sunda that instant, without care and seeing the lamentable end of ship, the time she split or respect of any man's life.

The long boat with great difficulty we got out being 128 souls left to God's mercy. [However, the long boat could carry only thirty-six of the crew.] We kept till day some quarter mile [400 metres] from the ship. Finding rocks in many places, the sea [was] then so high we dared not adventure to them for fear of endangering ourselves. We were so slenderly provided with provisions that it was impossible, without God's great providence, that we should arrive at our wished for port.

Upon sight of day we espied an island bearing south-east some five leagues [25 kilometres] at most from us, to which we went. [We] stayed thereon for seven days for the freshing of our boat and supplies of water (having when we left the ship but one barrecoe full, the rest empty there being none but what the Lord sent per rain). Not any inhabitants thereon. We travelled over all the island seeing nothing but islands, some small, some great, breaches and shoals every way as far as we could see. To the south-south-west of this island there lieth a great island near nine leagues [45 kilometres] off. [Bright was describing the Monte Bello group, with Barrow Island nearby.]

The full description of these islands I would have sent you but many things I want to lay down as truly as I could wish. I am not one that possesses a mariner's art or any skill therein worth noting yet this much I understand, by relation of journals and plans, that these islands were never discovered by any. [Brookes] would excuse [the loss] to say he followed directly Captain Humphrey Fitzherbert's journal. Had our journals been compared with his, he [possibly the EEIC governor in Batavia] should have found Brookes' 400 leagues [2000 kilometres] in the latitudes 38 degrees to 34 degrees more to the eastward than he or ever ship was again. We always feared the ship to be beyond [Brookes'] reckoning . . . the wind that present we struck south-south-east, he directing his course north-east and north-east and by east, when the Sunda Straits bore north-westerly of us.

Bright was exactly right but Brookes wasn't just wrong, he had to have known he was wrong. Green points out that he had to have steered due north to reach the east end of Java, then lied about the position of the Trial Rocks and the course he sailed to maintain the fiction that he'd done nothing wrong. He lied to save his skin, and in so doing consigned numerous vessels to fruitless searches, and many more to voyages fraught with fears of a shoal south of Sunda Strait that didn't exist. He may also have sent some ships to their doom, wrecked while they tried to steer courses to avoid the same nonexistent danger.

However, Bright wasn't finished.

It did seem strange to me that Brookes so cunningly excused the neglect of the company's letters, spangles and moneys. The moneys he confessed to the president and Mr Brockendon [a company official] to have transferred of me. [Yet] he for nigh two hours [did] nothing but convey from his cabin to his skiff to my knowledge both letters, moneys and spangles in his trunk, whereof many of these things, apparel, and other trifles he has by him now this present . . . the Black Box, wherein the company's letters were seen, left the ship also and [by] his own confession. Letters I conveyed into the skiff, some for the President, some for Mr Brockendon and others, were heaved overboard. His excuse was they were wet and yet not so wet but he perused the

contents thereof, which he well knew would have done him no good
if he had honestly delivered them.

The letter, dated 22 August 1622, exposes Brookes as a man who
wrecked his ship, stole its valuables and left most of his crew to die.
It may have been motivated by Bright's dismay that Brookes had
spun the EEIC an elaborate lie and gotten away with it. The EEIC letter of 27 August and the VOC's of September certainly indicate that
they'd swallowed Brookes' story hook, line and sinker, in spite of
Bright's testimony. But when Brookes was finally exposed, he'd been
dead for some 350 years.

If more confirmation of the story of the *Trial* was needed, the reason
for Green's closer investigation of the wreck was that, in 1969,
a group of divers from Perth had set out for Trial Rocks, 1500 kilometres north, hoping to find some sign of the wreck. The team was
led by Eric Christiansen and included Dr Naoom Haimson, Ellis
Alfred 'Alan' Robinson and Dave Nelly.

Like the final piece of the jigsaw falling perfectly into place, on the
first day of their underwater search the divers found what they were
looking for. The sea floor, rocks and a sand ridge yielded iron cannon, anchors, bronze pulleys and pieces of lead ballast and iron.
Some of the artefacts recovered provided evidence that the wreck
was extremely old – certainly old enough to be the *Trial* – though
there was nothing that established conclusively that the vessel was
the *Trial*. It was possible the wreck site was one of several Dutch
ships that were lost in the 17th century without trace. However, when
you find exactly what you are looking for exactly where you expect
to find it, the circumstantial evidence is almost overwhelming.

Yet it was almost as if the elusive *Trial* was going to replace one mystery with another. And it wasn't finished with tales of outrageous behaviour either: for the *Trial*'s modern story includes a character every bit as deceitful and self-serving as the *Trial*'s captain, John Brookes.

On a later visit to the wreck site, to search for some evidence that would confirm the *Trial*'s identification, Jeremy Green found that the site had been disturbed. A person or persons unknown had actually used dynamite to blast the site, hoping to break relics free from their coral encrustation and reveal any treasure that might be hidden.

The perpetrators have never been identified but the finger of suspicion points to a colourful member of the original team who discovered the wreck site. Ellis Alfred 'Alan' Robinson, a controversial, sometimes violent figure, was thought to have done the blasting, possibly out of pure vindictiveness, some time in mid-1971, working from a trawler called *The Four Aces*. He was charged, but eventually acquitted. Suspected of the plunder of several other wrecks – notably the *Batavia*, *Zuytdorp* and *Vergulde Draeck* – Robinson died (possibly suicided) in 1983 while on trial for conspiring to murder a former de facto using explosives and acid.

Several Western Australian writers have detailed the activities of Robinson at length. In *Carpet of Silver*, Dr Phillip Playford wrote of him:

> Even in 1994, eleven years after his death, the Select Committee on Ancient Shipwrecks denied him formal recognition as one of the discoverers of the *Vergulde Draeck* [the VOC ship *Gilt Dragon*] and the *Tryall* wrecks, despite the fact that he is known to have played a significant role in both discoveries.
>
> Robinson will be remembered as a highly controversial figure, who played a prominent role in the discovery and publicising of early wrecks on our coast. His destructive actions were responsible, albeit inadvertently, for much of the State and Commonwealth legislation that was enacted to protect our historic wrecks.

It is now illegal to disturb or remove material from any shipwreck in Australian waters prior to 1900.

Robinson and Brookes had quite a lot in common. For the latter's career didn't end with the *Trial*. In Batavia, in 1623 he took command of the *Moone*, voyaging to ports around South-East Asia, before returning to England in it in 1625. On board was the recently promoted EEIC East Indies President Brockendon, who died on the voyage. In September 1625 Brookes wrecked the ship on the coast of England. He and the master were flung into Dover Prison, accused of deliberately casting the ship away and of plundering the jewels and diamonds in Brockendon's chest. Not only did they manage to get off, largely due to the incompetence of the EEIC, Brookes secured a reward of £10, plus wages for his boy, who had stolen the diamonds and returned them to the EEIC.

To date, the earliest known records of a ship being wrecked in Australian waters are those of the *Trial*. However, older vessels could have been wrecked without trace or any note to acknowledge them, or the records of their loss may themselves be lost or forgotten in some organisation's files. And fuelling these possibilities is one mysterious wreck that may be much older than the *Trial*. Buried somewhere beneath the sand dunes halfway between Warrnambool and Port Fairy, on Victoria's 'Shipwreck Coast', what little is known of the 'Mahogany Ship' has given rise to wide-ranging theories and speculation.

First, the facts. In January 1836, two sealers named Wilson and Gibbs made it to shore after their boat capsized in heavy seas just off the mouth of the Hopkins River, drowning a third man, Captain Smith. The two started walking the 25 kilometres to Port Fairy (Warrnambool not having been settled at that time) and along the way they came across a substantial vessel almost completely buried by sand.

They reported their find, and the loss of their own boat, and a party set out in an attempt to recover the lost seal boat and to investigate the wreck. The party included Hugh Donnelly, Captain John Mills and his brother Charles. According to Hugh Donnelly: 'She lay well up on the beach, fast in the brow of the loose dry sand on the edge of the natural verdure, almost broadside on with her bow towards Port Fairy, her stern a trifle more seaward.' Captain Mills added: 'I stood on her deck, not knowing what timber she was built of, and tried to cut a splinter out of her timbers, but my clasp knife glanced over them as if they were bars of iron.'

When questioned about the wreck, local Aborigines are reported to have answered: 'She all time longa here.' It was sufficient to suggest the wreck was extremely old, certainly predating European settlement of the area, which had only begun in 1834. The site for Melbourne wasn't settled upon until March 1837.

In later years, the wreck became a local landmark. Captain John Mason wrote of it:

Riding along the beach from Port Fairy to Warrnambool in the summer of 1846, my attention was attracted to the hull of a vessel embedded high and dry in the hummocks, far above the reach of any tide. It appeared to be a vessel of about 100 tons burthen, and from its bleached and weather-beaten appearance must have been there for many years. The spars and deck are gone, and the hull full of drift sand. The timber of which she was built had the appearance of either mahogany or cedar.

Mason returned to the vessel the next year with a shipbuilder, after which he wrote: 'She had the appearance of a large lighter, but of a build which bespoke ignorance of the art of shipbuilding as we know it.'

The curious nature of the vessel was also described by the wife of
a magistrate, Mrs Thomas Manifold, in 1848: 'It was made of dark
red wood, but strangely designed and constructed. Instead of the
familiar planks along its sides it had wooden panels.'

Over the years the vessel gradually disappeared into the dunes,
scavenged for souvenirs and building materials, covered by shifting
sands that moved faster after the introduction of grazing animals. Captain Mason had been told the flooring of a local farm was mahogany
from the wreck. A chest in the Flagstaff Hill Museum, Warrnambool,
is made from timbers found in the vicinity of the wreck. They are
thought to have come from the tropics and are like mahogany.

In 1880, the wreck was seen by two people walking the beach,
Thomas Paton and Samuel Avery. They reported seeing a local
farmer, Henry Lyfield, piling brush around the wreck's timbers and
setting it alight to recover any metal fittings once the wood was
burned away. Since then, the wreck has not been sighted, despite
repeated and increasingly sophisticated searches, many of which
have been frustrated by the large amounts of timber that have been
buried naturally beneath the dunes.

Speculation on where the ship might have come from has continued
ever since. One of the most obvious possibilities is that the Mahogany
Ship was Dutch. Had it been following the Brouwer Route well to the
south it may have gone too far east, past Cape Leeuwin, and found
itself unable to turn back against the prevailing westerly winds. The
ship may well have been hugging the coast, looking for an end of the
Great South Land so it could head north. It could be one of the Dutch
ships that have disappeared without trace – including the *Ridderschap
van Holland* (1694), the *Fortuyn* (1724) and *Aagtekerke* (1726).

It has also been suggested that the ship could be Spanish or
Portuguese, from the 16th century (see Kenneth McIntyre's *The
Secret Discovery of Australia* and Lawrence Fitzgerald's *Java La
Grande – The Portuguese Discovery of Australia*). At the time both

these seafaring nations were in their golden ages of navigation and spent much of their time searching for a southern land, a counter-balance to the landmasses of the northern hemisphere.

An even more intriguing possibility is that the ship was Chinese. Between 1405 and 1433, Chinese Admiral Cheng Ho's massive fleets of junks embarked on seven voyages through the Indian Ocean and Western Pacific. Navigating with the aid of compasses (invented by the Chinese in the 11th century), some of the vessels were the largest ever built, over 122 metres long, and the fleets themselves consisted of dozens of vessels. The total number of people claimed to have embarked on some of these voyages is put at over 27 000.

In several of his books, the late Jack Loney goes considerably further. In *Wrecks on the Queensland Coast* he states that the Emperor Ying Tsung produced a map of Australia in 1620, after sixty-two ships circumnavigated the island continent. Loney's knowledge of Australian shipwrecks was encyclopaedic, but unfortunately he cites no references for the claim. Some Internet sites claim the map is held in the Beijing Museum. My efforts to locate it have proved fruitless. And even if found the map may be like many of those drawn by European cartographers before Australia's discovery – merely speculative, rather than a detailed representation of an actual voyage.

Nevertheless, a Chinese junk shipwrecked on the Victorian coast might explain the vessel 'of a build which bespoke ignorance of the art of shipbuilding as we know it' and 'strangely designed and constructed. Instead of the familiar planks along its sides it had wooden panels.'

In the absence of the wreck itself, the matter will now probably never be settled. If it could be found, whatever was left might point to its method of construction and country of origin. To confuse matters, over the years other vessels have come to grief in the vicinity. For example, a piece of wood purported to have been taken from the Mahogany Ship some time before 1890 is now held in the National Library, Canberra. It has been dated at between 1660 and 1710. However, it is now thought to be a species of eucalypt, and therefore originating in Australia. Unless the Aboriginal custodians of Australia have managed to keep the fact a huge secret, no-one was building ships out of eucalypts at that time. It's probably a very old piece of driftwood.

If anything, the Mahogany Ship highlights the importance of protecting shipwrecks for future generations. More than a century after the Mahogany Ship disappeared, we are reduced to guessing. What ship was she? Does she have as grim a tale to tell as does the *Trial*? Without the physical evidence, we may never know.

The wreck of the *Trial* has taken its place in history as the first recorded shipwreck in Australian waters, but not before causing centuries of navigational problems. In 1627 the VOC's *Heren XVII* issued new sailing orders for their ships that included instructions for the course to be taken between October and March:

> so that when you are at about 30 degrees latitude you estimate yourself to be 950 or 1000 mijlen [7000–7400 kilometres] east of the Cape of Good Hope. These 950 or 1000 mijlen being passed then it is permissible (if the conditions of wind and weather allow such) to run into sight of the Land of Eendracht at 27 degrees latitude or farther north, and from there to make such a course with which you may reckon to pass by the Triall rocks, which lie at about 20 degrees latitude south, without peril, and the south coast of Java can then be made conveniently so as to reach Sunda Strait.

Using the Land of Eendracht to avoid Trial Rocks in this way may have contributed to the loss of four VOC ships over the next century – *Batavia* (1629), *Vergulde Draeck* (1656), *Zuytdorp* (1712) and *Zeewyk*

(1727). The three other ships that disappeared without trace – *Ridder-schap van Holland, Fortuyn* and *Aagtekerke* – may also have foundered on the Western Australian coast thanks to Brookes and the *Trial*.

The VOC's new sailing orders bear a striking resemblance to the suggestion of Houtman, written in 1619, before the *Trial* had hit the rocks. In either case, it seemed an effective way of avoiding a potentially deadly obstacle that lay far to the west. The truth, as it turned out, was that it lay far to the east – so far east it needn't have been avoided at all.

Had anyone who had read Houtman's reports twigged that Brookes's 'island formerly seen by the Dutch' was actually Een-drachtsland, and that Brookes was a truly bad navigator, the game of Chinese Whispers might have ended much sooner. That, however, would have required an almost forensic analysis of all the accounts that were coming in from the increasing number of vessels probing the waters of north-west Australia. And it would have taken an abil-ity to discern what was right and what was wrong, while the truth of the waters in question was surrounded by a haze of distance and ignorance. Brookes banked on ignorance to save him, and it did.

Yet it also cost ninety of his crew their lives. And that was just the beginning. The loss of the *Trial* marks the start of the slow, pains-taking development of knowledge, mapping and navigation of the vast coastline of Australia. As the ensuing chapters show, much of that knowledge was gained at a terrible cost in human life, but also often in circumstances of extraordinary bravery and sacrifice. The history of Australia's shipwrecks, from 1622 to the present day, is the history of the discovery and deepening understanding of Australia.

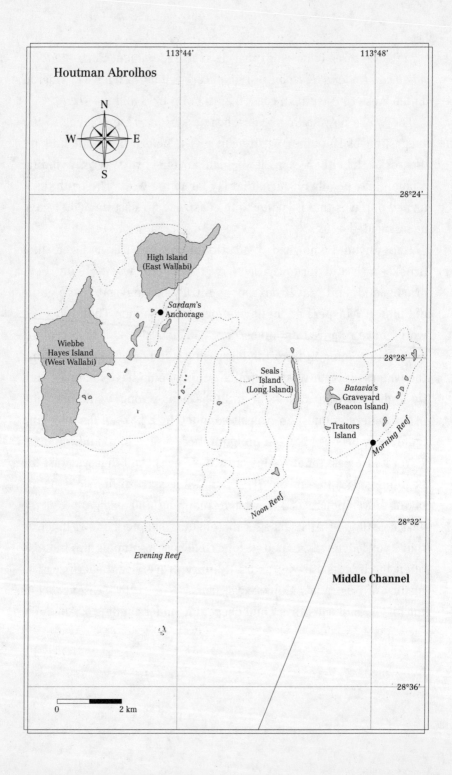

Houtman Abrolhos

113°44'

113°48'

N

W   E

S

28°24'

High Island
(East Wallabi)

Sardam's
Anchorage

Wiebbe
Hayes Island
(West Wallabi)

28°28'

Seals
Island
(Long Island)

Batavia's
Graveyard
(Beacon Island)

Traitors
Island

Morning Reef

28°32'

Noon Reef

Evening Reef

Middle Channel

28°36'

0   2 km

Batavia under sail, from *Ongeluckige Voyagie*
(Australian National Maritime Museum)

2. THE DEVIL AND THE DEEP BLUE SEA: *BATAVIA*, 1629

As she rode at anchor at the Cape of Good Hope in late April 1629, the Dutch ship *Batavia* was one of the most beautiful sailing vessels of her age. Freshly painted, adorned with finely sculpted figures from bow to stern, she had just completed the first leg of her maiden voyage, bound for the port in the Indies after which she'd been named. She was the flagship of a fleet of ships from the Dutch East India Company (the VOC), carrying 315 passengers, soldiers and crew, a rich cargo of trade goods and an absolute fortune in jewels and coins of silver and gold. Her skipper, Ariaen Jacobsz, should have been one of the proudest men alive, honoured with the command of such a spectacular vessel. Unfortunately, he was not. This particular evening he was roaring drunk – cutting a truly ugly swathe through the Cape's bars and the other ships at anchor.

With him were *Batavia*'s supercargo (the officer responsible for her cargo and commercial transactions), Jeronimus Cornelisz, and a female passenger, Zwaantie Hendrix. The three had little in common other than difficulties dealing with people in authority – that and a fondness for the fierce Cape liquor flatteringly described as 'gin.'

Cornelisz's problems with authority had begun in Holland. In his home town of Haarlem he'd become involved with the painter Johannes Torrentius van der Beeck, who'd come up with the doctrine that there was no such thing as the devil. He believed that only God existed, therefore it was impossible to do anything evil. His followers embraced the concept with enthusiasm and Torrentius, inspired by the ensuing scenes of immorality, excess and indulgence of the flesh, painted them. In the strict Dutch society the fun was never going to last long. After Torrentius was indicted there was a witch-hunt for anyone who shared his views. Cornelisz, an apothecary or chemist by training, decided an extended sea voyage would be a good career move.

Zwaantie Hendrix was no innocent either. She'd all but abandoned Lucretia Jansz, the woman who had hired her as maid for the voyage. Jacobsz would have preferred Lucretia's company. On the voyage to the Cape he had become extremely familiar with her, to the point of scandal. 'Her skin is beautiful and fair,' the skipper had confided to Cornelisz. His plan was to tempt her to his bed with gold; and if that didn't work, then there were 'other means.' It seemed to have escaped his attention that Lucretia was married, on her way to the Indies to join her husband. But presumably Lucretia had set him straight, so he had turned his attention to her servant, Zwaantie. He'd already heard from the wife of the ship's cook that she was a loose woman and the *Batavia* was soon riddled with rumours that she 'refused the skipper nothing.' Cornelisz knew it was more than rumour, having surprised Ariaen and Zwaantie in the skipper's cabin engaged in an activity Torrentius might have painted.

However, sexual scandal was the least of Jacobsz's problems. As the night wore on and he became increasingly drunk, that became obvious to all and sundry. His real problem was his commanding officer – Francisco Pelsaert. Pelsaert was a company man. He knew nothing about sailing a ship, yet the high and mighty VOC directors, the *Heren XVII*, had made him a commodore. It choked Jacobsz with rage that Pelsaert had been put in charge of the entire fleet. But what could you expect from the VOC directors? One of them was Pelsaert's brother-in-law, Hendrik Brouwer. Yes, Jacobsz thought, they knew how to look after each other. But none of those idiots knew a thing about sailing a ship. As Jacobsz and the others guzzled their way around the ships in Table Bay, Jacobsz cursed and spat venom at his commanding officer. The crew of the ship *Sardam* copped plenty of it. Not that anyone dared argue with the solidly built senior officer. The maelstrom of slander and outrage next moved on to the *Buren*, where things only got worse. It didn't end until the hopelessly drunken Jacobsz had started a particularly ugly brawl with the hapless ship's crew. Despite his condition, the skipper of the *Batavia* won the fight.

While Jacobsz was scandalising the Cape, Francisco Pelsaert was shopping. The morning after Jacobsz's spree, returning from a trip ashore to buy cattle, the commander of the fleet found messages waiting for him from the commanders of the *Sardam* and *Buren*. Several of the *Buren*'s crew had been injured, and her skipper described Jacobsz as 'very beastly with words as well as deeds.' If Pelsaert had any doubts about what he read, one look at his gin-soaked skipper was enough to dispel them.

The pampered company man confronted the hardened sailor in the ship's gangway. Jacobsz must have been expecting the worst. If Pelsaert had heard half of what had been said and done, he could have him flogged, or removed from command. And the two already had a history. Pelsaert and Jacobsz had sailed on a previous voyage – from Surat, in India, back to Holland. Before they'd even left port, they had clashed bitterly, Jacobsz using language only a sailor could really appreciate. Two such sailors, commandeur Griph and second merchant Wolebrant Geleijnsen, had taken Jacobsz to task over his behaviour. What particularly concerned them was that his unbridled animosity was no recipe for a peaceful voyage. They begged Jacobsz to treat the commodore with some respect or at least to maintain the pretence of decency for their sakes.

Pelsaert wouldn't have forgotten the trip from Surat, but now, instead of punishing Jacobsz, he merely threatened. The skipper's behaviour had been reckless, particularly taking Cornelisz and Hendrix with him. Pelsaert exhorted Jacobsz to remember his position and set a proper example. If he didn't then he, Pelsaert, would know what to do about it. Jacobsz faced demotion and public disgrace.

Jacobsz should have counted himself lucky. Pelsaert had been remarkably lenient. Perhaps he had a high regard for the rough man's skill, despite his faults. Perhaps, being a gentleman, he thought his kindness would be appreciated. Perhaps he was anxious about upsetting a hard-drinking, hard-brawling seaman.

Up on deck, Jacobsz found Cornelisz. 'By God,' he raged, 'if the other ships were not close by I'd give him such a hiding that he would not be able to leave his bunk for a fortnight; but I swear that as soon as we sail I'll get away from the ships and then I'll be my own master.'

'How would you manage that?' Jeronimus asked, in seeming innocence. 'The mates will be on watch.'

'That's nothing,' Jacobsz replied. 'I'll manage it during my own watch, for I haven't much faith in the first steersman, and less still in my brother-in-law [also a crew-member]. I don't think I could come to an understanding with them.'

The skipper of the treasure-laden *Batavia*, crammed with cargo and innocent people, was talking mutiny. Cornelisz listened, but didn't say a word to Pelsaert.

When *Batavia* took to the Indian Ocean on 22 April 1629, she followed the route pioneered by Pelsaert's brother-in-law some fifteen years earlier. As detailed in the previous chapter, the sailing instructions for the Brouwer Route had been refined and updated as the years passed and experience of the passage increased. By 1627, the sailing orders took account of the 'experience' with Trial Rocks. In addition the new instructions carried a stern warning:

> The way between the Cape and the Land of the Eendracht is in fact much shorter than shown by the plane chart and it may happen through the speed of the currents that the way is found to be even shorter than it actually is, so that the land could be sighted much earlier than could be expected. And the land of the Eendracht has south of 27 degrees many perilous shallows and sharp grounds, therefore cautious action is needed and timely watch must be kept, and at night and in darkness it is urgent to use the lead.

The warning referred to the Houtman Abrolhos, whose name meant 'Watch Out!' But the people on board the *Batavia* who should have been watching had other things on their minds. After leaving the Cape, Jacobsz succeeded in breaking convoy with the other ships of the VOC fleet without arousing suspicion. Having weathered a storm, they found themselves alone. Meanwhile, he and Cornelisz had been talking.

'All we need is the right opportunity,' Jacobsz murmured. 'Then we'll seize the ship and throw the commodore and all the people except 120 overboard.'

'Why are you so bitter against the commodore?' Cornelisz asked, though he was also wondering why the commodore put up with so much from his skipper. Jacobsz told him what had happened in Surat.

'So why don't you throw the commodore overboard secretly? Why cause so much loss to our lords and masters? Why kill so many innocent people?'

'It's not just the commodore. People like us can't gain much profit in India, but with the vessel we could do quite a deal.'

Cornelisz was tempted. He may have had the veneer of a cultivated man, but he had already been corrupted in his previous life. 'Don't you see any risk in the enterprise? Do you think you can carry it out?'

'Let me have my way,' came the reply. 'I'll manage it. I'm pretty sure of my cousin from the Schie [a river in Holland], but I have little faith in my brother-in-law, the second mate, or in the first mate either.'

The circle of conspirators widened. Cornelisz and the skipper carefully probed the loyalties of the crew, but they had to be careful. If they were caught plotting mutiny, they'd all be hanged. First, though, they'd be tortured and broken on the rack.

Cornelisz persuaded Allert Jansz, a musketeer, to join. Soon there were others: high boatswain Jan Evertsz, lance-corporal Jacop Pietersz Cosijn, Davidt Zevanck (an assistant to Cornelisz), cadet Coenraat van Huyssen, sailor Cornelis Jansz, musketeer Ryckert Woutersz and perhaps a dozen more. They had taken to sleeping with their swords in their bunks. The mutiny would come at night. At a signal they would nail down the hatch to the soldiers' quarters, then start throwing people to the sharks.

First, though, there was the matter of Lucretia. Jacobsz now hated her as much as he did Pelsaert, but for entirely different reasons.

He'd had Zwaantie released from her service. Now he was bent on the destruction of the woman he couldn't have.

On 14 May, at dusk, a group of men pounced on Lucretia in a companionway. A hand stifled her screams as they stripped her naked. A ribbon was torn from her hair and tightened around her throat. She was hung over the side of the ship by her ankles, molested, then smeared from head to toe in excrement and black pitch. Finally, she was dumped on deck, where she lay shaking and sobbing in distress until she was discovered by the officer of the watch.

Pelsaert was summoned. He had been confined to his cabin, suffering from a fever, probably malaria, which he'd picked up on his previous trip to the Indies. Now he was burning with rage. But Lucretia could identify only one of her assailants: Jan Evertsz, the high boatswain. In the darkness, his was the only voice she recognised. But it didn't take a genius to work out who else was responsible, or how long it would take the skilled and efficient inquisitors in the dungeons of Batavia Castle (the VOC's East India headquarters) to get a full list of names.

Pelsaert, however, hesitated to act. Evertsz was a senior member of the crew and he hadn't acted alone. To accuse only one man, and leave the others free to roam the ship wondering how long it would be before Evertsz was tortured and started screaming their names, was an invitation to mutiny. Pelsaert decided to wait until the ship sighted Eendrachtsland, and was in the last month of its voyage, before accusing Evertsz and having him put in chains. The mutineers, however, had decided that landfall would be their signal, too.

Jacobsz had a lot on his mind during the early hours of 4 June. *Batavia* was in latitude 28 degrees, steering north-east by north

under full sail before a light sou'-westerly. By his calculations they
would probably sight Eendrachtsland within a week. That idiot
Pelsaert was already getting jumpy, demanding they keep a lookout.
Jacobsz knew he was in the same latitude as the dreaded Abrolhos,
but he estimated he was still almost 1000 kilometres to the west, and
steering to miss them. Watch out? On a beautiful moonlit night, he
didn't see the need. Then, he thought he saw something.

'What's that white ahead?' he called to the lookout.

'It's the moon shining on the water,' came the reply.

Jacobsz relaxed. Now he was getting jumpy too – though he had
good reason. The mutiny was coming. As he'd said to Cornelisz,
'I shall go to the devil anyhow. If I reach India I shall get into trouble
whether or no.' But in a couple of days he'd be in possession of one
of the richest prizes on the high seas, and not just the *Batavia*. He'd
be a wealthy man with the beautiful Lucretia . . .

Batavia interrupted his reverie with a jolt. From below deck came
a grinding noise and the ship began to shake violently.

'She's struck!' the cry went up. The crew could feel *Batavia*'s keel
and rudder grinding over submerged rocks as she continued to force
her way forward, surrounded by foam.

Pelsaert had been below, in his cabin, still suffering from fever.
The impact threw him from his bunk and he immediately struggled
on deck. He saw the foaming water all around the stricken vessel.
Then he saw Jacobsz.

'You've brought us into this danger,' he snapped, 'by your reckless
negligence.'

He was more right than he knew.

'It wasn't my negligence. I was awake and carefully watching
everything.'

Pelsaert demanded to know what Jacobsz was going to do now,
and where he thought they were.

'God only knows,' said the skipper; 'this is an unknown dry bank, which must be a good distance from the mainland. I think we are on a shallow and perhaps it is low tide. Let us drop an anchor astern; possibly we may get off yet.'

'How deep is the water around us?'

Jacobsz didn't know that either.

Pelsaert got the lead out and they found only 17 or 18 feet (5 metres) of water at the ship's stern, less forward. They ordered the crew to lighten the ship by heaving several cannons overboard. They also tried to get some of the boats into the water. If they could use them to drop anchors some distance from the ship, they might be able to drag themselves back into deeper water.

It was then that the sea's mood changed. When *Batavia* had struck, it had been relatively smooth. It may have been a brief lull, which would have made the shoal harder to spot as *Batavia* ploughed forward in the darkness. Now, though, breakers came foaming at the ship, sending green water and spray flying across the decks. The first boat they tried to launch was hit by a heavy sea and washed overboard. To add to their woes, rain set in as the wind picked up. They struggled to get a small sloop into the water. This time they were lucky and it rowed after the drifting boat. Dawn was breaking before they got the two vessels back close to the ship.

The growing daylight showed they were surrounded by shallows. It also showed a few low islands in the distance. They were a small consolation. At least they weren't on an isolated rock in the middle of the ocean. If the ship was completely wrecked, they had some chance of escape.

Soon, though, they realised the tide was dropping. As it did the waves were making the ship lurch violently as she pounded against the rocks. With each wave, coming at intervals of between eight and ten seconds, *Batavia* lifted, then dropped on the reef; lifted, then dropped. She was solidly built, but not for this.

'We'll have to drop the mainmast,' Jacobsz shouted. 'This pounding will drive it through the bottom of the ship. She'll break her back.'

The crew grabbed axes and started to hack at the mast. When they lost their footing, hit by waves or thrown over by the ship's violent jarring, they rose and continued their desperate work. They had no way of knowing which blow would bring the mast down, or which way, and when they should dive for whatever cover they could find as the massive timber plunged to the deck. At last, with a terrifying splintering crack, it toppled and dropped.

To no avail. The mast fell across the ship, its weight pinning it to the rocks. The crew frantically tried to hack through the mesh of rigging that held it in place, but couldn't get the mast free. Hopes of saving the ship were fading fast.

The small boats trying to return to the ship also found that the mast and the breakers made it almost impossible to get alongside. But they had to try.

Pelsaert got Jacobsz aboard one of them and sent him to reconnoitre two small islands nearest to the ship, to see if they'd stay above water at high tide. He returned at nine o'clock saying they would, but that landing was difficult due to low rocky cliffs along the water's edge.

Meanwhile, Pelsaert was surrounded by a crush of terrified humanity. Women were wailing and crying. Children were wide-eyed with uncomprehending fear. Even the sick people had struggled on deck and were begging to be saved. Slowly, in the treacherous conditions, the little boats were filled and carried people to shore.

Only an hour later, the ship's fate was sealed. After constant pounding on the reef, she broke her back. Water flooded below. A few of the crew who had been trying to carry food and valuables onto deck frantically grabbed whatever bread they could lay their hands on before it was ruined by the swirling waters. They were hindered by many of their colleagues and some of the soldiers who had broken into the liquor. Pelsaert's authority had little effect on people who believed they were doomed. Soon, many of the people who could have saved much of the ship's supplies were roaring drunk. Among them was Cornelisz.

Still a few crewmen and soldiers persevered and managed to land some 180 people. They also managed to land twenty casks of bread and a casket of jewels, but only a few barrels of water. The two small islands had no drinkable water at all.

'It's no use taking food and water ashore,' Jacobsz told Pelsaert when he returned to the ship after sunset. 'The people devour it in the most lawless and ravenous manner. They drink as much as they like and my orders have no effect.'

Pelsaert leapt into the sloop and went ashore personally. On his arrival, exerting the full authority of a VOC commodore, he insisted that the food and water be rationed. Order was restored with the help of the soldiers on shore, but in truth there was hardly anything left. Pelsaert then attempted to return to the ship but a strong wind was throwing a huge sea around the disintegrating wreck. Pelsaert's boat crew soon found that they could make no headway. When they tried to get back on shore, they risked being swamped by the waves, and if they waited for a break in the waves, the current threatened to carry them away. Finally they got back on land, where they were obliged to stay for the remainder of the night.

On board the remains of *Batavia*, the crew's drunken debauch continued. One of the treasure chests was opened, and a fortune in coin spilled over the side of the ship. The sailors scooped up more of it and imagined themselves rich. Except they had nowhere to spend their wealth, and probably just a few hours left to live. They ended up throwing it at each other in their drunken ravings. They broke into Pelsaert's cabin, mocked the entries in his journal, then threw it over the side.

Cornelisz, however, still clung to the idea of seizing the ship. His ignorance of boats led him to think it still might be saved, despite

a conversation with Jacobsz during the day. The skipper had told the
merchant in no uncertain terms that the *Batavia* was finished.

On 5 June 1629, on a couple of tiny scraps of land – waterless,
covered only in low scrub and heath – more than 200 souls woke to
an uncertain dawn. In the distance they could just make out the
splintered remains of the great ship *Batavia*, wreathed in a mist
thrown up by the breakers that roared around her.

Yet already the industrious Dutch men and women were active.
The little food and water was rationed out for breakfast. Any wreckage that floated near was plucked from the waves. And the two little
vessels – the sloop and the ship's boat – were busy as Pelsaert
shuttled more people to the larger of the two small islands.

The two boats, one commanded by Pelsaert, the other by Jacobsz,
then headed back out to the ship. The seas were now so high that
only Pelsaert's oared sloop succeeded in getting to the ship, and
that after rowing hard for several hours. He found *Batavia* surrounded
by high seas that made it impossible to get alongside. Eventually,
while they waited for a break in the waves and a chance to get
aboard, a carpenter named Jan Egbertsz dived off the *Batavia* and
swam through the surf to reach the bobbing sloop.

'Please come to the rescue of the supercargo,' he implored them.
Cornelisz was still aboard with seventy other men. 'The ship is no
longer safe.'

A rescue attempt was suicidal. Instead Pelsaert asked Egbertsz if
he would attempt to return to the ship. He sent instructions to throw
overboard half a dozen planks so that more oars could be made for
the boats, and to begin building rafts with which to save themselves
if the ship broke up completely.

Back on the islands, they found carpenters already busy making oars from other pieces of wreckage. They added their planks to the meagre pile.

As the sun sank, the wind grew to a gale from the north-west. At times the ship seemed to be almost buried in the waves. That night, Pelsaert conducted a grim census. On the small island there were 40 people and about eighty cans of water. On the large island 180 people and even less water. Unless they found water quickly, they were all going to die of thirst.

There were anxious murmurings among the crew. 'Perhaps we should go looking for water on any islands nearby,' Jacobsz suggested. 'And the crew is restless. If you don't order a search, there's a danger of mutiny.'

He didn't mention that he'd quite likely lead it.

'We'll wait to see what the weather does and what becomes of the ship,' Pelsaert replied. 'We'd have to answer before God and the governors of Batavia if we leave those people, and the rich possessions of the company, without making sufficient attempts to save them.'

The commodore soon discovered he was almost alone in this belief. The skipper and others in the crew pressed Pelsaert to take the boats to the larger islands nearby or to the mainland in search of water. If they found any, they could return. If not, they could make all speed for the port of Batavia and return with a ship to rescue the survivors, assuming there were any.

Pelsaert reluctantly agreed, but insisted on going to the other island to tell the bulk of the people their intentions. The crew were wary of doing even this. They feared for the commodore's safety. More than that, they feared losing one of the boats. They didn't want to wait for rain, or for casks from the ship to float ashore. They wanted to save their skins.

Pelsaert persisted. 'If you don't consent,' he told them, 'I'll tell the people you don't intend to go out and find fresh water for everybody.

I'm ready to die with the people honourably and not leave the company's ship and goods.'

Reluctantly, the high boatswain, Jan Evertsz, and six men agreed to take the commodore to the larger island in the sloop, along with another cask of water, on condition that, if he was held there, they would leave with the boat. Pelsaert agreed and they set off. When they got near the shore, though, the crew took one look at the crowd lining the shore and refused to land. 'They will keep you and us there,' they cried, 'We don't wish to go nearer; if you have anything to say to them you can call out; we are not going to run any risk for your sake.'

Pelsaert was so indignant he tried to jump overboard and swim ashore, but Evertsz pulled him back. The men rowed further away from the shore, forcing Pelsaert to return to the smaller island.

Pelsaert reluctantly caved in to the demands of the crew. On the morning of 6 June, he wrote a letter explaining that the boats were going in search of water and then, fearful of the reaction, left it under a bread barrel for the people he left behind. Then the two boats sailed for the larger islands that lay about three kilometres to the north. There they searched all day but found only a little brackish water in some rock pools. The next day the two boats were made as ready as they could be for an extended voyage, and the following day, 8 June, the commodore read out to his crew a resolution, to which all consented with a solemn oath:

Since, on all the islands and cliffs round about our foundered ship *Batavia*, there is no freshwater to be found, in order to feed and keep the people who are saved, therefore the commodore has earnestly requested and proposed that an expedition should be made to the main southland to see whether it is God's gracious will that fresh water shall be found, of which so much may be taken to the people that they shall be certain of having enough provision for a considerable time; that then, meanwhile, someone shall be told off to go to [the port of] Batavia, in order to let the Lord-General and his councillors know of our disaster and to ask him for early assistance.

Then the two boats left for the mainland and Batavia with forty-seven on board. They included Jacobsz, who by now realised that if he'd spent as much time plotting his course as he had plotting a mutiny, he'd have known he was 1000 kilometres further east and right on top of the Abrolhos. With him were Zwaantie Hendrix and the man who was known to have interfered with Lucretia, Jan Evertsz, who now had an unpleasant date with the magistrates at Batavia Castle. Jacobsz and Pelsaert could expect an almost equally unpleasant experience when they arrived with news that they had managed to wreck the *Batavia*. Cornelisz was still clinging to what remained of the ship, though by now even he would have realised that it wasn't going anywhere.

All the people left behind, who four days after the wreck were already starting to die of thirst and becoming so desperate that some were drinking sea water, others their own urine, saw all this and named the island where Pelsaert had left his note 'Traitors Island.' They called the other island '*Batavia*'s Kerckhof' ('*Batavia*'s Graveyard').

Two days later, their luck finally turned. Rain fell steadily in the early hours of 10 June, replenishing the casks so well that the immediate danger to survival passed. Added to this were barrels of water floating in from the wreck, even a barrel of French wine, and four-and-a-half barrels of Spanish wine. It was calculated that with everyone receiving three cups of water and two cups of wine per day, they could survive for an extended period. Food wasn't a problem either. The islands were uninhabited, sufficiently distant from the mainland (some 30 kilometres east) not to have been reached by indigenous people from the mainland. The island had abundant birdlife that didn't know enough of men to fear them. There were

seals on a nearby island, referred to as 'Seals Island', which could
be reached in a small boat the carpenters had constructed. There
were plenty of fish in the sea and shellfish on the rocks. With sails
and spars washing ashore, they were able to construct basic shelters. Under the circumstances their prospects were starting to look
quite good. Even though winter was upon them, compared to the
climate the Dutch had come from, many of the survivors may have
mistaken the season for summer. All they needed to do was wait to
be rescued.

Out on the *Batavia*, the situation was far worse. The boats had
stopped coming to the ship, but it had continued to break apart. For
about a week she had mostly held together, then the prow and the
higher parts had washed away. The gales swept in almost daily, and
with them the waves, so that soon the port side was smashed away,
allowing more wreckage to float free. Crewmen were washed away too,
others tried to swim ashore and were drowned. A very few made
it through the breakers to one of the islands.

The last one left aboard was Cornelisz. His dreams of taking the
Batavia were now shattered into a million splinters of driftwood. On
10 June he'd taken refuge in what was left of the bow. He had little
option, because he couldn't swim. It was only when the bow broke
apart that he grabbed a piece of wreckage and floated away, half-
drowned. He was lucky enough to be washed ashore on *Batavia*'s
Graveyard, where there was considerable rejoicing that he'd survived.

Cornelisz learned that Jacobsz and Pelsaert had left for the mainland
and Batavia, which meant he was the senior officer. He was responsible
for the lives of about 250 people and all the VOC's valuables. The casket
containing the company's jewels was placed in his care. The young

apothecary had never had so much power in his life. Unfortunately, he also had a problem. One of the mutineers had talked.

When Ryckert Woutersz had come ashore, he'd got drunk and revealed everything, including many of the conspirators' names. The same night he'd disappeared in the darkness and was never seen again. Now the conspirators came to Cornelisz saying they had to act. They told him Woutersz had got a knife in his ribs, but now they had a wild plan to kill all the people on the islands and seize the rescue ship when it came. They could still get the money from the ship. And what was more, they were sure Ariaen Jacobsz was planning to stab Pelsaert and throw him overboard from the boats as soon as he got a chance. Pelsaert was probably already dead. Jacobsz would probably be in command of the rescue vessel.

Cornelisz looked at the odds. The mutineers numbered thirty at most, with a hard core of ten. Around them were nearly 200 people, including a squad of some forty soldiers who kept themselves apart from the rest, maintaining their military discipline. The soldiers' tents were neatly arranged with weapons stacked at the ready outside.

'Do nothing,' he said. 'I'll think of something.'

For the next three weeks, Cornelisz was the perfect model of a diligent company officer. He supervised the people constructing shelters, building small boats they could use for fishing and going to other islands to find food, and salvaging wreckage. One of his first acts was to send the contingent of soldiers, without their weapons, to the nearby high islands. The reason given: there were too many people on *Batavia*'s Graveyard. On the high islands they'd find more food and water, which Cornelisz told them an earlier exploration had discovered. When they found it, they should light three fires as a smoke signal and the boats would come to pick them up. Next, the remaining people were divided between Traitors Island (about twenty people) and Seals Island (a sandy spit with forty people). Little by little, the survivors were divided until only about ninety innocent people remained on *Batavia*'s

Graveyard with the thirty mutineers, who were practising their swords-manship. There was nothing unusual in that: many were cadet soldiers and junior officers honing their skills.

Everything changed on 3 July. Cornelisz called his men to his tent. To the hard core of his followers, Coenraat van Huyssen, Davidt Zevanck and Jacop Pietersz Cosijn, he gave his orders: 'Kill the strongest first.'

It started on *Batavia*'s Graveyard. The killing was done in secret, though it wasn't easy to do on a scrap of land no more than 200 metres long by 100 wide. Yet that night Coenraat van Huyssen and Davidt Zevanck took Jan Cornelis and Thomas Wensel, both sailors, and Hendrick Jansz, soldier, out on a raft one by one and drowned them. A cadet, Andries Liebent, was also taken, but begged for his life and was spared.

The next day, a gunner named Abraham Hendricks was an easy target for Cornelisz. He made the mistake of tapping a wine barrel, getting drunk, then offering some of the wine to another gunner, Arian Ariaanz. When they were caught, Cornelisz demanded they be put to death, but the council that had been organised to make deci-sions concerning affairs on the island refused to sentence the second man. Cornelisz flew into a rage and threatened the council, which had given him all the pretext he needed to dismiss it. Cornelisz had both the accused men killed anyway, plus two carpenters – Egbert Roelofsz and Warner Dircxsz – who were accused of trying to steal a small boat.

The next day, 5 July, Cornelisz dismissed the council and appointed new members: Coenraat van Huyssen, Davidt Zevanck and Jacop Pietersz Cosijn. The chief conspirators in the mutiny were now in control of *Batavia*'s Graveyard, and the number of men in a position to oppose them was shrinking rapidly. With them went the pretence of justice. Hans Radder, a cadet, Jacob Groenewaldt, the upper trumpeter, and Andries de Vries, an assistant, weren't accused of anything. The first two were taken to a small island on a raft, bound hand and foot, then carried into the sea and drowned; de Vries begged for his life and was spared.

The killing continued 'in secret' and anyone foolish enough to ask where the missing people had gone was told they'd been taken to the other islands. But it was glaringly obvious that something was wrong, not that there was much the people on *Batavia*'s Graveyard could do about it. The remaining men were outnumbered; the cut-throats had the only weapons. The name the survivors had given to their island had become the horrible literal truth.

On 8 July, the pretence of secret killing became gossamer-thin. In the evening, Cornelisz invited soldier Hans Hardens and his wife, Anneken, to dine with him. While they ate, another soldier, Jan Hendricxsz, went to their tent and strangled their six-year-old daughter, Hilletje. This episode showed Cornelisz's confidence in his growing power over the people, and the sadistic pleasure he and his men took in it.

The next day, though, the people on nearby Traitors Island, including the Provost Pieter Jansz and his family, had grown suspicious enough to build two rafts and attempt to escape to the high islands. Unfortunately, they were seen. The mutineers pursued them in the boats. When they were caught, they were tipped screaming into the water: the Provost and his wife and child, Claudine Patoys and her child, the wife of Claas Harmansz, soldiers Cristoffel Quist and Wouter Joel, and others. Claas Harmansz, Pauls Barentsz, Bessel Jansz and Nicklaas Winckelhaack swam for their lives, finally dragging themselves from the water on *Batavia*'s Graveyard. Seeing Cornelisz, they ran to him for aid. 'Kill them,' Cornelisz ordered.

All four were slaughtered. Rutger Fredericxsz hacked twice at Pauls Barentsz, then turned on Claas Harmansz and killed him. Barentsz was finally killed by Andries Jonas, a soldier from Liege, who pursued him into the water, then thrust a pike through his throat.

Some men became tools in the killing. After begging for his life on

5 July, five days later Andries de Vries was taken to a tent where
eleven people lay ill. 'Kill them,' he was told. It was an initiation of
sorts and failure to pass the test was death. Andries did as he was told.

On 12 July, the day the mutineers swore an oath of loyalty, Lenart
Michielsz, Hendricxsz and cadet Lucas Gellisz were ordered to go to
the tent of gunner Passchier van den Ende, carpenter Jacop Hendricks, and a sick boy. 'Cut their throats,' Cornelisz ordered. The
mutineers stormed into the tent, alleging that its inhabitants had
stolen some of the VOC's goods. Passchier was asked if he was hiding
anything. 'No,' he replied and begged to say his prayers, suspecting
his life was about to end. He wasn't given a chance.

'Get on with it,' Davidt Zevanck snarled, and Jan Hendricxsz threw
Passchier down and cut his throat. But the killers hesitated over
Jacop and the boy. Davidt Zevanck went to Cornelisz and asked him
to reconsider.

'He's a good carpenter,' Zevanck said. 'Let him live.'

Perhaps Cornelisz had all the boats he wanted. 'He's nothing but
a turncoat and quite unreliable,' he cried. 'He will only tell on us
some day; he must be put out of the way.'

The men returned to Jacop's tent, threw the terrified man to the
ground, Lenart Michielsz pinning him down. He was hard to kill.
Hendricxsz broke two knives stabbing Jacop in the chest, then two
more hacking at his neck. Finally, they grabbed a broken knife and
cut his throat. Then they killed the sick boy.

The next night the mutineers again forced Andries de Vries to kill
sick survivors. The next day, though, he made a mistake. He confided in Lucretia Jansz, but talking to her had been forbidden by
Cornelisz. Andries was seen. Cornelisz called Rutger Fredericxsz,
Jan Hendricxsz and Lenart Michielsz to his tent and gave them each
a sword. When they emerged and called to Andries, he ran. He got
as far as the water before he was caught. Lenart Michielsz was the
first to arrive and Andries died from two blows of his sword.

Lucretia was one of several women the men didn't kill. Judick Bastiaensz, Anneken Hardens (wife of Hans Hardens, who had joined the mutineers), Tryntgien and Zussie Fredricx, Anneken Bosschieters and Marretgie Louys – most of them married women, some of them recently widowed by the mutineers – were nevertheless taken to the tents of the men. Judick was the daughter of the minister Gijsbert Bastiaensz, but was forced to submit or face certain death. Only Lucretia received special treatment. She was not taken to the tent of Cornelisz, who flattered himself that he could win her over with charm where the skipper had failed. Despite the likelihood that it would cost her life, Lucretia spurned him just as she had Jacobsz.

On 15 July, Cornelisz turned his attention to the forty people on Seals Island. An expedition set out. They killed most of the men, and spared some of the women and children. Four men got away on pieces of timber, heading for the high islands; others hid. A few days later, the mutineers returned to finish off the survivors. One of them was Mayken Soers, at the time heavily pregnant. Andries Jonas took her by the hand and led her aside. 'Mayken, love, you must die,' he told her. Then he threw her to the ground and cut her throat. Three other women, Laurentia Thomasz, Janeken Gist and Gertje Willemsz, some of them still grieving for their recently murdered husbands, were also killed, as were fifteen children. Only three boys escaped by hiding in the desperately sparse vegetation.

Back on *Batavia*'s Graveyard, not even a cabin-boy was safe. Cornelisz ordered Andries de Bruyn to go out and catch some birds. Then he sent Allert Jansz after him, to cut his throat.

Cornelisz was now the master of all he surveyed, as long as he didn't look towards the high islands where the soldiers had been sent. Shortly after the killings had started the soldiers had lit three fires – the signal that they'd found water on the lower of the two high islands. Cornelisz had been sure there was no water on the islands and that he'd sent them to their deaths. Anyway, the men were too far away, and unarmed, to be able to check his unbridled slaughter. As for any other authority that might have restrained the descent into barbarity, the castaways knew they were on a tiny piece of coral as remote from civilisation as it was possible to get.

The descent reached rock bottom towards the end of July. On 20 July Cornelisz had been employing his skills as an apothecary by poisoning a babe in arms, but he must have been out of practice because by nightfall the child was still fighting for its life, cradled by its mother, Mayken Cardoes. Jacop Pietersz Cosijn went to the tent of one of the few surviving men, a senior officer of the VOC, undermerchant Salomon Deschamps, and called him to attend Mayken Cardoes. When they arrived, Davidt Zevanck, Jan Hendricxsz and Cornelis Pietersz were already there.

'Deschamps,' they told him. 'Here is a half-dead child. You are not a fighting man. Here is a little noose, go over there and fix it, so that we here on the island do not hear so much wailing.'

Faced with death himself, Deschamps did as he was told. The child was torn from its mother's arms, taken outside and strangled. The sounds of Mayken's grief haunted *Batavia*'s Graveyard all that night and into the next day.

Amid such scenes Coenraat van Huyssen invited the minister, Gijsbert Bastiaensz, to dinner. Also invited were Cornelisz and the woman Coenraat had made his concubine, the minister's daughter, Judick. The miserable preacher had no choice but to attend, and try to conceal his anguish. But the meal was only the appetiser. While they ate, Michielsz, Hendricxsz, Wouter Loos, Andries Jonas, Davidt Zevanck, Mattys Beer, Andries Liebent and Jacop Pietersz Cosijn stole to the tent where the preacher's wife, Maria Schepens, their six children and their serving maid, were preparing the evening meal.

First, the men lured the serving maid, Wybrecht Claasz, out of the tent. There Jan Hendricxsz stabbed her and the men watched as she bled to death. Then Davidt Zevanck and the others entered the tent, accusing the occupants of concealing goods stolen from the company. The tent was so crowded that some of the men had to wait outside. Moments later the candle was blown out and those inside the tent started swinging at Maria and the children using carpentry tools, adzes and axes. Lenart Michielsz hammered Maria's skull until she collapsed to the ground, then he turned on one of the children. Mattys Beer bludgeoned Willemyntgie, the middle daughter. When he tried to kill the youngest child, Roelant, the terrified infant ran between his legs. But there was no escape. In the darkness the child ran into another of the men, who killed him. Wouter Loos killed the eldest son. When the commotion was over, the sound was only broken by the groans of two victims who were still alive. Mattys Beer knelt beside Maria and finished battering her to death, then turned to work on the last of her children. Finally the men took the bodies and threw them into a hole they'd dug before the slaughter.

That night, though, the lives of eight innocent people weren't enough. Zevanck ordered Andries Jonas, who'd been left outside the tent, to take care of the grieving Mayken Cardoes. At her tent he called to her, 'Mayken. Are you asleep? Come, we'll go for a walk.'

The terrified woman replied, 'Andries, will you do me evil?'

'No, not at all,' Andries reassured her, so she left her tent and they strolled off across *Batavia*'s Graveyard. They hadn't gone far when Andries pulled out a knife. He threw Mayken to the ground and tried to cut her throat, but she fought back with all her strength. When Andries thrust the knife at her, she defended herself with her hand. The knife stuck straight through, but Mayken kept fighting. Her desperate struggles held off the assault, but the commotion attracted attention. Wouter Loos came running to the scene, armed with an adze. It took both men to overcome Mayken. Loos battered her about the head until she died, then he and Jonas dragged her to the hole where the bodies of the preacher's family were heaped.

Meanwhile, over at the tent of company assistant Hendrick Denys,

Jan Hendricxsz and the other men were calling to him to come outside. He refused, knowing what would happen if he did. So the men
dragged him out, and once again smashed their victim's head in with
adzes and axes.

Still they weren't finished. Allert Jansz called on under-barber
Aris Jansz. 'Aris, come,' he said, 'we have to go and search for birds
for the merchant.' It was a ridiculous pretext and Aris knew it, but
he stepped out of his tent and walked into the darkness with Jansz.
Down on the beach they came upon a group of men, armed with
swords. The first blow came from the man beside him. Jansz struck
him across the shoulders, then the others attacked. Aris ran, all the
time being hacked by his assailants. He got to the water, badly
injured and bleeding severely, and dived beneath the surface. The
men were upon him but in the water and darkness he managed to
stay under long enough to evade them. When he surfaced, he kept
lying low. 'He's had it,' he heard the men say as they turned away.

There may have been one more death that night. At some time
during the killings on *Batavia*'s Graveyard, a terrified boy had
crawled into the tent of Andries Jonas and Jacop Pietersz, on hands
and knees. He told Pietersz he'd seen people being killed that night.
Pietersz woke Jonas and said, 'Andries, drag that boy outside and
help him forth.' Outside the tent, Jonas cut the child's throat.

Later the preacher's cries were heard all over *Batavia*'s Graveyard. 'The parson won't live long either,' Cornelisz muttered.

The next day, the parson continued to grieve. He wrote of his loss:

> . . . some have come to me as I wept very much and said that I ought
> not to do so. [I] Said, that does not matter. [They said] be silent, or you
> go the same way . . . My daughter and I, we both went along as an Ox
> in front of the Axe. Every night I said to my Daughter, you have to look
> tomorrow morning, whether I have been murdered . . . Every day it
> was, What shall we do with that Man? The one would decapitate me,

the other poison me, which would have been the sweeter death; a third said, Let him live a little longer, we might make use of him to persuade the folk on the other Land to come over to us.

What to do about the soldiers was starting to prey on the villains' minds. Cornelisz, however, had other problems. He still couldn't get anywhere with Lucretia. When he could bear it no longer, he complained to Davidt Zevanck.

'And don't you know how to manage that?' Zevanck replied. 'I'll soon make her do it.'

He went to Lucretia's tent and said, 'I hear complaints about you.'

'On what account?' she asked.

'Because you do not comply with the Captain's wishes in kindness,' he replied. 'Now, however, you will have to make up your mind. Either you will go the same way as Wybrecht Claasz [the minister's serving maid], or else you must do that for which we have kept the women.'

He left her in no doubt that she wouldn't live to see another day if she didn't consent. The slaughter she'd seen was proof he'd do what he said. Where Cornelisz's imagined charms had failed, the horrible realities of *Batavia*'s Graveyard succeeded.

Not that Cornelisz's problems were over. There were two that pressed firmly on his state of mind. Sooner or later, a ship was probably going to appear. And over on the high islands, the soldiers steadfastly refused to lie down and die. Cornelisz suspected they now had a boat. The night they killed the preacher's family, a boat had gone missing, probably used by under-barber Aris Jansz to escape. Others had got away on rafts, so the soldiers probably had a strong inkling of what

had gone on in the weeks since they'd been dropped off. Nevertheless, Cornelisz decided to continue his policy of divide and rule. After
the theft of another boat, he sent Daniel Cornelisz with a letter on
23 July to a group of French soldiers on the high islands:

Dear Brethren and Friends, Jean Hongaar, Jean Reynouw de Mirinbry,
Thomas de Villiers, Jean Bonvier and Eduward Coo, the more we consider your faithful and fraternal friendship for us, the more we wonder
that you, who left willingly at the request of me, your merchant captain,
in order to take a survey of the High Island, do not return to report on
your mission, for we have always esteemed you and taken you for our
best and truest brethren and friends, and have continued and still continue to seek your alliance and comradeship, which we hold in as much
esteem as our own lives. But we think it strange that you seem to lean
an ear to the inventions of a few miscreants who had here deserved
death for mutiny, and were therefore sent to another island. They found
their way into your midst without our knowledge. We sent Jean Coos
deSally to the island merely on account of Jean Thiriou, who was sent
because he had drunk out of the casks. For we feared that Jean Coos
might help him. Afterwards we learnt that we misjudged in this, for
Jean Coos offered to stab Jean Thiriou if he might only be allowed to die
with us. Should he still be inclined to do this, it would be an act of
friendship and a service most agreeable to us. Well then, beloved
brethren and friends, return to us, together with Jean Coos, help us in
the cause of justice and in the punishment of the criminals. In particular try to deliver unto us alive those who robbed us so treacherously the
day before yesterday of our chief help, the boat, viz: Lucas, the bottler's
mate; Cornelis, the fat trumpeter; Cornelis, the assistant; deaf Jan
Michielsz, the musketeer; squinting Heynorick; Theumis Claesz, Cornelis Hellincks, and other ship mates who are with you; for unknown to
you they have a compass, with the help of which they intend to leave
secretly, with the boat, for the mainland. The merchant [Jeronimus

Cornelisz] has an especial liking for and confidence in Wiebbe Hayes and wishes that you shall secretly inform him of this. For further details we refer you to the report which bearer, your comrade, Daniel Cornelisz, will give you verbally, if you will give him a safe-guard. Dated the 23rd of July, 1629, on the island *Bataviae*'s Kerckhof.

Cornelisz got no reply. In fact, Daniel Cornelisz didn't return. Two days later, Jeronimus Cornelisz sent two boats with twenty-two armed men to the high islands. As on *Batavia*'s Graveyard, Traitors Island and Seals Island, they would be more than a match for the unarmed inhabitants, even though most of them were soldiers. Cornelisz had some muskets and powder, but he didn't want to waste powder on defenceless people. He had better save them for when the ship returned. So his men rowed into the shallows of the high islands and disembarked with swords drawn. It was hard going, though, as they staggered through the mud-flats around the island.

At last they got close to shore, where they were met by a group of soldiers and . . . they were armed! They'd made pikes from drift-wood, spiked with metal salvaged from barrel-hoops that had drifted ashore. They'd made clubs spiked with nails from the ship's timbers. Faced with such resistance, and the obvious readiness to join battle, the mutineers beat a hasty retreat to the boats.

Cornelisz led another attack before the end of July. Once again, he didn't use his muskets but he came in force – with three boats and thirty-seven men. Lucretia was taken along, to witness his bloody victory. Cornelisz dressed in finery salvaged from the wreck – a red cloak and a tall hat with a feather stuck in it. Many of his men were also gaudily turned out.

Once again, they grounded in the shallows, then staggered through the mudflats to the shore. This time they advanced to a low line of coral cliffs before they made contact with the soldiers.

Suddenly, there was a shout from behind the cliffs. Wiebbe Hayes, until then just a common soldier, yelled an order and the defenders rose from behind the walls and sent a volley of heavy rocks into the mutineers. They were thrown into disarray, gashed, bloodied and pelted as the fusillade continued. The defenders seemed to have an inexhaustible stock of rocks. The mutineers were forced back.

Hayes shouted another order. The defenders went over to the offensive, leaping over their coral walls and charging at the mutineers – stabbing and thrusting, swinging their terrible clubs. Those that survived the onslaught were sent howling back to the boats and rowed for their lives.

The defenders' hoots of derision sent them on their way. Enraged at their humiliation, Cornelisz's men vented their anger on the first defenceless person they found, a surgeon-barber Frans Jansz, who was surviving on a nearby small island.

> Lenart Michielsz has stabbed him right through with a pike, whereupon Hans Jacobsz struck him a blow on the head with a Morning Star, Mattys Beer has split his head with a sword, and Lucas Gellisz has stabbed him with a sword . . . which gruesomeness he could just as well have omitted because the man was already so hacked and stabbed.

Back on Wiebbe Hayes's Island there was jubilation, but the defenders maintained the lookouts and guards they'd stationed since they'd come to believe the horrific tales told by people struggling ashore from the other islands. Among them was Aris Jansz, who'd escaped his attackers despite his terrible wounds.

Wiebbe Hayes had emerged as a natural leader. A veteran VOC mercenary, he acted without hesitation, constructing weapons, piling coral into a stockade, amassing piles of rocks to be used as missiles. He'd intercepted the letter to the French soldiers and perceived that attack was imminent. His only fear was the muskets of the mutineers. He couldn't understand why they hadn't been used. As a soldier, he knew that even such unreliable weapons would be devastating if they were employed.

Now all Cornelisz could do was brood. He was a merchant, an apothecary, and the mutineers' leader, but he wasn't a soldier. He had no idea of how to lead his band of cutthroats against the well-drilled soldiery of Wiebbe Hayes Island. All he could do was continue murdering innocents. On the morning of 6 August, he was sitting in Davidt Zevanck's tent, when he noticed Stoffel Stoffelsz. He was working, despite being near exhaustion due to the demands and poor food given him by the mutineers. Cornelisz called Jan Hendricxsz to the tent, gave him a dagger and said: 'Go and cut out the heart of Stoffel Stoffelsz, that lazy lout, who stands there working as if his back was broken.'

On 16 August, Cornelisz gave his sword to Jan Pelgrom and said: 'Go and try whether it's sharp enough; cut off the head of Cornelisz Aldersz with it.' Pelgrom, hardly more than a boy, couldn't handle the sword so Mattys Beer took off the hapless man's head with a single blow. Pelgrom wept that he'd been denied the opportunity.

One of the few people left alive was the preacher, Bastiaensz. There may have been some sadistic pleasure in seeing the man of God's grief at the loss of his family and at the degradation of his daughter. His mental anguish was matched by his physical misery:

> I ate seal's skins and I put some salt water into the tot of water I was given, so that it would last a little longer. They forbade me to pray and to preach. Most of the time I sat on the beach reading, and there I plucked some salad or grass that was there, and then I had neither Oil nor Vinegar. For two months I tasted neither Bread nor Rice. I have been so weak that I could not get up.

They used him to negotiate with the soldiers on Wiebbe Hayes Island. Cornelisz's chief problem was the possibility that the soldiers could use their boats to warn the rescue ship. Bastiaensz was sent to offer food, clothing (the soldier's clothes were reduced to rags) and cloth for shelter. In exchange, all they had to do was return the little vessels.

While Bastiaensz shuttled back and forth, the bored mutineers took another oath. This time Cornelisz gave himself a promotion.

> We, the undersigned, all here present on this island, being councillors, soldiers, ship's mates and also our minister, nobody whomsoever excepted, accept as our chieftain, as captain-general, Jeronimus Cornelisz, to whom we swear severally and unanimously in the name of God to be faithful and obedient in whatever he shall command us; and whosoever shall do ought to the contrary shall be the Devil's own; herewith we cancel and restrict all previous public and private promises and oaths, comprising all secret comradeships, tent-mateships, and other alliances of whatever name or nature they may be. We further desire that the ship's crew among us shall no longer be called ship's mates, but shall equally with the other soldiers be named and reckoned as belonging to one and the same company. Thus given and signed on the island, named *Batavia*'s Kerckhof, on the 20th of August, 1629.

Clad in the gaudiest finery they had salvaged from the wreck of the *Batavia*, Cornelisz strutted in the grandiose manner of the commander of much more than thirty-six murderers and rapists.

Bastiaensz innocently negotiated with the soldiers who, though in a desperate situation, were still enjoying a better life than he.

> Water sweet as milk. Time would fail me to relate how miraculously God has blessed the good ones who were together with water, with fowls, with fish, with other beasts, with eggs in basketfuls. There were also some beasts they called Cats [small wallabies] with as nice a flavour as I have ever tasted.

During his visits, he managed to win Hayes over, until at the beginning of September, he agreed to the exchange. However, Davidt Zevanck improved on Cornelisz's plan. If he got the chance, he'd offer the French soldiers 6000 guilders each to change sides.

On 2 September, Cornelisz and five of his chiefs rowed to Wiebbe Hayes Island with cloth and lavish promises of good conduct. The ragged defenders accepted the cloth but didn't drop their guard. As Cornelisz dissembled, Zevanck chatted to the French. Offshore, the rest of the mutineers waited in the boats.

The Frenchmen listened for a while, then gave Hayes a signal. 'Treachery!' he cried, and the peace talks ended abruptly. The soldiers leapt on the six men with their pikes and clubs. They killed Zevanck, Coenraat van Huyssen, and two others. Wouter Loos escaped in the skiff. Jeronimus Cornelisz was taken alive. Kicking and screaming at a cunning he thought only he was capable of, he was taken and imprisoned in a compound built from coral blocks. From their boats, the mutineers could only watch as their plans were shattered. The defenders buried the dead and resumed their guard.

Back on *Batavia*'s Graveyard, the mutineers chose a leader from their diminished ranks. Wouter Loos was a soldier and in some ways a more capable leader than Cornelisz. In the absence of Cornelisz, he took possession of Lucretia, but left her to her tent, forbidding anyone to touch her on pain of death. Perhaps he had a sense of honour, perhaps he had a fear of what the viper Cornelisz might do to him if he managed to get free.

Two weeks later, on 17 September, Loos made his move. This time, unlike Cornelisz, he took the muskets. Hayes and the defenders were ready for them, but this time the battle wasn't so even. The mutineers advanced until the defenders came out to meet them, then fired a volley into them. Four men went down. Then the mutineers retreated. They started to reload for their next attack.

This was what Hayes had feared. The muskets could pick them off one by one and there was nothing they could do about it. It was now only a matter of time. Only a miracle could save them. And then there was a shout.

'A sail!' The defenders raised their eyes. 'Look! A sail.'

Some distance away, a ship had appeared.

'Quick, the boat,' Hayes cried. He and three others started running for their craft. They rowed, with the mutineers not far behind, but at least they had a lead. They rowed around the point of one of the small islands and saw a boat pulled up and people on the shore of the other high island. It was Pelsaert. Hayes rowed in and ran to the commodore. 'Return to your ship,' he cried. 'There's a band of miscreants coming in two boats intending to seize the yacht.'

The commodore was incredulous at first, being addressed by a man dressed in rags, but Hayes quickly related what had happened in the previous three months. He had become a captain of forty-seven people, who, to save their lives, had kept all that time on a little island, since some of the people who were left behind had turned scoundrels and murdered some 125 people, being men, women and children. They'd killed four of the villains and taken Cornelisz prisoner; they'd been attacked that day.

Pelsaert may still have had his doubts, but he decided to return to the ship, instructing Hayes to return to Wiebbe Hayes Island and fetch Cornelisz. Then, as the Commodore rowed for the ship, he saw one of the mutineers' boats. The people on board were rowing hard, clearly trying to overtake them. He exhorted his crew to pull faster, while preparing what weapons he had on board for defence. Even if they were caught, they might fight off their attackers.

Moments later the mutineers were close enough to take aim with their muskets. Pelsaert waited for the shot, but the powder burned away from the touchhole of the musket they'd fired. They poured more powder and tried again. Again it misfired. They kept trying, but the musket wouldn't fire. Still they rowed hard for the ship.

The Commodore reached the ship only moments before the mutineers. Pelsaert scrambled aboard the same yacht *Sardam* that had witnessed skipper Jacobsz's drunken spree back in Cape Town many months earlier. He cried to the crew to arm themselves and load the small cannon on deck. As the other boat approached it became increasingly obvious that something was very wrong. Everyone aboard the *Sardam* could see the outrageous dress of the mutineers. It looked like they were being attacked by a boatload of admirals, or the *Heren XVII* themselves.

Now armed to the teeth, Pelsaert called across the water, 'Why do you come on board armed?'

'We'll tell you when we're on deck,' came the reply. The commodore's doubts about Hayes' story evaporated with the insolence from this caricature of authority.

'Throw your weapons into the sea and come across,' the commodore ordered. 'I know how to force you to obedience.'

The thought of being raked by cannon made the attackers realise there was no escape. They did as they were told, and as they came on board, they were put in irons. The ordeal for the survivors of the *Batavia* was over. But for the mutineers, it had just begun.

Their interrogation started immediately and the telling of their story must have horrified Pelsaert. Jan Hendricxsz immediately confessed to killing or helping to kill seventeen or twenty people, under orders of the supercargo, Jeronimus Cornelisz. He confessed that the skipper, supercargo and first boatswain had planned to mutiny, kill the commodore, throw most of the people into the sea, then go pirating. After the ship was wrecked there had then been a plan to kill the commodore during the voyage to Batavia, and for those on the island to reduce the survivors to forty, who would then seize the rescue ship. They'd succeeded in doing this, except for the people with Wiebbe Hayes.

In a time when mutiny and death at sea from poor food and disease was commonplace, nothing Pelsaert had heard before came close to the unbridled barbarism that had occurred around the wreck of the *Batavia*. Of the original complement of some 315 people on the ship, 40 had died of privations, 47 had left for Batavia, 47 had got beyond the villains' reach on Wiebbe Hayes Island. The mutineers themselves numbered 37. Six to eight women had been kept alive to be sexually abused. Of the 135 who remained, they had killed 125. The killing had stopped only when they ran out of victims.

And then there was the mutiny. Back in Batavia, when they'd tortured Jan Evertsz over the assault on Lucretia, he had seemingly confessed everything. Yet he hadn't mentioned a word about mutiny. Evertsz knew they were going to hang him for Lucretia, but if he'd confessed to mutiny, they'd have broken him on the rack first.

The skipper, Ariaen Jacobsz, hadn't mentioned mutiny either. They'd thrown him in prison for 'negligently throwing away his ship.' Now it seemed he'd been plotting for months to kill his commanding officer. Pelsaert had been on the knife edge of death since *Batavia* left Cape Town.

In the afternoon, Jeronimus Cornelisz was brought to the yacht. 'Why have you let the devil lead you so far from all human feeling?' the commodore asked him, unable to comprehend how anyone could betray their position so completely. 'Why have you done that which had never been so cruelly perpetrated among Christians, without any real need of hunger or thirst, solely out of cold bloodthirstiness to attain your wicked ends?'

To which Cornelisz replied:

You shouldn't blame me for what happened. Davidt Zevanck, Coenraat van Huyssen and the others forced me to it, threatening otherwise to take my life. One has often to do a great deal to save oneself. I never intended to seize the vessel *Batavia*, and as to the project of seizing any yacht that should come to our rescue, Zevanck proposed it and I only consented, but without meaning it seriously, since I didn't think we would ever be delivered from these unfortunate islands. I'd heard Ryckert Woutersz say that skipper Ariaen had intended to seize the vessel, if it had not been wrecked, and to throw the commodore overboard, which made me think that they could never have reached Batavia, but that the skipper must have gone to Malacca. Should it have happened that the commodore had reached Batavia, and that a yacht were sent to our rescue, I would have tried to give warning.

Despite his protestations of innocence, and his appeals to the crew of the *Sardam*, they slung him into the hold with the other prisoners. During the night, though, the *Sardam*'s boatswain, Jan Willemsz, overheard Cornelisz talking to Jan Hendricxsz. 'When you were about to fight those on the yacht, why didn't you capture the commodore's boat? Why hadn't your muskets fired; had their powder been wet?'

Hendricxsz answered: 'If we could have fired a musket, we should have captured the boat for a certainty; but the powder burnt away from the touchhole three or four times.'

Then Cornelisz replied, 'If you had used cunning you would easily have conquered while on the water, and then we should have been all right.'

The next morning, Pelsaert took two boats to Wiebbe Hayes Island, armed Wiebbe Hayes and some of his men, and headed for *Batavia*'s Graveyard. When the remaining mutineers saw them approach, they offered no resistance. They threw down their weapons and prepared to die. Instead, Pelsaert took them prisoner. He gathered the company's valuables, which were scattered around the island. These included the contents of the casket of jewels, all of which were eventually recovered.

In the ensuing days, Pelsaert salvaged most of the treasure from the ship, scoured the islands for as much material from the wreck as he could find, hoping that his diligence would mitigate the storm that would erupt on his return to Batavia with news of the disaster that had taken place in part due to his absence. During the salvage, though, the high seas swept away one of the *Sardam*'s boats, and her skipper and three crew were never seen again.

Pelsaert decided it was too risky to take the worst offenders back to Batavia. The poisonous Cornelisz, in particular, might turn the *Sardam*'s crew to mutiny, especially with the extraordinary treasure from the *Batavia* wreck on board to tempt them. In a signed resolution, particular attention was given to the fact that: 'Jeronimus Cornelisz is not only tainted with abominable crimes, but has moreover adopted a most abominable creed, maintaining that there is neither devil nor hell, and trying to inculcate this belief on his comrades, thereby corrupting them all.' Pelsaert may have looked at Cornelisz and believed the devil was real, and had become flesh. And as the people of the *Batavia* had found, he was more deadly than any peril of the sea. Trial and sentence were to be carried out on the islands.

The Dutch system of justice was crude by modern standards, but effective. If there was sufficient presumption of guilt, torture was permitted to obtain the truth. However, guilt could only be established by a free confession, made at least a day after the torture. In addition the statements made under torture by several people had to be consistent with each other. The torture continued until they were.

On *Batavia*'s Graveyard, the torture was simpler than the rack, which dislocated the victim's joints, one by one. It was known as the water cure. A piece of canvas was tied around the victim's neck, then the fabric was pulled up around the face. Water was poured in and the victim was forced to drink or drown. But the more the victim drank, the more the torturers poured. The bodies of stubborn subjects eventually became hideously distended by the volume of water they drank. However, most of the prisoners confessed freely. There was little point in lying, given the evidence of their crimes strewn across the islands and the testimony of the few survivors, such as the minister Bastiaensz. The exception was Cornelisz.

He confessed under torture, then denied that which he'd confessed. He was tortured again. When he was confronted by his accomplices and their confessions, he called them liars. The torture and retractions continued from 19 September to 28 September. Then he was bound again, ready to be tortured and asked why he kept changing his story. He was confronted by his co-conspirators once more and they vowed that 'they had not aggravated his guilt in any way. If they had, they were willing to burden their own salvation with it; they would die for it and answer for it on the day of judgement.'

Pelsaert asked: 'Why have you mocked the council with your unpardonable vacillations, speaking the truth one moment and denying it the next?'

Cornelisz answered: 'I only did it to lengthen my life; but I have done enough wrong and cannot escape my punishment.'

Sentence was passed. Cornelisz was to be taken to Seals Island, have both hands cut off, then be hanged. Everything he owned was confiscated by the company. Jan Hendricxsz, Lenart Michielsz, Mattys Beer and Allert Jansz were to have their right hands cut off, then be hanged. Jan Pelgrom, Andries Jonas and Rutger Fredericxsz were to be hanged. Wouter Loos and many other minor mutineers were to be questioned and examined further, with sentence to be passed on the voyage and at Batavia. Pelsaert also decreed that Wiebbe Hayes receive a promotion, to the rank of sergeant, with a pay of 18 guilders a month.

The executions were to be carried out on 1 October, the day after the Sabbath. But they were delayed. First Cornelisz begged to be baptised, hoping this would buy him time. He was baptised but given no more time. Then he threatened that God would perform a miracle to save him from the gallows. During the night he took poison, but as with the child of Mayken Cardoes, it wasn't strong enough to kill him. As Pelsaert observed: 'He had to be got out of his prison certainly twenty times during the night because his so-called miracle was working from below as well as from above.'

Even so, Cornelisz got a brief reprieve. On the day of the executions the weather was so bad it wasn't possible to row across to the gallows that had been erected on Seals Island. They had to wait. The next day the weather was fine and the execution party assembled. On Seals Island, Cornelisz's accomplices demanded that he be hanged first, so they could see the death of the man who had tempted them to their fate. Some cried 'revenge.' Cornelisz cried that he would have his revenge on Judgement Day. They cut off his hands and hanged him anyway.

One of the condemned did manage to cheat the gallows. Jan Pelgrom, the eighteen-year-old steward who'd wept at his inability to behead a man became so distraught that he couldn't mount the gallows. He was such a pitiful sight that Pelsaert relented, much to the disgust of many of those present.

Most of the other prisoners begged to be sentenced on the islands. They feared what the governors in Batavia would do to them, with ample justification. Pelsaert did pass sentence on many, with punishments including keel-hauling, a hundred lashes, and dropping from the mast. Many considered this merciful.

The *Sardam* finally left the Abrolhos on 15 November 1629. Along the way many of the punishments were carried out. Wouter Loos (Cornelisz's successor as leader of the mutineers) and Jan Pelgrom were shown extraordinary leniency. They were marooned on the mainland, with a boat, supplies and gifts for the indigenous people. In subsequent years, ships were asked to look out for them, but they were never seen again.

The *Sardam* dropped anchor in the Batavia Roads on 5 December and the news she brought broke like a thunderclap that rolled around the world. The horrified governors retried most of the remaining prisoners and sentence was carried out on 30 January 1630. Jacop Pietersz Cosijn, for example, was 'broken from under upwards and the body exposed on a wheel.' Then they hanged him.

Scapegoats were sought. Antonio van Diemen, a councillor in Batavia who later became the Governor-General and sent Abel Tasman to explore the Australian coast, wrote: 'It is certain that a completely Godless and evil life has been conducted on the mentioned ship of which both the skipper and the President Pelsaert are greatly guilty.'

Jacobsz was in gaol, being tortured, and the last reference to him shows him resisting his gaolers two years later. There is no record of his eventual fate. Pelsaert died only a year after his return, in September 1630, from a combination of tropical disease, grief and overwork. Some 80 per cent of staff in the East Indies died from the hours they worked. However, Pelsaert's entitlements were withheld by the company when his mother applied for them in 1632.

The Batavia governors also overturned Pelsaert's promotion of Wiebbe Hayes to sergeant on 18 guilders a month. They made him a commissioned officer instead, on 40 guilders. He became a hero of his time, with a reputation that has endured to the present day. His ultimate fate is unknown.

Gijsbert Bastiaensz remarried in 1631, but died in 1633. His daughter, Judick, remarried twice in the two years following the wreck, but was widowed both times. She was eventually given 300 guilders by the *Heren XVII*, as widow's assistance, plus 300 guilders for her ordeal. Such generosity from the hard men of the VOC was unheard of.

Lucretia learned that her husband had died in the East Indies when Pelsaert arrived on the *Sardam*. She eventually remarried, but there is no record of her having any children. However, she is known to have lived to a ripe old age.

The story of the *Batavia* has become the most enduring in maritime history. The site lay undiscovered for nearly 340 years. However, in 1840 when British Navy surveyors on HMS *Beagle* mapped the Abrolhos, they found a very old wreck on one of the southern islands and accordingly named it Pelsaert's Island. In fact it was a different wreck (the *Zeewyk*, lost in 1727, which confused researchers for more than a century after).

In the 1950s, a Western Australian woman, Henrietta Drake-Brockman, conducted meticulous research into the *Batavia* that pointed searchers in the right direction. From the accounts she uncovered (and had translated from old Dutch), she pieced together the wreck's true location. One of her sources was Pelsaert's own journal. Through her research, Drake-Brockman concluded the wreck couldn't be in the southern Abrolhos. The 'cats' the survivors ate were wallabies, which were only found in the northern Wallabi Group. Plus Wiebbe Hayes had found water in wells on Wiebbe Hayes Island. This only existed on East and West Wallabi Island. Accordingly she thought the wreck site would be on Noon Reef, in the Wallabis. When it was located by Max Kramer in June 1963, it was on Morning Reef, only a few kilometres away.

The site was first explored by Hugh Edwards, David Johnson and others and has been extensively excavated by the Western Australian Maritime Museum. It has proved to be one of the most potent examples of the archaeological value of shipwrecks in Australian waters. Among the items found in and around the wreck, a 400-year-old time capsule, are early navigation instruments, ceramics and coins. Most spectacular, sandstone blocks for a portico for Batavia Castle have been recovered and pieced together in the Western Australian Maritime Museum in Geraldton, the fishing town on the mainland nearest the wreck site, which is 60 kilometres offshore. Timbers, including a large piece of the stern section, have been erected and are also on display in Fremantle. Other fascinating artefacts are Beardman or Bellarmine jugs. It was Cardinal Bellarmine (1542–1621) who instigated proceedings against Galileo for teaching that the earth was round and revolved around the sun. His efforts against Protestants led ale houses to lampoon him by casting jugs caricaturing his likeness. And the jugs found their way to the antipodes without sailing off the edge of the world.

Today the *Batavia* story has become a tangible experience in the form of a replica built in a dedicated shipyard in Holland between 1985 and 1995. A team of apprentices and master shipwright Willem Vos used traditional methods and historical research to construct the vessel, including the vital clues provided by the remains of the wreck found in the Abrolhos. Remarkably, the ship was built without the help of any original plans, because when the original *Batavia* was built, in only seven months, the shipwrights used their practical knowledge rather than blueprints. In 1999, the new ship was brought to Australia in a specially designed container vessel where she was rigged, ballasted and underwent sea trials.

In December 1999, the people of Sydney turned out to welcome *Batavia* for her extended visit to the Australian National Maritime Museum at Darling Harbour. As she passed up the Sydney Harbour, escorted by fire-tugs sending up curtains of water and dozens of spectator craft, she made a magnificent spectacle. Her mast was so tall she had to pass under the Harbour Bridge at dead low tide. She marked the occasion with shot from her cannon.

On her ill-fated maiden voyage she was one of the wonders of her age. Nothing had changed 400 years later. She can now be seen at *Batavia* Werf, at Lelystad in the Netherlands.

It is a comment on the ability of the Dutch navigators that after *Batavia*'s wreck only three other vessels are known to have come to

grief on Western Australia's coasts. They were highly skilled in reading the oceans' currents, depth, weed, the presence of sea and land
birds, and anything else that might give clues to their position.

In April 1656 the *Vergulde Draeck* (*Gilt Dragon*) was wrecked on
a reef six kilometres off the coast near the town of Ledge Point
(approximately 80 kilometres north of Perth). From a complement of
193, 118 drowned and 75 landed on the mainland. A ship's boat
with 7 survivors made it to Batavia on 7 June. Search vessels were
sent out, resulting in more casualties. The *Goede Hoop* lost eleven
crew when they went ashore and didn't return. The *Waeckende Boey*
abandoned fourteen crew in the ship's boat. The sixty-eight *Vergulde
Draeck* survivors left behind were never seen again. After the wreck
a standing order was given that commanders must stay with the
people at the wreck and send junior officers for help. The wreck was
ultimately discovered by Graeme, Jim and Alan Henderson, John
Cowen and Alan Robinson in April 1963.

In 1712, the *Zuytdorp* went onto the rocks of the mainland
60 kilometres north of the town of Kalbarri. She carried a fortune in
silver which fused to form a famous 'carpet of silver' on the ocean
bottom. The wreck site was known from the 1920s, but identified in
the 1950s and explored in the 1960s. Much of the silver was eventually plundered. No survivors from the wreck made it to Batavia,
but evidence at the site suggests many people made it to shore and
may have mingled with the local Aboriginal population. Two rare
genetic diseases, found only in some Dutch descendants at the Cape
and in Dutch-founded communities in the USA, have also been noted
in the local Aboriginal population.

The last wreck was the *Zeewyk* in July 1727, on the south-
western side of the Houtman Abrolhos. The longboat was sent to
Batavia to raise the alarm, but was never heard from again. In
October the *Zeewyk*'s officers despaired of its return, and having
salvaged all the ship's treasure, they built another boat from the

wreck of the ship and any timbers that came to hand. The *Sloepie* (*Little Sloop*) took four months to build and set sail on 26 March 1728, with eighty-eight crew and three tonnes of coin. It arrived in Batavia on 30 April, with eighty-two survivors.

There may be other ships lying undiscovered along the Western Australian coast. Ships that disappeared without trace include: the *Ridderschap van Holland*, lost in 1694; the *Fortuyn*, lost in 1724; and the *Aagtekerke*, in 1726. Expeditions were mounted to search for such vessels, notably in 1697 when Willem de Vlamingh led an expedition to find the *Ridderschap van Holland*. Such expeditions also sought to ascertain whether there were any places suitable for settlement or setting up trade, but, while de Vlamingh found the site of Perth and the Swan River, no report led to Dutch settlement. The experience further north was particularly daunting. The land was desolate, almost waterless and populated by a people who gave every appearance of waging a constant battle for survival. The north-west corner of Australia is the edge of one of the harshest environments on earth, one that hides its treasures well. Two centuries after the wreck of the *Batavia*, pearls, abalone, rock lobsters, iron ore, diamonds and stupendous quantities of gold were found in a country that brought ships in droves. And when they came they found that the coasts were as unforgiving as they'd been when the shipwrecked *Batavia* met her terrible fate.

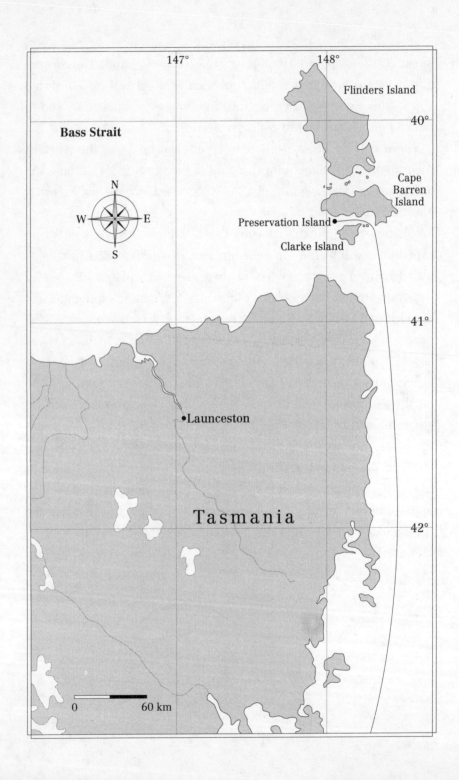

The supply vessel *Borrowdale*, believed
to be similar to the *Sydney Cove*
(Australian National Maritime Museum)

3. THE LONG GOODBYE: *SYDNEY COVE*, 1797

The merchant vessel *Sydney Cove* may well hold the record for the longest time a ship has taken to go to the bottom. She first sprang a leak on 13 December 1796, in the middle of the Indian Ocean. According to an account in Calcutta's *Asiatic Mirror* a year later:

In lat. 15 degrees 30 seconds south, [the vessel] experienced a severe gale of wind, with a heavy sea. The weather continued variable, generally with strong gales and a high sea, till towards the middle of January. During this time the ship laboured much from the violence of the weather, making from six to eight inches [15 to 20 centimetres] of water in an hour. The leak was judged to be under the starboard bow. In order to get at it the forehold was unstowed. The rushing in of the water was distinctly heard; but the leak could not be reached, owing to its being seated at the back of a timber.

The *Sydney Cove* was bound for the tiny colony at the port she was named after. At the time, Sydney, established in 1788, was the only European settlement in the entire continent, despite Australia having been known to Europeans for the previous 182 years. In all that time, the enormous distance, terrible calamities like that of the *Batavia* and the reports of the inhospitable terrain had meant that in European eyes it remained Terra Nullius – No Man's Land.

However, the world of the 1790s was very different from that of the 1620s. The word 'revolution' had entered the language and was changing the political map of the world. In England, the Industrial Revolution was causing massive population movement from the countryside to the rapidly swelling cities, bringing with it soaring crime rates.

On the high seas, English sea power had grown until it could claim that Britannia ruled the waves. The British Admiralty's offer of £20 000 as a prize for devising a method for determining longitude at sea had lead to John Harrison's development of the chronometer in 1761. James Cook came to call it 'my trusty friend the watch', but did not have its help on his first great voyage in 1770 when he went to observe the transit of Venus in Tahiti. While he was there he became the first navigator known to explore the east coast of Australia. Shipwrecked there, briefly, when he went aground in the midst of the Great Barrier Reef near Cooktown, Queensland, he managed to continue his voyage after jettisoning cannon, then beaching his ship, the barque *Endeavour*, for repairs.

Back in England, the changing social and political climate combined to give Cook's reports a ready audience. The British had been using the USA as a dumping ground for convicts, but the American Revolution had closed that avenue. The government was on the lookout for a godforsaken place to which it could send the refuse of England's society. The Great South Land beckoned.

The penal colony at Sydney Cove was established in 1788 with the arrival of the First Fleet, a motley collection of eleven vessels containing some 1350 soldiers and convicts. It is one of the great feats of maritime survival that every one of the leaky, worm-ridden ships made the distance. However, as soon as the colony was established, it struck its fundamental problem – supply. Vessels coming to the colony were few and far between, which in part explains why, in the years before the ship *Sydney Cove* got into trouble, there were only two shipwrecks. There weren't that many ships to wreck.

The first wreck was the First Fleet's flagship, HMS *Sirius*, Captain Hunter master, in 1790. However, her loss wasn't so much a question of if, as of when. Some years earlier, she'd caught fire and burnt to the waterline, but rather than abandon the ruined hulk, the Admiralty rebuilt her. The contractor who did the work cut plenty of corners. On her voyage to Sydney, the crew checked her planking below the waterline and found timbers that were supposed to be new were already rotten. Despite this, in October 1788, the *Sirius* was sent from Sydney Cove to Cape Town to procure supplies. Hunter extended the roaring forties strategy of the Brouwer Route, heading as far as 57 degrees south, and heading east across the Pacific to Cape Horn, then on across the Atlantic to Cape Town. *Sirius* made it back to Sydney, only to be blown onto a reef on Norfolk Island on 19 March 1790, while trying to land cargo. She'd tried to sail for open water, but her hull was so fouled with weed that she barely responded to the helm. The crew and most of the cargo was saved.

The second wreck didn't involve the colony at all. It was that of HMS *Pandora* in 1791. The twenty-four-gun frigate was carrying fourteen of HMS *Bounty*'s mutineers, captured in Tahiti after they'd obliged Captain William Bligh to undertake a 5750-kilometre voyage to Batavia, through Torres Strait, in an open boat. *Pandora*, under Captain

Edward Edwards, struck the Great Barrier Reef at what is now known as Pandora's Entrance (200 kilometres south of Cape York) and sank, drowning thirty-one crew and four mutineers. Seven more mutineers might have died, confined in a stifling cell on deck, but for a crew-member who disobeyed Edwards' orders and threw the doomed men the keys to the locks as the ship went down (the remaining three had already been released to man the pumps). There were ninety-nine survivors, most of whom eventually made it to Batavia in open boats.

What particularly discouraged trade with the colony, apart from the incredible distances, was that for the ships involved it was a one-way business. They brought goods in, but they sailed away empty, because the colony was barely able to support itself, let alone produce goods for export. To alleviate the situation, permission was given in 1790 for the colony in Sydney to trade with ports closer than England, which led to several vessels venturing from India with speculative cargoes. One of them was the *Sydney Cove*. Her voyage was prompted by reports received in 1796 from another vessel belonging to her agents, Campbell and Clark. Captain James Storey arrived at Calcutta from Sydney in May, reporting that the colony was prospering. The reality was quite different, but it didn't stop Campbell and Clark organising another ship and cargo to send to Sydney. The vessel was the *Begum Shaw*, renamed *Sydney Cove*, a two-decked, three-masted ship which, according to a 1794 sales notice in the *Calcutta Gazette*, was '500 bags of rice burthen, well found, a remarkably fast sailer, new sheathed and coppered up to the bends and having undergone very considerable repairs about twelve months before at Mr Glass's yard.'

Her skipper was Captain Guy Hamilton, who may also have had an interest in her as he'd been involved in the attempt to sell her in 1794. The crew included chief mate Hugh Thompson, six other European crew and assistant supercargo William Clark, nephew of one of the company's partners and only recently arrived in India.

ere forty-four Indian sailors, known as
mong shipowners because they were
en.

10 November 1796 with a cargo that
ohol – mainly rum (Campbell and Clark
beer, wines, champagne, gin and brandy.
ar, tobacco, salted meat, tea and china
m), tar, vinegar, shoes, soap, candles and
mber of live cattle and horses, plus one
uropean.

tarted on 13 December, *Sydney Cove* con-
nd even chose the longer, though fastest,
ld Brouwer Route, heading due south into
the giant sou........ng gales of the roaring forties before turning
east to track beneath Australia to Van Diemen's Land. As she went,
they attempted to 'fother' the leak, by spreading a piece of a sail with
a pad of thick material sown onto it over the leak from outside the
hull, then firmly lashing the sail to the boat so the action of the sea
wouldn't displace it. The first attempts to do this failed in the big
seas. The 'thrummed' sail was torn to shreds.

Meanwhile, the crew manned the pumps. The work was constant,
and the inefficient 'common' pump was so exhausting a crewman
could only work it for five minutes before needing relief. Yet the ship
sailed on through December and into January, in latitudes around
42 degrees south, with the crew working the pump around the clock.
Thousands of kilometres from land, it was a battle of endurance they
couldn't afford to lose.

At last, on 13 January: 'a thrummed sail was got over the starboard bow, and passed under the bottom, which reduced the leak
from 6 to 4 inches [15 to 10 centimetres] an hour.'

It didn't mean the crew had to stop pumping, but the work got
a little easier. Unfortunately, the respite was short-lived. On 25 January,

Sydney Cove was hit by 'a gale of extreme violence'. While furling sails, second mate Leisham was flung into the sea from the main topsail yardarm. The ship was blowing away from him and in the wild conditions it was impossible to turn back. He was never seen again; though, in the icy southern ocean, his survival time would have been mercifully short. Assuming he didn't drown, hypothermia would have taken him in a matter of hours.

Meanwhile, on *Sydney Cove* the wind was so strong it tore three sails that had been 'handed' (furled and securely stowed on the yards) to shreds. The ship now hove to without any sail, at the mercy of the sea.

> The gale continued, and the sea running dreadfully high, caused the ship to labour greatly and the leak to increase. The weather was intensely cold, with constant rain, from which the crew suffered considerably. The lascars were well supplied with blankets and warm clothing, shipped on purpose at Bengal; yet they were so benumbed by the severity of the weather that neither entreaty nor force could prevail on them to work on deck at the pumps.

Four weeks at the pump was taking its toll as well. The crew were eventually forced on deck and the hatches locked to stop them going back below, but they still refused to work in the appalling conditions. The water, however, was soon over a metre deep in the hold, so they didn't need to use the pump. They could go below and bail from there. Out of the weather, the crew threw themselves into the task and by noon the following day they'd got the water in the hold down to a depth of half a metre.

However, everyone had to keep pumping and bailing as the storm raged on. During the afternoon, one of the lascars at the pump collapsed from exhaustion. When he didn't get up, his colleagues tried to raise him, but to no avail: he was dead.

Sydney Cove had been at sea for two-and-a-half months, more than long enough for the symptoms of scurvy (caused by poor nutrition) to become obvious in the crew. One of its symptoms is circulatory failure. Consequently, a scurvy sufferer should avoid extreme physical exertion, but the crew of the *Sydney Cove* had no choice in the matter. They kept at the pumps all afternoon and into the night as crewman after crewman collapsed. During the long hours of that relentless storm, five men died.

Dawn on 27 January saw *Sydney Cove* still afloat and the gale easing enough that she was able to put up her foresail and continue on her course. The water was coming in at 25 to 30 centimetres an hour and the crew – barely able to help themselves, let alone the ship – were still far from any landfall. They managed to get another thrummed sail over the bow and the following day had got the leak down to 20 centimetres an hour. It was still too much, and the water in the hold slowly gained on the pumps and men.

Finally, on 1 February, *Sydney Cove* sighted land. According to accounts of the voyage, it was in latitude 40 degrees 1 minute south. If so, it could only be the south-west tip of King Island, at the opening of Bass Strait. Except in 1797 no-one knew the Strait was there. It was believed that Van Diemen's Land, now known as Tasmania, was the southern extremity of the mainland (the Dutchman Abel Tasman had mapped part of it during a voyage that circled the Great South Land and New Zealand in 1642 and, from his time to that of English navigator Matthew Flinders, the continent was known as 'New Holland').

Accordingly *Sydney Cove* turned south, to round Van Diemen's Land. When she did so, she was just over 1000 kilometres from Sydney. Rounding Van Diemen's Land added an extra 700 kilometres to the already ill-fated voyage, and took *Sydney Cove* into some of the most vicious seas on earth. Even so, she managed to round the south-east corner of Van Diemen's Land and finally started heading north. Limping into the teeth of yet another gale, she passed Maria Island, off the Van Diemen's Land coast, on 4 February.

From then until 7 February, another gale built until *Sydney Cove*
was again without sail. On 8 February:

> The gale now increased to a perfect hurricane, with a dreadful sea. At
> half-past 3 p.m. sprung a new leak, which gained so fast on the pumps
> as rendered it necessary to bear up for land to save the lives of the
> people, and, if possible, to get the ship into a place of security. Bore in
> accordingly for the land and made more sail, Cape Barras [Barren] by
> accounts West half North or West and by North, distant by accounts
> 90 miles [150 kilometres].

Below the waterline, *Sydney Cove* was literally falling to pieces.
The ad for the 1794 sale of the *Sydney Cove* (when she was known
as the *Begum Shaw*) had mentioned she'd had her timbers below the
waterline sheathed in copper (to deter marine borers). *Sydney Cove*
had been built with iron nails fixing her timbers. In seawater, copper
and iron react. Over time, the iron disintegrates. And once the nails
start to go, there's nothing holding the ship together.

As *Sydney Cove* headed for 'Van Diemen's Land' (on the eastern
side of Bass Strait, south of Flinders Island), the crew started throwing cargo overboard. 'At 5 p.m. there were 2½ feet [75 centimetres]
of water in the well, and hourly gaining. At 8 p.m. the water had
increased to 5 feet [1.5 metres], and the ship settling fast, the longboat was got clear – still running west and carrying a press of sail in
order to get in with the land.'

By midnight, the water had all but filled the lower deck. Half an
hour later, *Sydney Cove* sighted land about two miles (three kilometres) away. However, all the crew could make out was cliffs and
heavy surf. So they hove to and pumped all night. At dawn, the water
was over the hatches of the lower deck, the ship leaning to one side.
She barely answered the helm as the crew put on all sail and headed
for land, a group of islands close at hand. When they were close to

shore they hove the lead, but didn't find the bottom at 75 fathoms [137 metres]. A little closer in, they suddenly found bottom at 15 fathoms [27 metres]. The longboat was got out and sent ashore on one of the islands, with rice, ammunition and guns. The ship wallowed behind, finally fetching up on a sandy bottom. The rudder was torn off by the impact as the vessel ground to a halt. The men stopped working the pump. It was 9 February: *Sydney Cove* had taken two whole months to sink.

Ironically, since she'd turned south from King Island *Sydney Cove* had managed to cover 1000 kilometres of ocean, far enough to have reached Sydney if she'd known to keep going east through Bass Strait. Instead, she was still some 825 kilometres south-west of her destination, but she wasn't going anywhere.

The crew landed on the larger of two islands close at hand, which they called 'Preservation Island.' As they started salvaging what they could from the wreck, the rum was stored on the smaller island, out of temptation's way. It became known as 'Rum Island.' The islands were searched for water but none was found. Eventually a well was dug that supplied water – brackish but drinkable. The crew threw up makeshift tents, though most of their efforts were devoted to salvaging the wreck and preparing the longboat to go to Sydney for help.

On 27 February, the longboat was ready. Perhaps having learned the lessons of ships like *Batavia* 168 years before, Captain Hamilton stayed with the wreck. Chief mate Hugh Thompson, assistant supercargo William Clark, the ship's carpenter, two European seamen and twelve lascars set out across Bass Strait.

The disasters which had dogged *Sydney Cove* now followed the longboat. It managed to get across Bass Strait and on 1 March got an observation that put them at 38 degrees south. They had covered about 350 kilometres and were just off the coast of Ninety Mile Beach, 475 kilometres south-west of Sydney, when they were hit by yet another storm. 'On the evening of this day it began to blow, and

soon increased to a stormy gale, with a heavy sea, by which the boat
was in great danger of foundering. They were at an inconsiderable
distance from the shore, but the surf broke with such violence as to
prevent the possibility of approaching with safety.'

The crew dropped two anchors to try and hold the longboat out
of the breakers. They were right on the corner of the continent, where
the massive waves and current from the west met the counter-
current and mighty surge of the South Pacific. Where the two oceans
collide, the turbulence is monumental. The crew spent a terrifying
night on the fringe of the enormous breakers that were lifting out of
the depths and rolling onto the beach from hundreds of metres out.
Some broke over the longboat, but she managed to hang on.

Their luck held till morning, when the crew cut the anchor cables, set
sail and tried to make for the open sea. It was a disastrous move. The
boat was carried closer to shore, where it got caught by a breaking
wave, and completely filled. Though swamped, the crew tried to get in
to land through the surf. They managed to get ashore, but the boat was
lifted in the shore break and smashed into the sand. It broke up quickly.
The crew were able to salvage some supplies, but were left standing
on a beach 450 kilometres from Sydney as the crow flies. There were
no roads, the country around them was completely unexplored, and it
was peopled by indigenous Australians, most of whom had never seen
white people, but whose attitude could well be hostile. They lingered
on the beach for two weeks, collecting what they could from the longboat before deciding to walk to Sydney.

Assistant supercargo William Clark took notes, which provide
fascinating insights into the first contact many Aboriginal communities of the south coast had with Europeans passing through their
country. On 18 March, Clark writes:

We this day fell in with a party of natives, about fourteen, all of them
entirely naked. They were struck with astonishment at our appearance,

and were very anxious to examine every part of our clothes and body, in which we readily indulged them . . .

The natives of this part of the coast appear strong and muscular, with heads rather large in proportion to their bodies. The flat nose, the broad thick lips which characterise the African, also prevail amongst the people on this coast. Their hair is long and straight, but they are wholly inattentive to it, either as to cleanliness or in any other respect. It serves them in lieu of a towel to wipe their hands as often as they are daubed with blubber or shark oil, which is their principal article of food. This frequent application of grease to their heads and bodies renders their approach exceedingly offensive. Their ornaments consist chiefly of fish-bones or kangaroo-teeth, fastened with gum or glue to the hair of the temples and on the forehead. A piece of reed or bone is also worn through the septum, or cartilage, of the nose, which is pierced for the admission of this ornament.

The party journeyed on, sometimes passing through country they found park-like and beautiful, seeing in the distance the massive bulk of the Great Dividing Range. The principal obstacle was rivers, some of which necessitated constructing rafts to cross. On 29 March:

On crossing a narrow but deep river, one of the natives threatened to dispute our landing, but approaching with a determined appearance no actual resistance was attempted, and a reconciliation was effected by the distribution of a few strips of cloth. A good understanding being thus established, the men called to their wives and children, who were concealed behind the rocks, and who now ventured to shew themselves. These were the first women we had seen; from their cries and laughing it is evident they were greatly astonished at our appearance. The men did not think proper to admit of our coming sufficiently near to have a full or perfect view of their ladies, but we were near enough to discern that they were the most [w]retched objects we had ever seen.

[The next day] We came to a pretty large river, which, being too deep to ford, we began to prepare a raft, which we could not have completed till next day, had not three of our native friends, from whom we parted yesterday, rejoined us and assisted us over. We were much pleased with their attention, for the act was really kind, as they knew we had this river to cross, and appear to have followed us purposely to lend their assistance.

They met five Aborigines from the same group on 2 April. Not only were they friendly, they gave the straggling band some shellfish to supplement their diet. The next day they found themselves in difficult terrain: thick bush studded with sharp rocks and tree stumps that left them bruised and weary. Two of their party became separated as they struggled forward, sometimes on their hands and knees. The party waited for the missing two the next day and were overjoyed when they caught up.

On 8 April, they faced their most serious threat to date, after crossing yet another river.

We had scarce surmounted this difficulty when a greater danger stared us in the face, for here we were met by about fifty armed natives. Having never before seen so large a body collected, it is natural to conclude that we were much alarmed. However, we resolved to put the best appearance on the matter, and to betray no symptoms of fear. In consequence of the steps we took, and after some preliminary signs and gestures on both sides, we came to some understanding, and the natives were apparently amicable in their designs. We presented them with a few yards of calico, for they would not be satisfied with small strips, and, indeed, we were glad to get rid of them at any expense, for their looks and demeanour were not such as to invite greater intimacy.

[On 9 April] We were again alarmed at the approach of the party who detained us yesterday and whom we so justly suspected of treacherous intentions. They came on with dreadful shoutings, which gave us warning to prepare for defence, and to give them a warm reception in case violence should be offered. Fortunately, however, from the particular attention we paid to their old men, whom we supposed to be their chiefs, and making them some small presents, they soon left us.

The next day they were accosted again, by a smaller group from the party of the previous two days. Armed with a gun, two pistols, two small swords and a variety of clubs they prepared to defend themselves, but the attack still didn't come. They managed to exchange a piece of cloth for a kangaroo tail 'with which we endeavoured to make some soup, by adding a little of the rice we had remaining, from which we received great nourishment, being much weakened by the fatigue and want which we had suffered in these inhospitable regions.'

On 11 April, they fell in with a new group of Aborigines.

We met fourteen natives, who conducted us to their miserable abodes in the wood adjoining to a large lagoon, and kindly treated us with mussels . . . These people seemed better acquainted with the laws of hospitality than any of their countrymen whom we had yet seen, for to their benevolent treat was added an invitation to remain with them for the night . . . As far as we could understand, these natives were of a different tribe from those we had seen, and were then at war with them. They possessed a liberality to which the others were strangers, and freely gave us a part of the little they had . . .

Clark hadn't lost his sense of humour. The next day the party found a dead skate, 'which, though a little tainted, would not have been unacceptable to an epicure with our appetite.'

On 13 April, they met another group of Aborigines, who, over the next few days, took them across several rivers in canoes.

This was not accomplished without several duckings, for their rude little vehicles formed of bark, tied at both ends with twigs, and not exceeding 8 feet [2.4 metres] in length, by 2 [0.6 metres] in breadth, are precarious vessels for one unacquainted with them to embark in, though the natives, of whom they will carry three or four, paddle about in them with the greatest facility and security.

The help they received may have been offered because the party was by now obviously in desperate circumstances. Already worn down by three desperate months at sea, they were ill-fed and exhausted by the daily marches and river crossings. On 16 April, nine of the party were unable to go any further. Clark continued with those who could, all of them hoping the others would follow later, but knowing deep in their hearts that their chances of survival were practically nil. The stronger party loitered with the natives, collecting herbs and picking shellfish off the rocks, but the others were never seen again.

The next day they nearly lost the chief mate, Hugh Thompson, while crossing another river.

> We found an old canoe on the bank, in which three or four of our party got to the other side, and proceeded on their journey. Mr Thomson, who could not swim, in making an effort to cross, was left struggling in the water by the canoe sinking under him. This was witnessed by four Bengal blacks, who, though they were adepts at swimming, stood unmoved spectators. I instantly jumped in and flew to his relief, although very much fatigued and very cold. I seized him by the hair and drew him to the shore motionless. My first care was to place him over a rock with his head downwards, pressing him at the same time on the back, by which means he discharged much sea-water by the mouth, and in a little time recovered.

On 20 April, the group again fell in with Aborigines who fed the stricken men as much as they could. On 26 April they met another group to whom they indicated that they were hungry and exhausted. The locals brought them enough fish to satisfy their hunger, plus some to take with them. Later in the day, they met a war party of fifty, whom they managed to calm with gifts before passing on. Their relief was short-lived.

> We had not parted more than twenty or thirty minutes when a hundred more approached us, shouting and hallowing in a most hideous manner, at which we were all exceedingly alarmed. In a short time a few of them began throwing their spears, upon which we made signs to them to desist, giving them some presents, and appearing no ways dismayed at their conduct – any other demeanour on our part would have been quite superfluous, having only one musket unloaded and two pistols out of repair, and at best were only six opposed to such a multitude, for our little company were daily dropping off. No sooner had we turned our backs on this savage mob than they renewed hostilities and wounded three of us, viz, Mr Hugh Thompson, myself, and my servant. Notwithstanding this disaster, we, in our painful situation, proceeded 8 miles [13 kilometres], to get clear, if possible, of these savages; but just as we came up to a very deep bay they overtook us again. This pursuit induced us all to suppose they intended to murder us – as we were, however, to make a virtue of necessity, and to remain among them all that night, though it may be well supposed that the anguish of our minds and the pain of our wounds prevented the possibility of sleep.

They managed to separate from the war party the next day. Had they been aware of it, the increasingly aggressive contacts with the Aborigines meant they were getting closer to white settlement and Sydney. Having been pushed off their land or mistreated, the Aborigines were far less disposed to show any kindness. Reduced to only five – Clark, Thompson, the carpenter, one of the European seamen and a lascar – they struggled north until 14 May.

Thompson and the carpenter could go no further, so the others pressed on without them. The next day near Wattamolla Beach – in what is now the Royal National Park on Sydney's southern outskirts – the three remaining members of the party happened upon a fishing boat. They were picked up and carried back to Sydney, where a rescue party was sent back for Thompson and the carpenter. At first, a few bloodstained articles were found and it was assumed they'd been slain. Later, their remains were recovered.

Two weeks after the three men straggled into Sydney, the government schooner *Francis* and ten-tonne sloop *Eliza* set out for the wreck site. They left Sydney on 30 May, arriving on 10 June. The survivors on Preservation Island had fared considerably better than those on *Batavia*'s Graveyard. This was despite the fact that the fittest men had gone with the longboat, leaving behind those sick with scurvy. Mindful of the time it might take to be rescued, Captain Hamilton had concentrated every effort on salvaging as much as possible from the wreck, while rationing the men to a cup of rice per day. The abundant wildlife was ignored while the work went on, and during the salvage operations Captain Hamilton recorded the deaths of three lascars and the European passenger. With the approach of winter, the weather deteriorated.

From 23rd April til the 1st May was one continued storm, with thunder, lightening, rain, and extreme cold. The tents being soon dismantled and blown to pieces, the unfortunate sufferers were left exposed to the extremities of cold, wetness, and hunger, for during the continuance of this storm it was impossible to keep always fire to dress the pittance of rice on which their subsistence depended.

The crew of *Sydney Cove* still didn't know it, but they were getting a taste of the weather that was to make Bass Strait infamous. However, the storm did the remaining crew, and the fledgling colony, one big favour. It so badly damaged the ship that further salvage was impossible and the crew's efforts turned to building a small house and foraging for food. What they soon discovered was that the mutton birds that flocked around them were remarkably sustaining, the waters surrounding them full of fish, and the islands abounding in seals. No more deaths were recorded and the presence of so many seals suggested that here might be the basis of a sealing industry whose products could fill the hold of a ship on its return voyage from the colony of Sydney Cove.

The vessels *Francis* and *Eliza* were too small to carry all of the *Sydney Cove*'s salvaged cargo, so six lascars were left behind to guard the remaining cargo, until another ship could be found to pick it up. Still the *Sydney Cove*'s list of calamities weren't over. In a 1798 letter to his masters in England, Governor Hunter explained:

I beg their Lordships may be inform'd that the schooner returne'd in safety with the master of the wreck'd ship and a few lascars, but a heavy gale of wind having set in on the day of their leaving the island, the longboat [*Eliza*], which was commanded and navigated by Mr Armstrong, founder'd with all her crew and seven or eight lascars on board, together with such articles as had been put on board from the wreck.'

The wreck also focused interest on the waters around Van Diemen's Land. There had been speculation since Hunter himself had circumnavigated the world in the *Sirius*, that there might be a strait between Van Diemen's Land and New Holland. Passing up Van Diemen's Land's east coast, Hunter had detected a strong current coming from the west.

Why hadn't anyone tested the theory? With the roaring forties at his back, no skipper approaching from the west dared go exploring what would be a leeward shore. If there wasn't a strait, they'd be hammered into the coast by the wind and waves. So when the exploration of Bass Strait began, it came from the eastern side, the side where *Sydney Cove* had gone down.

In December 1797, George Bass (surgeon of HMS *Reliance*) set out in a well-supplied whaleboat to explore the south coast, and in particular investigate the coast between New Holland and Van Diemen's Land. In January, he rounded Wilsons Promontory and stretched off the coast as far as latitude 40 degrees south. This put him in the centre of the Strait and he might have gone further, but as Hunter put it: 'the wind shifting to the westward and blowing strong, he was oblig'd to run for land again, which he with difficulty reach'd. The sea rose to so mountainous a height that he had every reason to believe he was not covered by any land to the westward.'

Returning to Wilsons Promontory, Bass followed the coast for 100 kilometres, stretching to the west-north-west, away from Van Diemen's Land, until he surmised, correctly, that Wilsons Promontory was the southern tip of New Holland.

Then, at the furthest extent of his voyage, with his supplies running low, Bass was surprised to come across a group of Europeans. On a small island off the coast, he'd spied smoke from a fire and thinking he might be able to converse with a group of Aborigines, he'd gone to investigate. They turned out to be a group of seven convicts, marooned by seven other convicts with whom they'd stolen a boat on 2 October 1797. It had proved too small for them all. In fact they were one of two groups of convicts that had stolen boats after hearing of the beaching of the *Sydney Cove*. Both groups hoped to get to the wreck, refloat it, and escape the colony. The other group, having on 5 September stolen the vessel *Cumberland*, had been wrecked near Jervis Bay.

It wasn't the only escape attempt at sea. According to author Robert Hughes:

The fantasy of escape to China was one of the obsessive images of early transportation . . . As the settlement slowly moved outward and tracks were made through the raw bush, even the blindest optimist could see that the convict skeletons that kept turning up must mean something. The will to walk to Peking guttered out as it became clear that the logical escape route from this continental prison was not the land but the sea.

The sea route produced one epic escape in the early 1790s whose notoriety blossomed in London, reached back to Botany Bay and gave heart to would-be absconders for years to come. It was led by a woman, Mary Bryant (b. 1765) – 'the Girl from Botany Bay', as the English press later dubbed her – who, with her two small children, her husband William Bryant, and seven other convicts, managed to sail a stolen boat all the way north from Sydney to Timor, a distance of 3250 miles [5200 kilometres] in just under ten weeks.

Bass, meanwhile, was unable to take all the convicts in the little whaleboat, so he took two who were ill and gave what help he could to the others. He transferred them to the mainland, gave them a compass, fishing lines and directions on how to get back to Sydney, some 800 kilometres distant. They were never seen again, but it's believed they made it, stole another boat and escaped to the north.

In December 1797, and again in February 1798, the government schooner *Francis* returned to the *Sydney Cove*. On the last occasion it did so with the second lieutenant from the *Reliance*, Matthew Flinders, who was instructed by Hunter to make 'what observations he could amongst those islands.' His investigations around the *Sydney Cove*, combined with those of Bass, led to Hunter naming the strait in early March 1798. He then fitted out the sloop *Norfolk* and sent the two young navigators, Bass and Flinders, to explore Bass Strait completely.

On 16 December 1800 the *Lady Nelson* arrived in Sydney, having become the first vessel to pass through Bass Strait from west to east. The strategic importance of the Strait was obvious. It reduced the journey for vessels bound for Sydney by weeks, even though it was

studded with treacherous rocks. Consequently, when the French
navigator Baudin started investigating the uninhabited area in 1802,
the English were quick to move. They settled Risdon Cove on the
Derwent River on the south-east side of Van Diemen's Land in
September 1803, naming the new settlement 'Hobart'. In October,
the transport ship *Ocean* and the *Calcutta* entered Port Phillip Bay
on the northern side of Bass Strait, and searched for an appropriate
place to found a colony. Finding the natives hostile and their
impressions of the area that was to become the city of Melbourne
unfavourable, they moved on to Sydney. However, while they were in
Port Phillip, five convicts escaped, one of whom, William Buckley,
lived among the Aborigines for the next thirty-two years. On
4 November 1804, another colony was established on the southern
side of Bass Strait, on Van Diemen's Land, at Port Dalrymple, later
known as Launceston.

Finally, the wreck of the *Sydney Cove* brought Robert Campbell,
the principal of her agents, Campbell and Clark, to Sydney to super-
vise the sale of the cargo. Campbell was anything but deterred by the
wreck, and immediately set about organising a new ship to continue
the trade from Calcutta. He was to become the first merchant in the
colony who didn't come from its officer class, and after opening
a warehouse and import business in June 1800, he managed to break
the officers' monopoly on goods. Campbells Cove, on the western
side of Circular Quay in Sydney, and the warehouses that are still
sited there (now converted into fashionable restaurants) are part of
his legacy.

In 1807, he was active in stamping out illegal stills that were being
used to make rum. Empowered by Governor William Bligh, of
Bounty fame, he seized two stills illegally imported by former New
South Wales corps officer John Macarthur. Campbell's company,
as mentioned earlier, was itself extremely active in the rum trade.
The following year, 1808, the persecution of Macarthur and the

military monopolists led to Australia's only armed revolution, the Rum Rebellion.

When the last of the salvage ships sailed away from Preservation Island, the wreck of *Sydney Cove* was left to the mercy of time. For the next two centuries, the islands were visited only by sealers and mutton-birders. In 1856, Van Diemen's Land was officially renamed Tasmania, after the first European to sight it, Abel Tasman. The name was changed because of the original name's close association with its convict past.

On 1 January 1977, scuba divers rediscovered the wreck (with the help of a map drawn by Matthew Flinders). It was soon placed under the protection of the *Historic Shipwrecks Act*. The site has been stabilised to protect it from the currents, it has been extensively excavated and has yielded numerous artefacts, many of which are on display at the Queen Victoria Museum and Art Gallery, Launceston. Marine archaeologists have learned many of the vessel's secrets, some of which contributed to its demise. Research has also established how the wreck was crucial to developments in the colony's history. Indeed, it was one of the men sent to investigate the area around the wreck of the *Sydney Cove*, Matthew Flinders, who was soon to be sent to circumnavigate the continent and who subsequently gave New Holland the name by which it is now known – Australia.

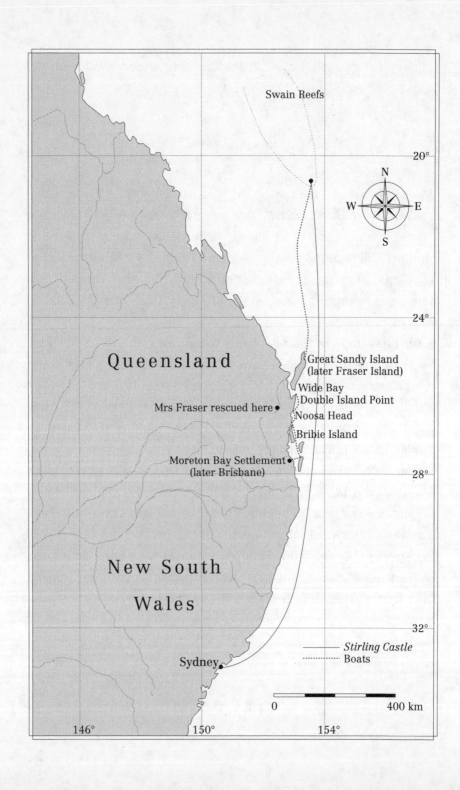

Swain Reefs

20°

N
W ★ E
S

24°

Queensland

Great Sandy Island
(later Fraser Island)

Wide Bay
Double Island Point

Mrs Fraser rescued here •

Noosa Head

Bribie Island

Moreton Bay Settlement
(later Brisbane) •

28°

New South

Wales

32°

——— Stirling Castle
········· Boats

Sydney •

0   400 km

146°   150°   154°

Illustration from John Curtis's
Shipwreck of the Stirling Castle, 1838
(Mitchell Library, State Library of
New South Wales)

4. HEART OF DARKNESS: *STIRLING CASTLE*, 1836

The colonies of Australia were still in their infancy in the year that the merchant brig *Stirling Castle*, James Fraser master, set sail from Sydney Cove. The year was 1836, a time when Sydney, Hobart (where the ship had delivered its cargo) and Fremantle were the only settlements of note. The site for Melbourne had been chosen only the year before – and bought with a few trinkets – and a settlement at Adelaide was in the final stages of planning. Near the coasts farming communities were spreading, but most of the other settlements were penal colonies. On the site of present-day Brisbane, for example, the convict settlement of Moreton Bay had become the largest, and one of the cruellest, in the colony.

In Britain, the source of all those convicts, William IV was in the final year of his reign and the radical Chartist Movement was being formed as part of a wider push for political and social reform that was eventually to reduce the flow of the country's unwanted classes. Coincidentally, 1836 was also the year that Sweden's John Ericsson patented a screw propeller for ships that was to see steam-powered vessels challenge the dominance of sail in the next few decades.

Meanwhile, despite its size, Australia was starting to prosper, climbing onto the sheep's back that was to bring the country immense wealth for more than a century. Nevertheless, on 15 May 1836, the *Stirling Castle* left Sydney without a cargo, bound for Singapore, where the trade prospects were brighter. Rather than head south and beat into the westerlies of the roaring forties, she sailed north for the tricky navigational challenges of the Torres Strait, but moderate south-easterly trade winds.

On board was Fraser's wife, Eliza Anne, who was heavy with child. Most of the crew were new to the ship, those coming out on the voyage from England having opted to try their luck in the colonies. The voyage was uneventful until 21 May when, as Eliza described it: 'on Saturday, about 9 o'clock [p.m.], I was in the passage leading out of the cabin when Captain Fraser came down . . . having given over charge to Mr Brown the first mate; he had not been down more than two or three minutes, when the vessel struck. At the first shock he uttered an exclamation of surprise and rushed on deck.'

The *Stirling Castle* had struck on one of the outermost of the Swain Reefs, some 280 kilometres north-north-west of Sandy Cape, itself 300 kilometres north of the nearest civilisation at Moreton Bay. Up on deck Captain Fraser quickly saw that the ship could not be sailed off the reef, so he ordered the sails to be taken down. Without them, though, the vessel swung around until it was side on to the waves, which started breaking over her. Fraser ordered the masts cut away to ease the ship, but, according to one of the seamen, Robert Hodge, after the brig struck, she stove in her bottom and broke her back in two places.

'He [Captain Fraser] then came below and found that the sea was crashing through the stern ports and had filled the whole place with water,' Eliza wrote. The vessel was doomed, but their problems were only beginning. Up on deck the sea had washed away the jolly boat and badly damaged the longboat and pinnace.

As Sunday dawned, Fraser gave orders that no-one was to leave the ship, which he believed would hold together until the next day. His main objective was to repair the remaining boats and prepare them for an extended voyage south to Moreton Bay. But the crew openly disobeyed him. They wanted to abandon the *Stirling Castle* as soon as possible. When Fraser insisted they at least bring up beef, bread and water from the hold, they told him he was welcome to do it himself. 'The boats were now got over the side, though with great difficulty being both stove in consequence of the heavy sea which was breaking across the vessel,' wrote Eliza.

All the ship's complement of eighteen managed to escape the wreck. Eliza was in the longboat with her husband and his young nephew John, first mate Charles Brown and seven of the crew. The pinnace carried second mate John Baxter, the boatswain and five crew. Both vessels immediately required constant bailing, indicating their unseaworthy condition.

Another reason for Fraser's reluctance to leave the ship may have been his wife's delicate condition. An open boat on the high seas, with scant food or water, was no place for a woman approaching full term. As the days wore on the stress took its toll and Eliza, trying to help bail, went into labour prematurely. However, the boat was so full of water that as the baby was being delivered it was impossible to keep its head above the surface. After it was born, it managed to gasp for breath a few times and then died. Eliza cradled it for some time until the first mate, Charles Brown, took it from her, wrapped it in a piece of shirt and consigned it to the deep.

Nine days after the ship was wrecked, on 30 May, the boats came to an island where they put in. They found water to replenish their casks, but little food. Nevertheless, they spent two days there, trying to caulk the boats with soap and blankets. It had little effect and, returning to sea, both crews needed to bail constantly to stay afloat.

As they slowly made their way south, the boats became separated. The pinnace, being the faster sailer, had been going off in search of water, but on one excursion, according to crewman Robert Hodge, it missed the longboat on its return at night. Her crew then decided to hasten southward. According to the second mate, John Baxter:

> The pinnace afterwards parted company with the launch [longboat], leaving us with one piece of beef, weighing 4 pounds [1.8 kilos], 13 gallons [59 litres] of beer and water mixed, 1 gallon [4.54 litres] brandy and 7 pounds [3.2 kilos] of wet bread. In the pinnace were Edward Stone, boatswain; James Major; Robert Hodge; John Copeland, seaman; Jacob Allen, cook; a boy named John Fraser [Captain Fraser's nephew]; and the carpenter.

According to Eliza, the boats parted company 'in spite of the Captain's orders to the contrary taking the Captain's nephew with them for the purpose of navigating their boat and leaving the second mate with us.'

Whatever happened, the pinnace was eventually wrecked somewhere on the coast south of Moreton Bay. By then, according to Hodge, John Fraser had already drowned after slipping from a rock while gathering oysters. The remaining men had continued south along the coast, living on grasses and wild herbs. One of the sailors, James Major, died of burns received while sleeping in a hut. Another, John Copeland, drowned attempting to cross a river. The boatswain, Edward Stone, and the carpenter were left on an island north of the Macleay River because the natives they'd met refused to take them in their canoes due to an argument over a waistcoat. The cook, Jacob Allen, collapsed 15 miles [24 kilometres] from the Macleay. Hodge was the only survivor. *The Sydney Gazette* described Hodge, who arrived in Sydney in mid-September, as being in a 'deplorable condition; being nearly covered with sores, and dreadfully scorched with the sun.'

Yet the ordeal for those in the longboat was to be far worse. Having parted with the pinnace around 10 June, Captain Fraser asked the men not to insist on going ashore again until they reached Moreton Bay – their reduced numbers being no match if they met hostile natives. But dogged by hunger and thirst, the men were becoming increasingly mutinous. When the boat was about 20 miles (32 kilometres) south of Sandy Cape (the northern tip of what was to become known as Fraser Island) the men saw smoke and insisted on going ashore.

Eliza tells us: 'Directly we landed the natives came down in crowds but were prevented at first from using any violence from the sight of our Fire Arms. We procured some fish from them in exchange for articles of wearing apparel.'

Fraser, Baxter and Brown again tried to repair the longboat, but the crew refused to help. Some ten days later, when the officers considered the boat seaworthy, they called the crew to get aboard. According to Eliza, they told her husband, 'He might go if he liked but they would walk to Moreton Bay.' When he asked them to at least help launch the heavy vessel, they refused, took all the guns and left.

The remaining party comprised the officers, Eliza, Michael Doyle and the steward Joseph Corralis. Unable to launch the longboat, whose timbers were shrinking as they dried in the sun, opening the cracks between them even wider, they had no choice but to follow the crew along the beach. They took the few items they'd salvaged from the ship (the chronometer, sextant, compass and some clothing) and started walking. They didn't get far, as Eliza recounts: 'The next day we met with a numerous tribe of natives, who finding us unarmed took every thing from us with the exception of the clothes on our backs, beating us severely at the least resistance.'

Appreciation of their danger grew when they noticed a piece of

a woman's dress on one of the natives. They asked if any white people
had been there before, hoping that perhaps missionaries might be
nearby. 'To which they replied by signs . . . that a man, woman and
child had been wrecked there, and massacred.'

The tiny party managed to get away and travelled constantly for
the next five days, hoping to find safety. Around 26 June:

> We . . . fell in with another tribe who stripped us perfectly naked and
> forced us to follow them into their camp. We were now portioned off to
> different masters, who employed us in carrying wood, water and bark,
> and treated us with the greatest cruelty. With the exception of a small
> portion of Fish which we but very seldom got, all we had to subsist
> upon was a kind of Fern root which we were obliged to procure our-
> selves in the swamps.

Captain Fraser, who had been unwell while on board the *Stirling
Castle*, declined rapidly, but was still forced to work. Kept apart during most of their enslavement, Eliza met her husband when he was
near the end of his endurance.

> On one occasion through debility to carry a large log of wood one of the
> natives threw a spear at him which entered his shoulder a little below
> the blade bone. Of this wound he never recovered, and being soon after
> seized with a spitting of blood he gradually pined away until his death –
> which took place eight or nine days afterwards. During this time whilst
> he was laying on the ground incapable of moving, I was always pre-
> vented from approaching him or sending him any assistance – when he
> died they dragged him away by the legs and buried him.
>
> The first mate Mr Brown having likewise become too weak to carry
> wood the natives burnt his legs and back in a most dreadful manner
> by rubbing them with fire brands. Three days after my husband's
> death one of the natives put Mr Brown and myself over to the main

land in a canoe. Mr Baxter the second mate being too weak to accompany us. Three or four days after we had crossed Mr Brown died from the frightful sufferings he had undergone. For some days he had been totally unable to walk as the flesh had fallen from his feet, and the bones of his knees protruded through the skin. He was left without any food or assistance, and on one occasion when I endeavoured to take a few cockles to him, some of the natives came up and after taking them from me, they knocked me down and dragged me along the ground by the arms and legs. After this I saw him no more.

On Tuesday afternoon, 9 August 1836, on leave from his duties at the Moreton Bay penal settlement, an officer of the 4th (King's Own) Regiment was out and about on Bribie Island, on the northern side of Moreton Bay, getting in a spot of shooting. However, Lieutenant C.J. Otter was abruptly interrupted when:

Two men were brought up to me whom I at first took to be Natives as they were quite black and perfectly naked. They told me that they belonged to the Brig *Stirling Castle* . . . that they had subsequently been stripped and cruelly used by the Natives, that two of their number had been drowned endeavouring to swim the channel which separated them from the Main, and that they themselves with another man (who had been forced to stop about 25 miles [40 kilometres] behind had proceeded along the beach from tribe to tribe for five weeks, and after undergoing a variety of hardships, arrived at Breiby's [sic] Island and most fortunately fell in with us. I immediately sent two of the boat's crew in quest of the man who had been left behind and they brought him back about 12 o'clock the following day when I immediately returned to the Settlement.

The commandant of the settlement at Moreton Bay, Captain Foster Fyans, wasted no time on hearing from Otter that at least half-a-dozen people, among them a woman, could be lost somewhere to the north of his station. In fact, he already knew about them. One of his prisoners was an Irish convict, John Graham, who had absconded from Moreton Bay in 1827 and lived for six years among the people north of the settlement. In 1833 he'd returned to Moreton Bay and given himself up, hoping to become a free man. While Otter was banging away at the wildlife, Graham was being visited by a group of young Aboriginal men who told him they'd seen other 'ghosts' like him. They'd even seen a 'she-ghost.' The local Aborigines readily explained the existence of white people as the returned ghosts of dead black men. They'd sometimes go so far as to identify the ghost as a particular person, giving the white person the rights to lands and kinship that were enjoyed by the supposed predecessor during their lifetime. In fact, this is what had happened to Graham. Now, however, Graham realised that the people his Aboriginal friends were talking about were shipwreck survivors – who'd fallen into the hands of one of the fiercest tribes on the coast. Graham was trying to convince Fyans of the story when Otter arrived with the three survivors: Robert Darge, Henry Youlden and Joseph Corralis.

Hearing that other people were still alive, Darge and Youlden were reluctant to tell much of their story. With the assistance of Corralis and the information from the young tribesmen, Graham believed he had a good idea where the people would be found.

The next day, Thursday, 11 August, Fyans despatched Otter, leading a party of twenty soldiers and convicts in two whaleboats, to mount what they all knew might be a dangerous rescue. Much of the land north of Moreton Bay is extremely fertile (nowadays it produces a dazzling range of high-quality produce), and in 1836 it supported a large population of Aboriginal people. With his knowledge of the country and the local language, Graham was appointed as 'interpreter' and 'guide'.

Two days after leaving Moreton Bay, Otter's party reached the sheltered mouth of 'Huon Mundy's River', now the site of the tourist resort of Noosa Heads. Huon Mundy was a famous local warrior, who has since given his name to the nearby town of Eumundi.

Otter wrote in his official report: 'As we expected some intelligence at this place, and as no natives appeared [Graham had arranged to rendezvous with the young warriors there], I dispatched the prisoner Graham to one of their camps, with the situation of which he was well acquainted.'

Actually, the expedition was Graham's idea. Heading off alone, he took with him some bread, potatoes and a hatchet. Not long after he appeared at the camp. There the Aborigines were surprised to be confronted by a ghost who, unlike the others they'd recently encountered, spoke their language. Graham, however, noted the presence of two other ghosts, ship's boy Robert Carey and crewman Robert Dayman. Graham gave the Aborigines the items he'd had the foresight to bring with him and said that he would give them more if they brought the two ghosts with them to his camp. The Aborigines readily agreed.

When Carey and Dayman reached Otter's camp, according to a letter Otter wrote to relatives in England: 'The poor fellows were wild with joy at seeing us, and they could hardly believe their senses, as they never expected to be liberated.'

The men said they'd seen Eliza Fraser only five days before, on the beach at Wide Bay, about 65 kilometres to the north. She was still alive, though 'suffering dreadfully from the cruelty of the natives.' The Captain and first mate were dead, but they thought the second mate, Baxter, was still on the island (Fraser Island), with the natives who worried Graham the most.

Graham also surmised that the tribes were moving south to a well-known corroboree ground near Lake Cootharaba, a few miles north of Huon Mundy's River. He'd ascertained as much from his Aboriginal friends. Some of the white ghosts, especially Eliza, were being brought there to be shown off.

The next day Otter sent one of the boats about 50 kilometres north to Double Island Point. He, Graham and two others proceeded up the beach, hoping to hear news of Eliza. They'd gone only 10 kilometres when the natives, who were following them at a distance, became hostile. Noting that they had passed their road home, Graham had grown wary of their motives and told them to turn back. They responded by throwing their waddies (killing sticks) from a distance. After a show of force the natives retreated, but Graham, suspecting they'd be back with spears and more warriors, convinced Otter to return to the remaining boat. Or as Otter put it in his report:

> We were obliged to return to the boat, as they shewed very little fear of our pistols though we fired two or three shots.
>   When we got back I started directly for Wide Bay, which I reached before night and joined the other boat. The following morning [Monday, 15 August] Graham started off to obtain intelligence and returned the following day with the second mate whom he had brought off the island in a native canoe.

In his letter home, Otter wrote of John Baxter's condition: 'Such a miserable skeleton I never beheld, quite black, and naked. The account of his sufferings was horrible, as he had been tortured in a variety of ways because he was too weak to drag the heavy logs of fire-wood.'

While Baxter's story was harrowing, Graham's was courageous. Seeking information about the *Stirling Castle*'s crew, he'd come across two Aboriginal women by a waterhole. Initially terrified by the appearance of a ghost, he calmed them by speaking their language and asking sociably after various relatives they might have in common. Soon Graham and the women were exchanging gossip about people they knew in this life and the next, and Graham learned where the other two ghosts were. Eliza was at the corroboree ground. Baxter was on the southern tip of Fraser Island, just a few kilometres away.

Graham decided to go after Baxter first. He covered the short distance north to Inskip Point, where he faced the treacherous 5-kilometre strait between the mainland and the island. Wondering how to cross, he noticed a dilapidated canoe and set about repairing it, while waiting for slack tide. Once the fierce current abated, he got across and soon located the native camp. He was shocked by what he found. At least twenty men were gathered there, and when he asked to see the other ghost they brought out Baxter. As Otter had described him, Baxter was near death, certainly in no state to make a quick dash for freedom. The only option was to talk the Aborigines, the most aggressive in the area, into helping him take Baxter to safety.

August is the time of year when food is scarce in the seas around Fraser Island, and Graham noticed that Baxter wasn't the only person in camp who was going hungry. So he told the warriors that he'd come from the south, where there were plenty of fish. He'd come to take the other ghost down there for a feed, but there was plenty for everyone. Plus, there was a whale on the beach a little further south. It was all the bait the hungry men needed. Eight canoes recrossed the strait, with Baxter and Graham among the passengers. Along the way, Baxter told Graham that he'd seen what had happened when the two other men – Michael Doyle and William Elliott – who were supposedly drowned, had tried to swim the strait. The natives hadn't lifted a finger to stop them. They'd watched as the men swam out. Then the dorsal fin of a shark had appeared and the men were taken under.

As the party marched south, Graham grew increasingly apprehensive about how far he'd get before the Aborigines realised they'd been conned. Then he had a stroke of luck. The band came upon a big school of fish swimming right near the shore. Soon they had a good catch; and after they'd all eaten well – including Baxter, who no longer cared whether he lived or died – it was easy to convince the men to continue south to Otter's party.

Now there only remained the most difficult prize of all: the she-ghost

Eliza. An armed attack would almost certainly see her killed or carried further into the bush. Taking hostages would lead to bloodshed
on both sides. So once again, Graham decided to set off alone to the
spot where he was sure he'd find her, leaving instructions where to
meet him with Otter, who later wrote: 'I followed him early the next
morning with the two Corporals [Campbell and McGuire] and
Mitchell the cockswain, all of us well armed for the purpose of rendering any assistance that might be required. After walking about 25
miles [40 kilometres] we found a mark in the sand, which had been
previously agreed upon as a sign to halt.'

And there they waited. Graham tells us: 'On the 17th of August
1836, he [Graham] freed Mrs Fraser from seven hundred cannibals
and savages who had her in the mountains (as a show) west of
Cousk's Wide Lake [Lake Cootharaba] Where he went and getting the
tribes that claimed him as There [sic] friend to Stand by him while
he claimed her as him or the (Spirit of his wife).'

Graham makes it sound simple. While living among the Aborigines he had been married to a woman who had since died. He was
claiming Eliza as the spirit of the woman the natives knew was dead.
The trouble was, a member of the tribe holding Eliza claimed she
was the spirit of his sister. In either case, Graham pointed out that
the tribe wasn't taking good care of the she-ghost and that he
wanted to take her to his country and feed her up. The people could
see more of the she-ghost after she'd been taken care of.

Eliza recounts: 'A white man whose name I have since heard is
Graham came up and told me he had been sent for me, and that
there was succour at hand. He spoke to the natives for some time
and after a good deal of altercation managed to get me away. After
travelling nine or ten miles [16 kilometres] we got to the beach
where we found a party of three men and an officer.'

Otter records:

I went up to meet him [Graham], and you may conceive my joy and sat-
isfaction when he told me that Mrs Fraser was waiting on the top of the
hill until I sent her a cloak. I immediately gave him a cloak and petti-
coat, and shortly afterwards she appeared. You never saw such an
object. Although only thirty-eight years of age, she looked like an old
woman of seventy, perfectly black, and dreadfully crippled from the sufferings she had undergone. I went to meet her, and she caught my
hand, burst into tears, and sunk down quite exhausted. She was a mere
skeleton, the skin literally hanging upon her bones, whilst her legs were
a mass of sores, where the savages had tortured her with firebrands.
Notwithstanding her miserable plight, it was absolutely necessary for us
to start homewards, though she had already come nine or ten miles, as
there were 300 natives in the camp, who, Graham said, would most
likely attack us in the night, for many of them had been unwilling to give
her up. He had fortunately met with one of his former friends, a kind of
chief, through whose influence he had succeeded. So treacherous are
the natives, that it is impossible to trust one of them for a moment.

The boats were still some 40 kilometres along the coast and
despite her condition, Eliza insisted on setting out immediately. After
giving her a little port wine, the party moved on, though half-way
through the journey Eliza was unable to walk and the men took
turns carrying her. As they went, she recounted her experiences:
seeing her husband's death and that of the first mate, being constantly beaten, and being forced to sleep in the open, seldom being
allowed inside the natives' shelters, even in the heaviest rains.

The concerns about the natives were well-founded. The party
managed to reach the boats on Thursday, 18 August, but
unfavourable winds kept them ashore for the next four days. During
that time, one of the men, John Shannon, was speared through the
thigh while collecting firewood within 100 metres of the camp.

On the Sunday, the boats finally got away and, after sailing all night and the following day, reached Moreton Bay and the settlement on Monday evening. The joy on their arrival was not universal. On hearing news of the *Stirling Castle* crew's mutinous behaviour, Captain Fyans threw Darge and Youlden out of their comfortable lodgings and put them on poorer-quality rations.

While Eliza and the men recovered, a vessel was obtained to take them back to Sydney. Efforts were made to ease Eliza's mind about her affairs – as she was now destitute, with three young children to support back in England.

Various members of the rescue party wrote their reports, none of them omitting mention of the extraordinary courage of James Graham. Otter wrote:

> I cannot conclude without requesting that I may be allowed to recommend to His Excellency's [the Governor of New South Wales] notice, the prisoner Graham to whose indefatigable exertions we are indebted for our success. He shunned neither danger nor fatigue, and on the last occasion he was exposed to very imminent risk, by venturing into the large Camp where Mrs Fraser was detained, as had he met there any of the natives who attacked us a few days before it might have been fatal to him – as he was obliged not only to go unarmed, but to strip himself perfectly naked when he went amongst them.

Fyans added his admiration in his communication to his superiors, who stopped short of giving Graham complete freedom, eventually giving him a ticket-of-leave and £10, which effectively set him free until his term expired.

In October, Eliza and the rest of the crew sailed for Sydney aboard the *Prince George*, stopping at points along the coast to search for signs of the crew of the pinnace. The burned remains of James Major were found and identified by the crew, thanks to the distinctive waistcoat he had on. The presence of the waistcoat aroused some suspicions about his fate. Had any 'cannibal natives' been involved in his death, they would have taken it. It was not impossible that his crewmates may have been responsible, cannibalism among shipwrecked sailors having occurred in other such instances. The body of the cook '15 miles north of the Macleay River' was never found.

When the *Prince George* reached Sydney, Eliza's story caused a sensation. Church services were held and a subscription was opened that raised £400, equivalent to three years of her husband's income. When she was sufficiently recovered, she took ship to England, arriving at Liverpool in the *Mediterranean Packet* on 16 July 1837. There her story took another twist.

Eliza went to Liverpool's Commissioner of Police, Mr Dowling, asking for assistance to get to London where she had friends who would contribute to her support. According to Dowling's report:

> In reply to some questions put to her respecting the savages with whom she professed to have been so long domiciled, she detailed few particulars, compared with which the marvels witnessed by the renowned Mr Lemuel Gulliver would be very common-place matters indeed. Among other singularities she said that the barbarians had large tufts of blue hair growing upon their shoulders in the form of epaulets, and that their heads were quite denuded of hair, with the exception of the crown of the head from which streamed a large portion of the same texture and colour as the material forming their shoulder ornaments.

A dubious Dowling suspended all assistance and summoned the skipper of the vessel, Captain Alexander John Greene. He was reported to be away on business, so the first mate was summoned. 'After a good deal of hesitation, however, he admitted that she was in no distress whatever; that she had an abundance of clothes of a very superior description; and moreover that she was married to the captain, whose name was Greene, and consequently could want for nothing any woman in her sphere of life had a right to expect.'

The police considered her application as an attempted fraud and dismissed her. So Eliza and Greene (whom she'd married in Sydney on 23 February 1837) moved on to London, where they approached the Secretary of State for the Colonies, Lord Glenelg. Greene wrote to him: 'During the said widow's stay at Sydney very little was done for her in a pecuniary point of view, further than enabling her to purchase a few articles of clothing, paying this for her passage and purchasing the necessaries for her subsistence during this passage.'

The Secretary of State refused to see her, so she went to the Lord Mayor of London who brought her plight to the attention of the media, including her eventual biographer, John Curtis of *The Times*. The Lord Mayor also opened a subscription for her and more than £500 was raised before the police in Liverpool heard of the appeal and exposed her.

In her defence, which appears to have been run by the Lord Mayor and the media to head off personal embarrassment, she admitted being married to Greene but that she only sought assistance for her children (who were living in Britain), rather than herself. She was further excused by her state of mind, as described by Curtis, who wrote of her:

> . . . it appears evident that the unfortunate woman, notwithstanding her
> kind treatment at the settlement, had evinced symptoms of aberration
> of mind, and as we have before gently hinted, we think we have seen
> a tendency that way ourselves. And if it be so, who can wonder? Many a
> lady has found an asylum in a mad-house for life in consequence of
> bereavements less painful – who have never experienced the pains,
> privations, and insults of the female we are alluding to.

However, no mention was made of the substantial sum collected in Sydney. Eventually as much as £1000 was collected in London and distributed to her children. Back in Sydney, the newspapers were far less charitable when news of Eliza Fraser/Greene's activities in the mother country arrived. *The Sydney Gazette* wrote on Thursday, 25 January 1838.

> The recently received British Journals teem with the most horrible accounts of the disastrous wreck of the ship *Stirling Castle* on her voyage from this colony to Singapore, in May, 1836 . . . Our object . . . in referring to the matter now, is not to retrace ground we have already trod, but to undeceive the British public with regard to the statements that, we perceive, have been made before the Lord Mayor of London, and, also to relieve our fellow-colonists from the odium of having displayed an utter want of sympathy for the surviving sufferers, for such is the conclusion which cannot fail to be deduced by the British reader from the narrative published in the British Journals . . . It is not our wish to deprecate the sufferings endured by the wretched survivors . . . We do blame Mrs Fraser, however, (and her husband Capt. Greene, late of the *Mediterranean Packet*, at whose instance, doubtless, Mrs F. has gone to London, to lay this statement before the Lord Mayor), for her inexcusable ingratitude in concealing the kindness she met with in Sydney and the very liberal subscription which was made on her behalf previous to her departure . . .
>
> Captain Greene's conduct in the matter is highly reprehensible if he, as is stated in the Journals before us, not only concealed the fact of his marriage altogether, but stated that 'the unfortunate lady was not mistress to a farthing.'

However, that wasn't the end of Eliza's and Captain Greene's moneymaking ventures. In 1837 Eliza's own account of her ordeal was published in the USA, but was more fiction than fact. And Henry Stuart Russell writes in his not entirely reliable memoir, *Genesis of Queensland*, of an experience he had in London:

Walking down Hyde Park from Oxford Street, I observed a man who
was carrying over his shoulder one of those show advertisements . . .
a bright daub which represented savages with bows and arrows, some
dead bodies of white men and women, which other savages were cutting up on the ground, and another squad were holding 'spits' to
a large fire. It was amusing enough to stop my walk: horrible enough
to impress the writing beneath the picture on my mind – '*STIRLING CASTLE'*
WRECKED OFF THE COAST OF NEW HOLLAND, BOTANY BAY, ALL KILLED AND
EATEN BY SAVAGES; ONLY SURVIVOR A WOMAN: TO BE SEEN; 6D. ADMISSION.

Yet Eliza Fraser's ordeal, as we've seen from the account she gave
immediately upon her arrival in Moreton Bay, and from those of
others involved in her rescue, was harrowing enough not to require
embellishment. And its consequences extended far beyond the lives
of the immediate participants. As the Rev. Dr Lang wrote to Sir
George Grey in London on 12 May 1837, regarding establishing missionary stations:

I beg most respectfully to submit to your attention and consideration
the extreme importance of Moreton Bay as an additional station, as
well as endeavouring, by a comparatively extensive and well-directed
missionary agency, to make a strong impression on the tribes to the
northward. While the natives are comparatively numerous in the vicinity of Moreton Bay, the frequency of shipwrecks on the reefs, to the
northward of that settlement, is ever and anon exposing the helpless
Europeans who survive these disasters to the savage brutality of the
tribes on the coast; and it is only by extending missionary operations
from Moreton Bay, as the point of departure, along the coast to the
northwards, that these tribes can be subjected to the humanising influences of Christian civilisation. The *Stirling Castle*, a vessel in which
I made a voyage to the colony, and [which] carried several ministers of
religion and instructors of youth, has recently been wrecked on a reef,

and the captain and first officer, and several of the crew, barbarously murdered by the black natives to the northward of that settlement, after escaping safely in their boats to the shore.

Of course, if 'the humanising influences of Christian civilisation' didn't work, there were some brutal alternatives. Only two years after Eliza Fraser arrived in Sydney with her frightful tale of shipwreck and mistreatment, the colony of New South Wales was shocked by what has become the most widely known massacre of Aborigines, at Myall Creek, in what is now central New South Wales, on 10 June 1838. A band of a dozen white men slaughtered at least twenty-eight Aborigines, leading to such outrage that several men were tried and convicted.

Meanwhile, John Lang got his way in the same year, 1838, arriving in Moreton Bay with twelve missionaries, Lutherans, who were the first free settlers of what was eventually to become the state of Queensland (Queen Victoria having ascended the throne the previous year). Yet the widely held attitude to the Aboriginal population had become malevolent, especially if the sentiment expressed in the slender volume *A Mother's Offering to Her Children* by 'a Lady long resident in New South Wales' is anything to go by. Published in 1841 and dedicated by permission to the son of the Governor of New South Wales, it describes the wreck of the *Stirling Castle* and Eliza's ordeal, and concludes: 'Such wanton barbarities fill one with horror and indignation; and a wish to exterminate the perpetrators.'

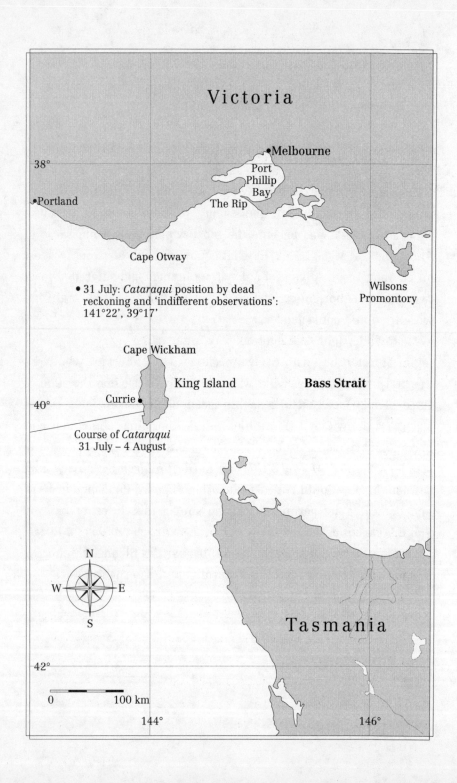

Victoria

•Melbourne

Port
Phillip
Bay

The Rip

•Portland

Cape Otway

38°

• 31 July: *Cataraqui* position by dead
reckoning and 'indifferent observations':
141°22', 39°17'

Wilsons
Promontory

Cape Wickham

King Island   **Bass Strait**

Currie

40°

Course of *Cataraqui*
31 July – 4 August

N

W   E

S

Tasmania

42°

0   100 km

144°   146°

Imminent Danger, a recent watercolour of
the *Cataraqui* by Barry Collis, King Island

5. THREADING
THE NEEDLE:
CATARAQUI, 1845

On the night of 3 August 1845, the biggest problem for Captain
Christopher Finlay, master of the emigrant ship *Cataraqui*, was that
despite all the advances in navigation that had occurred since Australia's first shipwrecks, he still didn't know exactly where he was. And
the little he did know about his position only made matters worse.

The 802-tonne sailing vessel was en route from Liverpool to the
recently established town of Melbourne with 369 emigrants and
a crew of 46, and Finlay was approaching the treacherous western
entrance of Bass Strait, just a day or two from his ultimate destination. Up to that point, the five-month voyage had seen little incident.

The first 10 000-kilometre leg from England to Cape Town had passed smoothly. On the second leg from Cape Town to Australia there had been one fatality among the crew, when seaman Robert Harvey fell overboard on 4 July. Among the emigrants, five babies had been born and five had died. Yet, by the standards of the day, the losses were unremarkable.

Then, after passing the midway point of her second leg at St Paul's Island on 19 July, following the route pioneered by Brouwer some 230 years previously, the *Cataraqui* was overtaken by one of the roaring forties' vicious winter gales. For the rest of the month it blew, veering from north-west to south-west, but always driving the vessel onward across the Indian and Southern oceans. The storm was accompanied by heavy cloud and constant rain, so that from then on the weather made the sightings of the sun and stars, which were vital for navigation, impossible.

The ship ploughed on, her hatches battened and passengers forced to stay below. There the conditions pushed the limits of endurance. The close atmosphere was full of sea damp mixed with the stench of unwashed bodies, rotting food, soiled babies, and the residue left by people too seasick to leave their bunks. The skills of the ship's medical officers, Dr Carpenter and his brother, Edward, were sorely tested.

At the end of July, Finlay still couldn't get an accurate fix on his position: 'Upon the 31st July, latitude by indifferent observation 39 degrees 20', according to a subsequent report in the *Melbourne Courier*. Without the longitude, however, he had no idea how far east the *Cataraqui* had come, so was forced to rely on dead reckoning – the method Dutch ships had used to avoid the Australian continent's extensive west coast, with mixed success. The problem was that Finlay was attempting to thread a passage into Bass Strait and the entrance was a mere 90 kilometres wide. The 'indifferent observation' had Finlay on a latitude that ran almost dead-centre through what mariners had dubbed 'the eye of the needle', but if it was wrong . . .

On the northern flank of the Strait lay Cape Otway, the tip of a mountain range that protruded from the mainland before ending with a dramatic plunge into the foaming Southern Ocean. The shore-line stretching north-west of Cape Otway had earned a grim title: 'The Shipwreck Coast.' Over the years it was to claim eighty vessels, blown onto the lee shore by the relentless westerly gales. Today there are twenty-five sites marked on the short stretch from Port Fairy to Moonlight Head, where the nature of the coast makes the chances of survival for shipwreck victims slim indeed. Much of it is sheer limestone cliffs gouged and furrowed by century upon century of ocean storms. Anyone not drowned or dashed to pieces on the rocks literally had nowhere to get ashore.

The southern flank of Bass Strait was guarded by King Island, which has claimed some sixty vessels. One word keeps cropping up in descriptions of its west coast: fear. The zoologist on Baudin's exploration of 1802, François Peron, commented:

All the western side of the island, being without shelter from the waves of the vast Southern Ocean, bristles with dangerous reefs . . . The bot-tom, almost everywhere, is muddy black sand, very suitable for anchorage; but unfortunately, this layer is so thin, and it covers such sharp rocks that there are perhaps no places more to be feared by sailors. Apart from this first handicap King Island has also the disad-vantage of being exposed to the South-west winds, the strongest and most formidable of these latitudes; and its position at the opening of the strait submits it to the deadly influence of these terrible currents . . .

Of all the rocks peculiar to King Island there is none more remark-able than that of which I have still to speak . . . each of these masses presents a trihedral pyramid, of which the summit points upward, and of which the edges are sharp and cutting . . .

116   SHIPWRECKS

It is to this strange characteristic that the granite that we are describing owes the unfortunate property of being the terror of sailors on these coasts.

Captain John Lort Stokes, surveying the straits aboard the famous HMS *Beagle*, wrote of his visit there in 1838: 'The most remarkable circumstance we noticed in this part of our cruise was the leafless appearance of the trees on the higher parts of the island. It seemed as though a hurricane had stripped them of their verdure.'

In 1841, Sir John Franklin, Lieutenant-Governor of Van Diemen's Land, wrote to the governor of New South Wales:

The prevalence of strong winds, the uncertainty of either the set or force of the currents, the number of small rocks, islets, and shoals, which, though they appear on the chart, have been imperfectly surveyed, combine to render Bass's Strait under any circumstances an anxious passage for a seaman to enter; and I will venture to say that the master of any merchant ship trading from the northern hemisphere to Sydney, or in the opposite direction, looks upon this portion of his voyage with the greatest apprehension.

Franklin was asking for lighthouses to be built in the strait. Their lack was another of Captain Finlay's problems. If he came within sight of land by day, even in bad weather he had a good chance of avoiding it, as well as of getting a fix on his position. At night, however, there was no light on uninhabited Cape Otway and virtually uninhabited King Island. He wouldn't see land until it was too late.

The need for lighthouses was well recognised; however, amid numerous competing priorities, they remained unbuilt. Even large loss of life hadn't brought action. On 13 May 1835, the convict ship *Neva*, Captain Peck master, from Cork in Ireland, struck the island. Of 239 people aboard, mostly female convicts and their children,

only twenty-two made it ashore. There six convicts and a child succumbed to the effects of exposure (some also to the consumption of
rum washed ashore). Only nine of the crew, including Peck, survived.

In 1842, the Legislative Council of New South Wales did appoint
a committee to look into building lighthouses in Bass Strait. It examined Captain Stokes, among others, and eventually recommended
the erection of lighthouses at several points. However, due to a lack
of funds, nothing was done. That was still the case as Captain Finlay
approached Bass Strait at the beginning of August 1845.

On 1 August, the day after Finlay had got his 'indifferent observation', there was, according to the account in the *Melbourne Courier*,
a 'strong gale from north-west, increasing to a perfect hurricane; ran
under close reefed topsails, and reefed foresail, until Sunday the 3rd,
at 7 p.m., when we hove to under a close reefed main topsail and
fore topmast staysail.'

By the *Port Phillip Herald*'s account: 'No opportunity had offered
for taking an observation to enable the captain to ascertain the ship's
course for four days . . . and from the dead reckoning kept, it was
presumed that the vessel was in 141 degrees 22' east longitude, and
39 degrees 17' south, which would make her between 60 or 70 miles
[100 kilometres] from King's Island.'

When the ship hove to (put its bow into the wind and so stopped
going anywhere), Finlay effectively conceded his uncertainty about
his position. By his reckoning he was still more than 100 kilometres
from the entrance to the Strait, but had he kept going, during a long
winter's night the ship could cover that distance and more, and it
would be suicide to thread the needle into Bass Strait virtually blind.

It was a prudent decision, but one that also underlined Finlay's
fundamental problem. During the night of 3 August, Finlay must
have considered his options countless times, as well as the conditions both outside and inside the *Cataraqui*. How great was the
margin of error in the estimate of their position? Might they be

50 kilometres further north, south, east or west? What if it was
100 kilometres? What if they got under way again at daylight and
failed to make landfall by night the next day? Then they'd certainly
be much closer to land, possibly dangerously so. What if they got
into Bass Strait and were forced to weather another night in its narrow confines before reaching the safety of Port Phillip Bay? Even the
3-kilometre-wide entrance to Port Phillip, the notorious Rip, was
a hazard in its own right, with a tidal flow that had swept many vessels to their destruction. What if they came up to it during the night?
Perhaps when morning dawned they could just head north until they
made a landfall that would fix their position, but this might put them
on a lee shore with the dreaded Shipwreck Coast. And the longer he
spent debating his options, the longer he prolonged the suffering of
his passengers, cost the ship's owners money, and increased the possibility of disaster.

According to the *Port Phillip Gazette*, that night it was 'raining
hard, blowing a fearful gale, and the sea running mountains high.'
And these are some of the biggest waves in the world. They start as
tiny ripples off the coast of Patagonia, but soon they are whipped and
driven west by the constant winds, growing ever larger. The ocean
swells can circle more than half the planet before they reach the
coasts of Victoria and Tasmania, there to rise even higher as they
strike the continental shelf, and finally break and crash onto the
rocks and cliffs. The largest wave measured off the west coast of Tasmania, by a Waverider buoy anchored in 100 metres of water
between 1985 and 1992, was 20 metres from crest to trough. That's
a wave the size of a six-storey building. The organisation that
measured it, the CSIRO's Division of Marine Research, described it
as a once-in-ten-years event.

Finlay was in something more than a one-in-ten-year event. He
might have wanted to stop going anywhere, but the universe around
the *Cataraqui* continued its utterly chaotic motion. Below decks

Finlay was confronted by the stricken faces of his passengers, pale in the dim candlelight, crying and sobbing in mortal fear as the ship pitched and rolled in the giant seas, groaning and shuddering with the strain, the rigging whining, breaking waves roaring and crashing against the hull.

Some idea of the conditions *Cataraqui* endured comes from another vessel that was in these waters at that time. On 23 July the cutter *William* left Launceston, Tasmania, for Adelaide, South Australia, with thirty-three passengers and a cargo of horses on board. Normally it was a journey of just a few days. Five weeks of 'fearful weather' later, she put into Portland Bay, only halfway to her intended destination.

At three o'clock on the morning of 4 August, just eight hours after the *Cataraqui* had turned into the wind, Captain Finlay decided to act. He had spent most of that fearful night at the mercy of wind and current. Then, according to the *Melbourne Courier*, 'about three, gale moderated, set the close-reefed main topsail and fore topmast staysail, bore away steering east by north, expecting to make the land about Cape Otway.'

It seemed an odd time of the night to be setting sail, but there was logic to this decision. If Finlay was where he thought he was, he should sight Cape Otway during the afternoon on 4 August. Then he'd have a firm fix on his position and could set a safe course for Port Phillip, storm or no storm, and arrive at the mouth of the bay just after daylight on 5 August. Finlay was relying on his dead reckoning being correct, or at least reasonably so. If it was slightly wrong (less than 100 kilometres), he might sight land during the morning. If the error was greater, it meant he would be sailing towards unseen dangers for the next three to four hours.

Chief mate Thomas Guthery (also spelled Guthrie in various accounts) came on watch at 4 a.m.:

I found the ship running free under three close-reefed topsails and reefed foresail. The captain was on deck at the time, and gave me orders to continue the course east by north, to keep a good look-out, and let him know at daylight.

About half-past four o'clock a.m., the tempest still continuing, rain falling in torrents, and the darkness of the night such as not to allow any object to be seen within a few hundred yards of the vessel, the ship struck, going at the rate, I suppose, of about seven knots through the water. The man at the wheel was, from the violence of the concussion, on the ship striking, knocked from it. I went forward to look over the bows; the ship continued her course through the water for the space of about 15 minutes, when she struck the second time, after which she ran a-head for a few minutes, and, striking the third time, she struck and fell over on her larboard side.

Cataraqui had run onto the jagged teeth of a reef off King Island. She was actually almost 150 kilometres south of the Captain's esti-mated position – the error in his reckoning being so great that he thought he'd run onto Cape Otway. Not that estimates of position were of importance any more.

As the ship ground against the bottom the crew begged Finlay to give the order to cut away the masts. 'I will not,' he replied. 'Keep every rag of canvas spread. It's our only chance of getting the ship over the reef.'

The *Port Phillip Herald* reported that 'all the passengers attempted to rush on deck, and many succeeded in doing so, until the ladders were knocked away by the workings of the vessel; when the shrieks from men, women and children, from below were ter-rific, calling on the watch on deck to assist them. The crew to a man were on deck the moment the ship struck, and were instantly employed in handing up the passengers.'

Soon more than 300 people were swarming over the decks, with more begging to be helped up from below. Although the water was rising around them, they may have been better off. Every wave that broke over the ship carried away some of the people who'd made it up from the cabins.

Amid the mounting chaos, the crew tried to get the longboat over the side. It was an impossible task. As they fought to get the boat clear, another wave broke over them. It swept across the ship, picked up the longboat, booms and spars, and smashed them over the side, taking with them anyone in their path.

Not long after, the battered ship fell over further onto her weakened larboard side, exposing the decks even more. Most of the remaining boats were smashed; the bulwarks, spars and a part of the cuddy were washed away. The weight of the masts, now leaning at an acute angle, held the ship over even further.

'Cut away the masts,' Finlay at last gave the order. He was hoping his action might help the ship right herself, and buy them some time. It might also help the crew bring up the passengers still trapped below. The crew sprang to the task and quickly succeeded, but it made no difference. *Cataraqui* was too badly broken to lift herself out of the raging seas.

The *Courier*'s account read: 'No-one being able to do anything further, the survivors clinging to such parts of the wreck as they were able to lay hold of. Up to this time about 200 souls perished, and at daylight we found about 200 still clinging to the wreck. Saw the land and the position of the vessel, and gave up all hopes of being able to reach the shore.'

By then the stern of the vessel was shattered. The ship was surrounded by dead bodies, some floating in the water, others strewn over the needle-sharp rocks. Yet Captain Finlay still wouldn't give up. He shouted to his crew, 'My lads, go below and get hold of as many coils of rope as possible. We'll try and get it on shore. If once we had it fastened there, we could all haul ourselves on shore.'

Half a dozen of the crew who still remained on board obeyed and headed down into the hold. If such a thing was possible, it was now worse there than being on deck. The surging waters had dislodged the cargo, which was being rolled and tossed in the confined spaces. All the men were at risk of being crushed at any moment. Yet they stuck to their search until they found four coils of rope. It was all they could manage before being forced to retreat and struggle back on deck.

They'd almost all made it when one of them, a ship's boy named William Blackstock, realised he was trapped. He couldn't climb out of the hold without a ladder, and left alone it was only a matter of time before the heaving cargo was sure to crush him. Hearing his cries, another crewman managed to throw him a rope, and the desperate lad was hauled to safety.

On deck the ropes were joined and tied to a buoy that was thrown over the side. The wind and waves quickly washed it away from the ship, towards the distant shore, and for a moment, hopes of success ran high. Then, while it was still well out from shore the buoy became entangled in masses of kelp (*Durvillea potatorum*) that swept back and forth in thick beds all around the rocks. No matter how they tugged at the ropes, then let them go, the buoy got no closer to shore.

It was 10 a.m. when another attempt was made to launch a boat. The starboard quarter boat was the only one still intact. The crew managed to get it into the water, then four men and the doctor got aboard. Yet they'd not even got clear of the ship when they were caught by another breaking wave. The boat was capsized and the occupants thrown into the water. As the helpless survivors looked on, all five men and the boat were lost.

The *Herald* resumes:

Those who were able continued to cling to the wreck until about four in the afternoon [other accounts suggest midday], when she parted midships at the forepart of the main rigging, when immediately some seventy or a hundred were launched into the tumultuous and remorse-less waves! The survivors on the deck still, however, continued to exert themselves to recover back all they could; but many of them were dead, although but momentarily immersed. Ridge lines were also stretched along the side of the wreck, to enable them to hold on.

Exposed to the icy waters of the Southern Ocean in the depths of winter, hypothermia was taking those that the sea hadn't yet claimed. In conditions of extreme cold, combined with wet clothing, victims can succumb in a matter of hours, slipping into uncon-sciousness, then death.

All through the afternoon, the storm continued without respite. People clung to the disintegrating ship as best they could until, just as the light was beginning to fade at around 5 p.m., the vessel parted by the forerigging. As she literally broke into pieces, most of those who were left were washed away. Only seventy remained, a huddled mass of misery, crowded together in the forecastle.

As night fell, all they could do was drag in the ropes that stretched to the kelp-fouled buoy, and use them to lash themselves to the remains of the wreck. The sea broke over them and a freezing wind cut through their soaking clothes. All through the night rain came down in sheets. As the hours passed, some died from the cold; others were drowned where they were lashed to the ship.

The *Gazette* continues the sad account:

One of the number named Blackstock, already alluded to, relates that on the night of the Monday he was sitting on the anchor holding on along with another boy named Robertson, at this time there were about twenty-five on the wreck, who had given up all hopes of being saved, and sat calmly awaiting their fate. Blackstock and his compan-ion were at one time during the night washed off the anchor, but Blackstock by a wonderful exertion, regained his position, and stooping down drew his companion again on the anchor. He had not been up more than five minutes when he died, and Blackstock pushed him down into the water again.

The forecastle barely held together until the morning, by which time the waves were washing freely through it. Captain Finlay was among the few still left, and realised that remaining on board was certain death. He decided to try and swim ashore, and dived off the wreck. He struggled in the sea, but soon became exhausted as he fought through the kelp, and was forced back. A few of the survivors who still had some strength left managed to get him back aboard.

Soon though, the little protection the forecastle afforded them evaporated. The bowsprit was washed away, and it was obvious that the time had come to swim or die. The lashings were undone and everyone who could get hold of anything that could float took to the water. The captain, second mate and steward still clung to the almost submerged bow, along with eighteen or twenty others, surrounded by the bodies of the dead.

According to the *Gazette*, the last words Captain Finlay was heard to utter were: 'God grant some one may be saved to tell the tale.'

One of those who'd managed to grab hold of a spar was the chief mate. The *Herald* reported:

Mr Guthrie was driven to a detached part of the wreck, but soon found it was impossible to live with such a sea breaking over, seized a piece of plank under his arm, and leaping into the water, was carried over the reef, and thus got on shore. He found a passenger who had got ashore during the night, and one of the crew (Robinson) who got ashore in the morning. John Roberts, a seaman, plunged in when he saw the mate ashore, and partly swimming, partly driven, reached the land. Five other seamen followed, and got ashore dreadfully bruised and exhausted. Almost immediately afterwards, the vessel disappeared.

Only nine people out of 415 escaped the terrible wreck of the *Cataraqui* and lived. Battered against the rocks, they'd also struggled through the almost impenetrable kelp, which had helped drown many as it wrapped itself around their bodies and dragged them under. Some of the survivors were at risk from hypothermia after two days of immersion and bitter cold. Many were virtually naked, their clothes having been torn from their bodies by the surging waves. Among the forlorn party there was only one emigrant, Solomon Brown, whose wife, daughter and three stepdaughters had drowned. Blackstock also made it ashore, having cheated death twice already on the disintegrating ship. All survivors were men.

The prospects on shore were only slightly better than on the ship. It was not until the afternoon that they found any sustenance: a small tin of preserved fowl and some scraps of blanket, soaking wet.

According to the *Port Phillip Herald*: 'The shore was strewed with pieces of the wreck and portions of dead corpses in horrible profusion. After a vain search for water, and being unable to find any more survivors, they slept that night in the bush.'

The men were parched with thirst and numbed by cold. They were unable to make a fire and the shore adjacent to the wreck, being low scrub and grasses, afforded little protection from the biting winter cold and damp blowing in off the sea.

King Island is a substantial piece of land, yet in 1845 its 50 kilometre by 20 kilometre extent was home to only four people: a wallaby hunter and sealer named David Howie, another European named Oakley, and two Aborigines, Maria and Georgia. They had been delivered to the island by the *Thalia*, out of Melbourne, with a small boat and supplies for three months. But during the afternoon of Tuesday, 5 August, Howie and the others suspected they were no longer alone. Along the western coast, they started seeing wreckage drifting in the current. Realising a ship must have gone ashore, they started searching the coast, but by darkness had found nothing and made camp.

The next morning, while their campfire was still burning, they
were found by the nine survivors. The *Port Phillip Herald* reports:

> About 9 or 10 o'clock in the forenoon, [the survivors] observed
> a smoke, which presuming they were on the mainland (according to the
> captain's calculations) imagined it was a fire of the natives. However,
> they shortly saw a white man approaching them, who turned out to be
> Mr David Howie, residing upon the island . . . fortunate, indeed, was it
> for the poor exhausted and benumbed survivors, to whom he instantly
> afforded fire and food, and constructed a shed against the weather.

For the survivors, the worst was over, but some idea of their condition comes from the fact that they were unable to cover the 40-odd
kilometres back to Howie's main camp at Yellow Rock. Howie had to
leave them and go back for supplies. He and the others returned on
8 August, hauling a large amount of food and clothing, having left
a note on the door of the hut at Yellow Rock. It detailed the tragedy
for any vessel that might call in their absence.

For almost five weeks, Howie and the others ferried supplies to
the stricken survivors, plucked bodies from the waters and buried
them as best they could, while waiting for a vessel to call. It was
a month after the wreck that a small cutter, the 10-tonne *Midge*,
John Fletcher master, cruising the island, called at Yellow Rock. What
Fletcher read sent him to the side of the island he had deliberately
been avoiding. His account was reported in the *Melbourne Courier*:

> The whole of the west coast of King's Island is one of the wildest and
> most dangerous that can be imagined. I was prepared by the small
> chart I carried with me, to find it a wild-looking coast; and I had no
> intention of attempting a cruise along it during the late severe weather,
> had I not observed upon landing at a sealing station [Yellow Rock],
> opposite New Year's Island, a notice of wreck being upon the coast

thirty miles [48 kilometres] to the southward. The whole line, from the latitude 39 degrees 40' to 40 degrees 7' is belted by rocks at irregular distances from the shore outwards, for about seven or eight miles [11 or 12 kilometres], and in running from New Year's to the position of the wreck, you find reefs extending nine miles [14 kilometres] seaward, and at this distance off one or two of the points, a wall of enormous rollers breaking towards the shore. We luckily ran down during a heavy gale from N.E. and by keeping a hand at the mast head, we were barely enabled to reach the wreck in tolerable safety.

We were unable to anchor for more than one hour during the three days we were off the coast, and at night had to run out to sea, alternately fill and lie to till daylight. During a breeze the surf upon the shore is tremendous, near the position of the wreck of the *Cataraqui*. I stood upon a ledge of rock 40 feet [12 metres] above the level of the sea, and found that over this had been driven by the sea the whole of the midship part of the vessel, from the after main to the mizen, a mass of about 40 feet by 15 [12 x 4.6 metres].

Opposite to where the *Cataraqui* struck, rises gradually from shore, a long rugged reef, about 40 feet high, and at a distance of about 20 fathoms [35 metres] run lower and parallel belts of rocks, on the outermost of those reefs the ship struck; and I am told the majority of the people were dashed to pieces by the break upon the second. There are, however, chasms upon each side through which some were providentially washed, and enabled to make the larger reef; when the chance of a few moments enabled them to escape. Numbers, however, perished upon this larger reef, upon which at short periods the sea broke very heavily.

. . . Perhaps in the annals of shipwreck, a more calamitous event is not to be found – nine souls of a complement of 423 [sic] being the sole survivors, and the ship herself, one of 802 tons, almost smashed into matchwood. The beach for about one mile [1.6 kilometres] above and three miles [5 kilometres] below the spot where she first struck, presented a most dreadful sight, strewed with bodies, fragments of booms, spars and tattered wearing apparel.

A mark of the difficulty of getting the survivors to the cutter was that it took three days. Around 10 September, she finally set sail for Melbourne, her cargo the tale of the fate of the *Cataraqui*. By now the ship was long overdue and in Melbourne concern was growing daily regarding her safety.

On Tuesday, 9 September 1845, while the *Midge* was plucking *Cataraqui*'s survivors from the shores of King Island, in Sydney, at a meeting of the Legislative Council of New South Wales, the member for Melbourne, Mr Robinson, moved the following motion: 'That a Select Committee be appointed to enquire and report as to the best positions for Light Houses or Beacons, in Bass's Straits, or on the coasts adjacent.'

Robinson acknowledged that a select committee had already done the same thing in 1842 and nothing had come of it, due to lack of funds. However, as the *Sydney Morning Herald* reported the next day, when the *Midge* was leaving King Island:

He should deem it a disgrace upon that House if another session was suffered to pass over without some further steps being taken in the matter.

Mr Lamb, in seconding the motion, remarked that he entirely agreed with the hon. member for Melbourne, as to the great want of lighthouses in Bass's Straits, conceiving, as he did, that many of the disasters which had taken place in that quarter might be traced to this want. He much doubted, however, whether, in the present state of the revenue it would be possible to proceed with an undertaking which would involve so large an expenditure as the erection of the proposed lighthouses.

The seemingly toothless motion was carried without further debate. It was only three days later, in the early hours of 13 September, that the *Midge* arrived in Melbourne. News of the loss of the *Cataraqui* struck the fledgling city with a shock that was unprecedented in its short history. As word spread, crowds gathered at newspaper offices desperate for news of what was then, and still is, the worst civil disaster in the history of Australia's European settlement. Extraordinary editions were put out during the Saturday, based on the accounts of chief mate Guthery and John Fletcher of the *Midge*. They included inevitable calls for lighthouses.

The *Port Phillip Herald* wrote: 'How terribly does this catastrophe give weight to the observations we made in our last number upon the imperative necessity of constructing lighthouses on the shores of Bass Straits, whilst daily and hourly hundreds of valuable lives are incurring the same dangers as those who have thus been sacrificed.'

Two weeks later, the news reached Sydney, where the *Sydney Morning Herald* reprinted accounts from all the Melbourne papers and joined the growing chorus for lighthouses: 'Had there been a lighthouse on King's Island, it is probable this wreck would not have occurred, and we hope Mr Robinson's Committee on Lighthouses, which is now sitting, will especially direct their attention to the importance of placing lighthouses on Cape Otway and King's Island.'

News of the tragic end of the *Cataraqui* rolled around the world, breaking most heavily in a handful of towns in the English Midlands. It was widely reported that most of the emigrants came from Bedfordshire, Staffordshire, Yorkshire and Nottinghamshire. In fact the origins of two-thirds of the emigrants (transported under a bounty system paid for by the government of New South Wales) were concentrated in two small areas – one between Bedford and Cambridge, the other near Oxford.

The public was swift to condemn. The *Sydney Morning Herald* didn't hold back the Monday after it first received news of the tragedy: 'this awful event was caused by a gross error in judgment of her ill-fated Captain. The ship had been hove to on the Sunday evening at seven o'clock and had this prudent measure been adhered to until daylight, all would have been well, and this calamitous accident not have occurred.'

Yet a subsequent inquiry exonerated Captain Finlay and the blame was put on the lack of lighthouses. In any case, the need to do something was considered imperative in the labour-starved colony. Who would attempt to relocate in Australia if it meant there was a good chance of being dashed to pieces on a rocky shore instead?

Lighthouses had sprung up around Bass Strait by the end of the 1840s, though King Island's proved inadequate and was replaced by a larger one in 1861, now the tallest in the southern hemisphere. Not that this stopped ships being wrecked. In 1865 the *Arrow* mistook the light on King Island for Cape Otway and ran aground with no loss of life. In 1875 the *Blencathra* made the same mistake. In 1867, the lighthouse-keepers at Cape Wickham found themselves caring for 450 emigrants when the *Netherby* ran aground. In 1871, another light was built at Currie, further south on King Island, to make it clear to vessels that they were approaching King Island's deadly west coast.

David Howie returned to King Island with a contract to bury the remaining dead. Over 340 bodies were eventually identified and buried in several graves. In 1848 a memorial to the victims was erected on instructions from Melbourne's Governor Latrobe. It eventually rusted away. A stone cairn was erected in 1956 and in 1995 the King Island Community and Tasmania's Parks and Wildlife Service erected permanent information markers and signage near the graves and at a point overlooking the wreck site. There is an excellent web site with details on the *Cataraqui* at http://www.parks.tas.gov.au/historic/shipw/cat.html

The exposed position of the *Cataraqui* means very little is left of the wreck itself – part of the capstan, an anchor and chain, and fragments of the slate cargo. Other items that have been recovered from the site are in the King Island Historical Society Museum at Currie. The wreck remains the largest civil disaster in Australia's history, only exceeded in loss of life by the sinking of HMAS *Sydney* in World War II. And while it underlined the pressing need for lighthouses around Australia's coasts, only twelve years later the government responsible faced a catastrophe caused by a lighthouse in its own front yard.

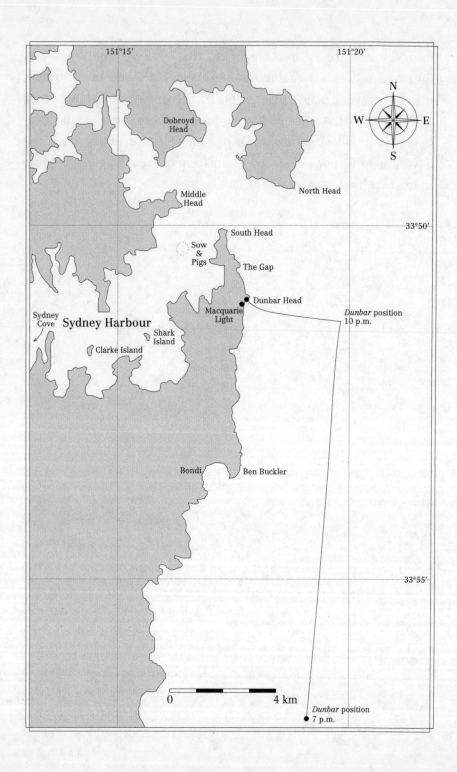

151°15'

151°20'

N

W ← → E

S

Dobroyd
Head

North Head

Middle
Head

33°50'

South Head

Sow
&
Pigs

The Gap

Dunbar Head

Dunbar position
10 p.m.

Macquarie
Light

Sydney
Cove

Sydney Harbour

Shark
Island

Clarke Island

Bondi   Ben Buckler

33°55'

0   4 km

Dunbar position
7 p.m.

The *Dunbar*
(Australian National Maritime Museum)

6. THE PORT OF SHAME: *DUNBAR*, 1857

The chain of events that leads to Sydney's worst shipwreck is one of the longest in the history of maritime disasters. It begins before the vessel was built, before most of its victims were even born, with a decision made by desperate people some sixty-five years before the merchant vessel *Dunbar*, Captain James Green master, struck the cliffs in the vicinity of Macquarie Lighthouse on the night of 20 August 1857. She was two kilometres south of the entrance to the harbour she was making for and the presence of the lighthouse should have made the *Dunbar*'s navigation safe, as lighthouses are usually placed so that they either guide vessels into harbour or warn them of danger. However, the Macquarie Lighthouse – Australia's first and at the time Sydney's only lighthouse – has a unique quality. It does neither.

The role of the Macquarie Lighthouse is bound to the circumstances that Australia's first European settlers confronted after
establishing their colony at Sydney Cove in 1788. As Captain Watkin
Tench, an officer in the English marines, wrote in his diary in 1790:

> From intelligence of our friends and connections we had been entirely
> cut off, no communication whatever having passed with our native
> country since the 13th of May 1787, the day of our departure from
> Portsmouth. Famine besides was approaching with gigantic strides,
> and gloom and dejection overspread every countenance . . . For eight-
> een months after we had landed in the country, a party of marines used
> to go weekly to Botany Bay to see whether any vessel, ignorant of
> our removal to Port Jackson, might be arrived there. But a better plan
> was now devised on the suggestion of [naval] Captain Hunter. A party
> of seamen were fixed on a high bluff, called the South Head, at the
> entrance of the harbour, on which a flag was ordered to be hoisted
> whenever a ship might appear, which should serve as a direction to
> her, and as a signal of approach to us.

The Signal Station is still on the site that was chosen, but Tench
wasn't exactly correct in his description of its position. The high bluff
that affords a view down the coast to the entrance of Botany Bay *and*
is in sight of Sydney Cove is 2.25 kilometres south of the entrance to
the harbour. Even today, the Signal Station is clearly visible eight
kilometres beyond the Opera House and the buildings of Circular
Quay. What can't be seen is the low-lying headland at the mouth of
the harbour. A signal station built there might have been able to
guide vessels into the harbour, but it couldn't have signalled the
supply-ship-starved colonists.

Nevertheless, the chosen site was considered so good by the colonists
that it was soon enhanced. Tench writes on 7 September 1790: 'His
Excellency [Governor Phillip] had this day gone to a landmark, which

was building on South Head, near the flagstaff, to serve as a direction to ships at sea.'

For the next 28 years, the Signal Station operated on the site, with
a wood- and coal-fired beacon used to guide vessels at night. However, after his arrival in the colony in 1810, Governor Lachlan
Macquarie identified the need to build a proper lighthouse. Lack of
funds (and for a time the lack of an architect) meant that construction wasn't begun until 1816, supervised by convict architect Francis
Greenway. Work was completed in 1818 although Greenway was
scornful of the quality of the sandstone used and didn't believe the
lighthouse would last long. The building was 25 metres high,
perched on the cliffs 80 metres above the sea.

Little consideration seems to have been given to locating the lighthouse nearer to the mouth of the harbour. Guiding ships to the
harbour, rather than into it, was still more important. And the site
certainly does that. The light is visible from south of Botany Bay.
Approaching from the north, it is only obscured by towering North
Head if a vessel is close in to shore.

Despite Greenway's doubts about its durability, for the next thirty-
seven years the Macquarie Light remained the first and only
lighthouse on Sydney's coast, guiding ships to the port which Governor Phillip had described, when he became the first European to
enter it on 21 January 1788, as 'the finest harbour in the world,
where a thousand Sail of the line may ride in the most perfect security.' First, though, they had to get there.

The *Dunbar* wasn't the first vessel to come to grief entering the
harbour. On the night of 25 August 1834, the 307-tonne wooden
barque *Edward Lombe*, Captain Stroyan master, coming up from
Hobart, ran for the harbour without a pilot as a fierce sou'-easter
built the swell at her back. She got inside the safety of the Heads and
turned south into the main harbour only to be confronted by the
small rocky reef of the Sow and Pigs. The Sow and Pigs is usually

a minor inconvenience, rather than an obstacle, but the *Edward Lombe* found it restricting her room to manoeuvre as she now had to tack into the wind. Sow and Pigs had long been recognised as a hazard, and a lightship was placed adjacent to it, which could help vessels find their way once they were inside the Heads. Stroyan dropped anchor only two boat-lengths from the Sow and Pigs, but in the howling wind the chain parted almost immediately. The gale blew the ship backwards towards the harbour's rocky western shore. Another anchor was dropped, to no avail. The ship was thrown onto Middle Head (an inner harbour headland), where the swell coming in the Heads was crashing ashore. The ship was completely wrecked and, of the forty-six on board, twenty-nine were lost. At the time there were calls for improvements to the harbour entrance, but as in Bass Strait, nothing was done due to a lack of funds and political will.

Almost to the day twenty-three years later the arrangements at Sydney Heads hadn't changed when the *Dunbar* sighted the coast off Botany Bay. The *Dunbar* was one of the biggest sailing vessels of her day, 1321 tonnes, and one of the fastest, built in 1853 for the Dunbar Line to compete with the American clippers. She had left Plymouth, England, on 31 May 1857, and less than three months later, at dusk on Thursday, 20 August, she was just 20 kilometres from her destination, having safely passed through the Brouwer Route's roaring forties and having successfully threaded the needle of the now well-lit Bass Strait.

Though Sydney's navigation aids had changed little in the sixty-nine years since European settlement, the city itself was unrecognisable. The desperate struggle for survival in its early years as a penal colony had given way to prosperity as it became the major port for the region. During the 1830s and 1840s in particular, it was the clearing house for rural exports from the flourishing inland. The growing demand for labour that lead to the introduction of the emigrant bounty schemes and the relocation of many of Britain's dislocated masses made Sydney the arrival point for successive generations of new Australians. At the start of the 1850s, the existence of the inland gold-fields finally leaked out (pastoralists had known of them since the 1830s but kept the knowledge to themselves for fear of worsening their labour shortages) and the tide of migration became a flood. Sydney's population rapidly grew and in 1856 it had reached 56 394.

The *Dunbar*, however, wasn't an immigrant ship. Many of her passengers were from Sydney, prosperous citizens returning from trips to the mother country, England. Even *Dunbar's* captain had deep Sydney connections. The *Sydney Morning Herald* described him as 'well known and much esteemed by a large number of the inhabitants of the colony. For several voyages in the *Agincourt* and *Waterloo*, he was mate with Captain Neatby. For two voyages he commanded the *Waterloo*; subsequently he has been in the *Vimeira*; and this was his second trip as master of the *Dunbar*.' Many of the crew were eager to get to Australia, too – several were working for their passage, with pay of a shilling a month.

At Botany Bay all hands saw the land distinctly. According to the account of Seaman James Johnson:

> After that the Captain ordered us to close reef the topsails, and we were close hauled to the wind; the wind was then about east and by south; we were close to the wind and lying about north-east and by north and lying along the coast.
>
> At the time we made this land to the best of my opinion we were about 10 or 12 miles [16 or 20 kilometres] off. We were under easy sail, sail having been shortened after we saw the land; we had on no topgallant-sails, and we had three reefs in the main, and four reefs in the fore-topsail. When night came on, we still kept our course, and shortly afterwards we saw the Sydney light; I saw it about seven o'clock, shortly after getting supper; it was known to be the Sydney Head light.

The watch on deck was sent below according to orders, and were relieved at eight o'clock; it was raining hard; the light was only seen at intervals, but distinctly. I was on deck at eight o'clock, as I belonged to the chief officer's watch; the captain remained on deck when the watch was relieved, and gave orders the same as usual; everything was attended to, and his orders were punctually obeyed; we stood along the coast till we fetched the light up to the lee mizen rigging [the aftermost mast on the three-masted ship]; the vessel was not labouring, she came to her helm willingly.

Johnson hadn't visited Sydney before and in darkness had no idea of the coastline he was passing. Approaching the harbour mouth from the south in daylight, it's an awesome spectacle. From Ben Buckler, at the northern end of Bondi Beach, to South Head, the cliffs extend in an almost unbroken line for nearly 6 kilometres. For much of the way they are vertical ramparts of yellow sandstone up to 100 metres high, only sloping down towards the water at South Head itself. In a sou'-easter the waves rebound off the rocks, doubling up with the incoming waves and creating a churning mass of water. The waves also rebound off North Head, an even more forbidding mass of rock. Its southern face, 1.5 kilometres away across the harbour, extends 100-metre cliffs for 1.6 kilometres out to sea. It then turns north and runs in an unbroken line of cliffs for another 3 kilometres.

Coming up from the south, the view into the harbour is daunting. From outside the Heads it appears to be all cliffs – the massive bulk of Dobroyd Head on one side of Middle Harbour extends south-west to Grotto Point, with Gowland Bombora breaking offshore in a sou'-easter. There's a little gap at the opening to Middle Harbour, then there are the cliffs of Middle Head, the same that claimed the unfortunate *Edward Lombe*. If you didn't know there was 'the world's finest harbour' tucked behind South Head, you wouldn't risk being embayed against such an unforgiving coast.

In the darkness, James Johnson and the rest of the *Dunbar*'s crew saw nothing of this. All they could see was the Macquarie Light, halfway along the line of cliffs leading to South Head, neither guiding them to safety nor warning them of danger.

The same night, Archibald Fletcher was the master of the steamer *Nora Creina*, plying between Shoalhaven and Sydney, which was on its way to the harbour:

When off the Heads, it being then ten o'clock, I saw a large ship; she was off the Heads about 2 miles [3 kilometres] having her head to the northward, she was going very slow, with easy sail; I saw the lights through her stern-windows, which appeared very large; when I came abreast of her, I saw her lights fore and aft; I was between the ship and the land, my vessel having clear mast light, and it is my opinion they must have seen me from the ship; no signals passed between us; the ship was then about two-and-a-half miles [4 kilometres] from the entrance into the port; I saw no signal of distress or lights burning to attract attention; I considered the ship perfectly safe; it was blowing in heavy squalls, the weather stormy, with torrents of rain; there was a heavy sea on; the wind was blowing about east, varying about two points to the north, the vessel was on her starboard tack, and appeared clear of all danger; the captain of the other vessel must have shortly made the Heads after I had passed had it kept its proper course; I saw the Heads when I was abreast of the ship; I was closer in than the ship; I am sure the captain of the strange vessel could not have seen the Heads; I was standing on the bridge of the steamer keeping a strict lookout, the light was observable, but the other ship, standing further off, had not so good an opportunity of seeing it . . .

It would not have taken an hour for her to reach the Heads from that time; I passed her pretty quick; the time requiring the vessel to reach the port would depend upon the way she was worked; if not hove to or delayed she might make the Heads in a short time after I passed her;

from my experience of the coast I do not think that a master acquainted with the coast, and having seen the light, could mistake what is known as the Gap [a low point in the South Head cliff line] for the entrance to the harbour; it is my opinion that if the captain had seen his danger in time, he could have avoided it by going out to sea, there being nothing to prevent his doing so.

James Johnson, aboard the *Dunbar*, never saw the *Nora Creina*:

The lee mizzen rigging was on the port side of the ship; the captain was on the weather side of the deck; he had no night glass, but the second mate had a case of what we call opera glasses; when the light was brought to bear upon the lee mizzen rigging all hands were piped up by the boatswain; the hands turned up; the boatswain sang out for 'All hands to wear ship'; these were the words that were passed along; the usual orders were given; when we came on deck orders were given to square away the yards; we got the orders to square away; after a short time the captain gave orders to haul up the foresail; it was then reefed; the ship then kept before the wind; the light was clearly visible at times; when the words were given to square the yards the light had previously been seen; the vessel was running in on a heavy sea; it was blowing very fresh in squalls, with thick small rain; it was about eleven o'clock when the hands were called up; there were two men on the forecastle with the third mate, on the look-out for the land; the third mate was on the forecastle with the two men, and the second mate was afterwards sent there also.

The captain sang out, 'Do you see anything of the North Head?'

And the mate said, 'No, I see nothing of it.'

I was on the poop at this time, standing by the braces; she had the light a bit on her port bow when I saw it at this time; then the captain sang out to the man at the wheel to keep his luff; the yards were about a point or so to port; I heard these words – it was done; the course of the ship was changed a small bit by this.

Shortly after this the second mate sang out 'Breakers ahead.'

The captain sung out to the man at the wheel to port his helm [turn to starboard]. We were all at the braces; he told us to haul in the port braces, and brace the yards sharp up; it was done, and done quickly, without delay; there were thirteen able seamen in each watch; there was no want of hands; we were well manned, and we could see the light; it appeared to be right over us.

I heard no further orders given; a few minutes after we hauled the yards round – about two minutes after – she went side on to the rocks; she was trying to stretch out to the eastward, her head lying along the land to the north; then we struck, and then the screaming began, the passengers running about the deck screaming for mercy.

The captain was on the poop; he was cool and collected; there was great confusion and uproar on the deck with the shrieks of the passengers. With the first bump the three topmasts fell; the first sea that came over us stove in the quarterboats; none were lowered; the mizzen-mast went first, then the mainmast. The fore-mast stood a long time; it was not more than five minutes after she struck that she began to break up; I was on the poop at the time; I caught hold of a stanchion, then laid hold of the mizzen chains; when these gave way, I made for the cabin, but the sea was coming down there enough to smother one . . . saw some of the young ladies, when going into the cabin, running about in their chemises, screaming, screeching and crying, and calling on Mr Spence [the second officer] to know if there was any possibility of being saved . . . I went below and got out of the cabin skylight to leeward, and got up the side of the chainplates of the fore-rigging; this broke up at last, and I was thrown over still holding by the chain-plates, which held some four planks together; and I was thrown upon the rocks in a heap of timber and rubbish . . . no-one was near me when I was washed away; she kept breaking up from aft, and I kept getting forward until at last I reached the chain-plates of the fore-rigging; I was washed away with planks and broken timber upon a shelf of rock, but immediately on the sea receding

I got up a bit higher out of reach of the back current . . . I had on a blue shirt, a singlet, and drawers, I hove everything off – boots, trousers, and pea coat, when the first alarm was given.

The *Dunbar* was carrying 59 crew, 30 passengers, and 33 more in steerage, making a total complement of 122. Johnson was the only survivor.

Friday morning dawned in Sydney with low heavy clouds scudding in over the coast from the south-east, laden with rain. It was windy and still quite dark at 7 a.m. as Mr Hydes, a harbour pilot, walked along the cliff tops near the lighthouse. According to *Bradshaw's Narrative of the Wreck of the Dunbar*, he

discovered under the Rocks near the lighthouse on the South Head, the wreck [debris] of some large ship. Search was immediately made along the coast, and about a mile and a half from where some floating spars were observed, at the Gap – which is a deep rocky shelving (crescent shaped) forming a perfect bit, which has on more occasion than one been taken for the entrance to the Heads, especially at a distance, it is situated at the extreme end or curve of the South Head – human bodies washing about, too truly told the sad tale.

Hydes and another pilot, Robson, searched along the coast until they found the wreck itself, half-way between the Gap and the Macquarie Light. As the *Herald* reported the following day:

They thought her a ship of 1000 tons, very heavily timbered, masts and bowsprits hooped; figure, a gilt scroll; had the appearance of an

American-built ship, with copper fastenings, and her internal fittings consisted of a large quantity of unpainted light wood, such as is used in immigrant ships.

Captain Charles Wiseman, commander of the paddle-steamer *Grafton*, en route from the Clarence River to Sydney, was one of the first vessels near the scene: 'On entering the Heads, about half-past nine o'clock Friday morning, noticed portions of wreck floating about; they belonged to some large vessel; knew at once that some large vessel must have been wrecked near at hand.'

He had been obliged to stop to clear debris from the *Grafton*'s paddles – timbers, bales of goods and bedding.

News of the disaster spread through the city, amid growing fears as to what ship it might be. One opinion was that it was a North American ship, another that it was British. Some of the pilots descended the cliffs to try to find something with the vessel's name on it among the apparel being tossed in the breakers. According to *Bradshaw's Narrative*:

By three o'clock some hundreds of cabs from Sydney, as well as several omnibuses, loaded to excess, had brought people to view the heart-rending scene of destruction going on at the Gap. Dead bodies by dozens were every minute being dashed upon the rocks by each wave, mountainous in themselves. Presently bodies without hands, legs, arms, bale goods, bedding, beams, ship's knees, and every imaginable article was being hurled in the air some 60 or 70 feet [20 metres] by the violence of the waves.

It was impossible to retrieve anything from the wreck site and extremely hazardous to reach it by boat, but by the afternoon much of the wreckage had floated ashore in Middle Harbour. On Edwards Beach, at Balmoral in Middle Harbour, about 12 metres of the keel was washed up, along with flooring timbers, and two sheets of copper still attached to the planking. The beach was littered with cargo. Near the Spit, two or three beer cask-heads with the Tooths brand were picked up, as were the bodies of two respectably-dressed men and a woman with a ring on her finger. And Bradshaw reported that 'on George's Beach', which probably refers to one of the small sandy beaches near George's Head on the western side of the harbour, 'the body of a little boy, quite naked, and apparently about four years of age, with black hair, was picked up; also a cow, red with white spots, and short horns, was floating near this spot, surrounded by sharks, who were devouring the animal.'

At South Head, the *Herald*'s correspondent reported:

> We found the residents of that locality watching with great horror the dead and mutilated bodies as they were thrown upon the rocks, the succeeding waves washing off again the naked remains. There were men, women, and children – their number was variously estimated at from twenty to fifty. But it was difficult to ascertain the number, as the bodies were thrown up on the ledges of the rocks and again taken off by the violence of the surf.

'The South Head was now one mass of people, anxious to view the wreck, and, if possible, to learn the slightest tidings as to what ship,' reported *Bradshaw's Narrative*. 'Darkness alone put an end to the horrid scene enacting beneath the rocks. The multitude returning home to Sydney, sickened at the sight, and maddened with the uncertainty overhanging the wreck.'

Sydney descended into severe shock. It transacted almost all of its business by sea and now it was seeing first-hand exactly what happens when a ship is wrecked.

At 3.25 p.m., 21 August, the Speaker of the New South Wales Legislative Assembly, Sir Daniel Cooper, had taken his chair in the Parliament in Macquarie Street. After dealing with a petition from the people of Moreton Bay to form the State of Queensland, a petition to incorporate Catholic St John's College into Sydney University and a question on the establishment of grammar schools in large rural centres, the attention of the House was turned to the terrible drama taking place 8 kilometres from the building.

Mr Holroyd broached the subject that was on everyone's mind: 'It is currently reported about town that a large vessel has been shipwrecked at the Heads during the gale last night. I desire to know whether the Government has received any information on the subject, and if so, what steps have been taken in consequence?'

The Premier and Colonial Secretary, Mr Parker, rose to reply:

I have not received any really authentic information upon the subject, and to detail mere rumours might be to agonise feelings for no purpose whatever. I can assure the honourable member, however, that the Government has taken the earliest opportunity, upon hearing of the disaster, to procure correct information, and to afford such relief as might be necessary. Owing to the thickness of the weather the signals at South Head could not be distinctly understood, and the consequence was that Captain Pockley [the Portmaster] went down himself to the scene of the wreck; but the only information that has been furnished to the Government, and that, as I said before, could not be relied on, was to the effect that a vessel had been wrecked last night on the outside of South Head. Later in the day the captain of the *Grafton*, steamer, reported that whilst entering the harbour, he saw the topmast of what appeared a very large vessel standing out of the water in the fairway, between the Heads. From this it would seem that the first report was correct, and that the wreck seen on the outside of South Head had subsequently drifted into the fairway of the Heads. There had also been seen floating about the wreck several human bodies, a large quantity of bedding, the carcasses of three bulls, together with a variety of other articles that had evidently been washed from the vessel. Of course this information not being authentic, I do not put it forth as being worthy of implicit confidence.

During the evening the Portmaster Captain Pockley returned to the city. There he was finally able to report that twelve bodies were ashore at Middle Harbour. One was the body of an officer, with gilt buttons on the coat marked 'W.B.W.' A mail bag was found marked '*Dunbar*, Plymouth, May 29', also a cask of tripe marked '*Dunbar*.' Among other articles found were several boys' cricket bats that corresponded with an expected shipment on the *Dunbar*.

Late on Friday night, despite this report, the *Herald* still entertained the possibility that the wreck might be some other ship:

> There is evidence sufficient to excite the most anxious and painful concern regarding the *Dunbar*; but we demur, with the present proofs, to declare positively that that fine ship, with her greatly respected commander, Captain Green, and a large number of passengers, many of them old and much respected colonists, is really lost.

Yet another part of the paper, presumably typeset later, told a different story. It was the report of parliamentary proceedings:

> Adjournment of the house. Mr Cowper [leader of the Opposition] said, the House had, within the last few minutes, been made acquainted with a most melancholy event, that had so shocked them all, that they felt utterly incompetent to the transaction of any further business. Under these circumstances it was the feeling of hon. members who ordinarily acted with him that the House should adjourn. Under any circumstances a wreck such as the one that had recently occurred would be most deplorable, since the unfortunate passengers must in many instances have relatives and connections amongst those resident here, but in this instance it was the more so, since it was known that

persons closely connected with a member of that House were passengers by this luckless vessel. Seeing this, he and his friends considered it would be but right that the House should suspend its proceedings.

The motion was carried and the House adjourned at 9.20 p.m. The member of the House referred to, Daniel Egan, had just learned that his wife, son and daughter, passengers on the *Dunbar*, were probably dead.

On Saturday morning both the *Sydney Morning Herald* and the *Empire* newspapers carried supplements confirming the loss of the *Dunbar*. Out at South Head, a crowd estimated at 10 000, nearly a fifth of the city's population, gathered above the scene of devastation. The *Herald* reporter wrote:

Having arrived at the scene of this melancholy disaster about a quarter to eleven this morning, I, like most of the spectators, mingled in the general excitement then prevalent, which may be far more easily imagined than described; and after walking about for some time, listening to fears here and hopes there, hopes that some one or more might yet be found living to clear up the awful mystery that must ever hang over such a disaster, uncleared by such testimony, when, behold, the joy of everybody was expressed by a shout of 'A man on the rocks! A live man on the rocks. There he is! There he is!'

It was James Johnson, still alive after nearly thirty-six hours clinging to the cliff above the waves. The Mayor of Sydney, George Thornton, interviewed Johnson shortly after his rescue:

On Saturday morning he endeavoured to get along the rocks; he could see people on the cliffs above, but could not make himself seen, until a brave lad (Antonio Wollier, an Icelander [actually Norwegian]), who had gone down 'Jacob's Ladder' [a fissure in the cliffs], and along the rocks, noticed Johnson waving a handkerchief; relief came, and he was soon after hauled up to the top of the cliffs, which are there about 200 feet [60 metres] high. The noble fellow (Wollier) was then hauled up, and received the hearty manifestations of the thousands there assembled. I opened a subscription, which was suggested by Captain Loring of HM ship *Iris*, and in a few minutes about £10 was collected and handed over to this courageous boy, who, in answer to my compliment when handing him the money, said, in broken English, 'He did not go down for the money, but for the feelings of his heart.'

Afterwards at the Gap, another brave fellow, whose name I have not yet learned, volunteered to go down to send up some of the mangled corpses, now and then lodging on the rocks beneath us – now a trunk of a female from the waist upwards – then the legs of a male, the body of an infant, the right arm, shoulder, and head of a female, the bleached arm and extended hand with the wash of the receding water, almost as 'twere in life, beckoning for help! then a leg, a thigh, a human head would be hurled along, the sea dashing most furiously as if in angry derision of our efforts to rescue its prey; one figure, a female, tightly clasping an infant to the breast, both locked in firm embrace in death, was for a moment seen, then the legs of some trunkless body would leap from the foaming cataract caused by the receding sea, leaping wildly, with feet seen plainly upward in the air, to the abyss below, to be again and again tossed up to the gaze of the sorrowing throng above. We procured a rope, lowered the man, with some brave stout hearts holding on to the rope above, and in this manner several portions of the mutilated remains were hauled up to the top of the cliff, until a huge sea suddenly came, and nearly smothered those on the cliff, wetting them all to the skin. I caused the man to be hauled up, thinking it too dangerous to continue. It was a heart-rending scene, and I was glad to leave it.

While Johnson received medical attention and gave a disjointed account of the fate of the *Dunbar*, the macabre work of recovering bodies continued inside the harbour. Captain Pockley and the Inspector-General of the Water Police, Captain McLerie, had chartered the steamer *Black Swan*. When it was due to leave on Saturday morning, it had been nearly overwhelmed by citizens, many seeking lost relatives, desperate to accompany her. In the company of the steamer *Pelican*, the vessel reached North Harbour at 11 a.m., carrying Pockley, McLerie, the Health Officer, Coroner, 'a large number of gentlemen' and a quantity of coffin shells. They proceeded around the shores, picking up bodies from several places where they'd been found, scouring the rocks for signs of any more. At the Quarantine Ground three bodies were picked up from HMS *Herald*, which had recovered them off North Head. One was identified as Mr I. Simmons, the other two, seamen, had been badly mutilated by sharks.

The *Black Swan* returned to Sydney with nineteen bodies and numerous body parts, which were taken to the Water Police deadhouse at Circular Quay. The steamer *Washington* and several other vessels went out of the Heads and down the coast, close inshore, looking for more survivors. There were none.

While the search for bodies continued on the harbour, and the crowds continued to throng South Head, at 10 a.m. on Sunday a jury was sworn in for the inquest into the deaths of the people recovered so far. The same day the proprietor of the Manly Beach Hotel, Phillip Cohen, who had pulled several bodies from the water, was prevented from recovering two more by the ferocity of the sharks, one of which dragged one body under when he'd tried to take it. Most of the wreck was now washed ashore at Middle Harbour.

'The shore is literally white with candles, and the rocks are covered a foot [30 centimetres] or more deep with articles of every kind –

boots, panama hats, and bonnets are here in abundance,' the *Herald* reported. 'Drums of figs, hams, pork, raisins, drapery, boots, and pieces of timber, piled in heaps and lining the shore for a considerable distance, give a vivid idea of the havoc created.'

At Watson's Bay, the *Black Swan* took on board another three bodies, which were described by the *Herald* in extraordinary detail: 'One, with the exception of the top of the scull [*sic*], and the loss of part of the left arm, was entirely whole, and seems to have been a fine man. The other two were only trunks, the mutilated remains of unfortunate sailors.'

Over at the inquest, it was proving too much for some of the jurors. The identification of the bodies was so harrowing that one juror fainted and several others had to leave the deadhouse to recover.

By Monday morning, the horror and grief over the disaster had been joined by anger. On Friday night, the *Herald* writers could hardly believe the *Dunbar* under Captain Green could come to grief. By Monday, they'd changed their tune.

> Whole families are plunged into mourning. Re-unions, fondly anticipated and momentarily expected to be realised, have been abruptly hindered, and hindered forever. Instead of the warm and loving welcome come tidings of a terrible catastrophe and then the cold, mutilated, half unrecognisable forms of those who will never cheer the social circle more. Almost at the threshold of their own homes they perished – so near once more to their friends and relatives – and yet so far . . .
>
> If we had dared to predict a safe voyage for any vessel it would have been the *Dunbar* under Captain Green. Yet, after a successful voyage it has been flung on shore almost in sight of the anchorage at the base of the lighthouse and with the loss of every soul on board but one. So fallible are the calculations of mortals! . . .
>
> But it seems to be tolerably clear that Captain Green mistook the Gap for the entrance to The Heads and thought the breakers reported

in front to be the waves dashing against the North Head. If so, it adds confirmation to an opinion often expressed by nautical men that the entrance to Port Jackson is not properly lighted.

In the evidence given recently before the commission which sat at Melbourne to inquire into the lighting of the Australian coast more than one witness stated that the lighthouse should be on the North Head. It [the Macquarie Light] is an excellent sea light and is seen far off, but it affords but little help to a vessel close in. It is a satisfactory guide *to* the harbour, but not a guide *into* it.

. . . We are entitled to expect that the Light and Navigation Board recently constituted will give attention to this matter without delay and either urge forward the necessary work or else produce such evidence of its undesirableness as shall satisfactorily disabuse the public mind of the prevalent impression that the guidance into the harbour is insufficient. It is due to the reputation of the port not only that there should be no such deficiency but that there should not be even any justification for asserting it.

The inquest, which had adjourned on Sunday after identifying bodies, reconvened on Monday to examine the witnesses – seaman James Johnson, Charles Wiseman of the *Grafton*, and Archibald Fletcher of the *Nora Creina*. Naturally, most of the interest focussed on Johnson.

Since his rescue, Johnson had been telling and retelling multitudes of people what had happened. The consequence was that much of the story was garbled and confused as it was repeated, misunderstood or interpreted. On the day of his testimony, for example, the Sydney newspapers carried the Mayor's account of what Johnson told him had happened. There were some interesting contradictions with the testimony he gave. The most interesting was the order Captain Green gave after hearing the cry 'Breakers ahead.' In the mayor's account, based on what Johnson told him immediately upon being rescued on the Saturday, 'The captain ordered the helm to be put hard to star-board to bring the ship round.' At the inquest on Monday he said, 'The captain sung out to the man at the wheel to port his helm.'

It's possible that one of the versions of the story was simply gar-bled in translation. But it's also possible that, for whatever reason, Johnson changed his story. What is certain is that Captain Green's last order was crucial. If he'd thought the 'breakers ahead' were on North Head, the right thing to do was to order the helm to starboard which would have turned the *Dunbar* to port, towards the entrance to the harbour. However, as he was actually facing South Head, that order would have turned the ship straight towards the rocks. The right thing to do, and what Johnson eventually testified, was to turn the ship to starboard. Green may well have done so and still been wrecked.

It's understandable that Johnson's testimony was shaky. On Thurs-day he'd been shipwrecked and seen over a hundred people die. All through Friday he'd clung to rocks in the cold winter air, watching bodies being smashed to pieces all around him. On Saturday he was rescued and besieged by frantic people desperate for news of their loved ones. On Monday, he fronted an official enquiry. The effects of shock and post-traumatic stress were unknown at the time, but his inconsistent story may be symptomatic of a man unready to give a coherent version of events. Or, Sydney being Sydney, the fixers had gone to work and covered up Green's fatal mistakes.

The haste with which the inquiry went ahead is underlined by its adjournment on Monday afternoon so the jurors could attend the funeral for the victims. The depth of the city's trauma was on open display, as the *Herald* reported:

The footpaths throughout the streets were literally walled with people. In proportion to the number of inhabitants, never can we recollect a scene in which the feeling of the people was so keenly and manifestly exhibited. The shops were, with only one or two exceptions, closed along the whole line of road.

After a prolonged journey from the city to the Cemetery, in the course of which, owing to the unfavourable condition of the road, one of the mourning coaches was considerably damaged, the procession reached its destination.

The bodies that couldn't be identified or were unclaimed, and the numerous body parts, were interred in a mass grave at St Stephen's Cemetery, Camperdown. The site was on the then outskirts of town, well south of the harbour and west of the sea, far from the roar of the surf and the cry of the gull. Moreover, the grave site is in the south-west corner, as far from the sea as it can possibly be. Yet even there it couldn't escape a connection with the sea and shipwrecks. The cemetery is on land that was formerly part of the estate of Governor William Bligh, captain of the *Bounty*, which was wrecked by the mutineers, some of whom were then wrecked on the Great Barrier Reef in HMS *Pandora*.

After the funeral, the inquest reconvened and finished questioning witnesses. Then the jurors adjourned to consider their verdict. After 'some deliberation' they delivered it that night.

The jury find that the bodies viewed are those of some of the passengers and crew of the ship *Dunbar*, out of London, commanded by Captain Green, and bound to this port, and that the ship *Dunbar* was wrecked outside the Sydney Heads, close to the Gap, on the night of Thursday, the 20th August last, causing the death of the said parties; there may have been an error of judgement in the vessel being so close to the shore at night in such bad weather, but the jury do not attach any blame to Captain Green or his officers for the loss of the *Dunbar*. The jury consider it their duty to put on record their opinion that the present pilot arrangements for this port are most inadequate, and desire to draw the attention of the Government to the matter.

That was it, just 141 words explaining the deaths of 121 people. Compared to modern inquests, which may convene after months of preparation and run for many months more, with voluminous findings, it was brutally brief. But even in its day, it wasn't enough for most people. If the *Herald*'s editorial on Monday had seemed scathing, Tuesday's showed they were just warming up.

No generous man will refuse a tear to the memory of Captain Green . . .
He had seen much of ocean life; had a reputation as a bold, generous, and successful sailor; had often cast anchor amidst the gratulations of his nautical friends and the grateful acknowledgements of his passengers. He was a favourite in this port.

Here we should be glad to stop. A noble maxim on every man's lips . . . is 'nothing but good of the dead.' To this maxim we should be the first to bow, were it not set aside by the higher interests of the living . . .

Influenced, there is reason to believe, by a determination to anchor within a given hour, he ventured when prudence and the commonest nautical experience would have made retirement imperative. With the same wind and weather others stood out to sea, whilst he madly approached a coast where a false manoeuvre or miscalculation would leave no chance of recovery or retreat.

The commentary on this sad instance of rashness and folly is a dark and full one. It is charged with every incident of sorrow and sacrifice. We have seen on the shore the fragments of fellow-beings which reproach this cruelty; we have collected from every rock the items of this awful indictment. Had Captain Green reflected for a moment on the solemnity of his charge, he would have cast to the winds his chance of a remarkable nautical success . . .

The system of betting on the speed of vessels [Captains vied to break the record for various voyages, and could even be rewarded by their company for doing so] is mischievous in the extreme. It puts life upon a game, and stimulates to ventures, which no man would encounter if left to his own reflections. It was not of the smallest moment to the colony, to the owners of the *Dunbar*, or to the passengers, whether the ship remained twenty-four hours longer at sea or not. The Captain was the only person to whom it could be of consequence; not, we are assured, to win a bet, but to keep an appointment to the day.

We notice these facts with reluctance and sadness. Captain Green is beyond the reach of human reproach. Those who died with him had not time for complaint. In that agonising instant, other thoughts, we may suppose, occupied their minds. Could we imagine that every cry of anguish and despair fell on the ear of this unfortunate commander as an accusation, he paid a fearful penalty – far more bitter than the bitterness of death!

Only in its conclusion did the editorial relent, as it reflected on the terrible impact of the wreck on the city.

If public sympathy with the bereaved could alleviate such sorrow, surely it has not been wanting. Such sad interest we have not witnessed for years. The catastrophe has been felt as a colonial misfortune. It could not be otherwise. It presented all those touching incidents of human woe which come home to the heart. Parent and child – stem and flower, have been laid low by one blast – a thousand cherished thoughts, warm affections, and glowing hopes were wrecked together.

Over at Macquarie Street, the Legislative Assembly met for the first time since it had adjourned the previous Friday on learning of the wreck of the *Dunbar*. If the Government thought the inquest had been the end of the matter, it was wrong. After taking the chair, the Speaker started to report that he'd approached the Governor-General regarding impediments to the purchase of Crown Lands, but the Leader of the Opposition was immediately on his feet, asking questions of the

Leader of the Government. Had the staff at the Signal Station been doing their duty? Were steps being taken to improve the pilot service, as the inquest recommended? Would the Government be erecting a lighthouse on the North Head? Would the Government finally get around to putting in an electric telegraph between the city and the South Head, as it had virtually promised to do the previous year?

Mr Parker rose to reply. The staff had acted properly, though little could be done. As for a light on North Head: 'With a lighthouse there, and a beacon on the South Head, the harbour would be at once perfect in that respect.' In his reply he made two other points.

> As I have been informed by persons living in the neighbourhood, the night was so dark, and so obscured by the storms of rain that passed over, that at such times even the light in the lighthouse was scarcely visible . . . I am sorry also to have to say that the conduct of Captain Green was somewhat rash. I would rather not make such a remark, but the true point to which the enquiry ought to be directed compels me to the remark.

The Treasurer, Mr Donaldson, then rose to defend Captain Green (with scant regard for what actually happened).

> No-one has lost a nearer or dearer friend than I have done in this ill-fated vessel. Captain Green has been a most intimate friend of mine and I am perfectly convinced that that person must have been in a perfect agony from the time of their first sighting the land off Botany. Everything went to prove this; the vessel was close-hauled to the wind, and he was trying to dodge off the land. I am perfectly convinced then, that when Captain Green gave the orders to square away, it had been with the hope, faint though it might have been, that he should be able to stretch in.

As for the electric telegraph (the early sign of the revolution in communications that was to change shipping forever), Mr Donaldson added in a rather convoluted way, 'I would not, though it would not have been of service in the present instance, pretend to say that it would not be very desirable to establish a line between the Heads and Sydney.' He added: 'That it would have been useful in this case would have been impossible, because, with the exception of the dog of Mr Siddons [at the pilot station], not one living creature was aware of the fearful tragedy that was enacting on the face of the waters.' Apparently, Siddon's dog had started barking into the darkness at the time the vessel was thought to have struck.

In the Parliament the debate degenerated until Mr Robertson suggested 'the whole affair was highly discreditable to the country' at which point the Speaker called the House to order as it was provoking 'irregular debate.' But the wreck was another nail in the coffin of a Government already teetering on the brink of collapse.

The next day, the Government brought in the second reading of the Light, Navigation and Pilot Board Bill, to empower the committee recently formed to expedite the lighting of the Heads, along with other sites around the coast. However, the Opposition howled it down, saying that instead of acting, the Government was simply providing jobs for the boys. They wanted construction, not committees, and in a vote of 21 to 15 that signalled real trouble for Parker's Government, the bill's reading was postponed for six months. While the politicians were arguing, the body of Mrs Myers, from the wreck, was being identified and released to her relatives and friends. The body of a two-and-a-half-year-old boy was being recovered in Chowder Bay. Elsewhere mutilated remains were still being picked up and conveyed to the deadhouse.

Amid the claims and counterclaims, one voice spoke up and told the truth about the safety of Sydney's much-vaunted harbour. In a letter to the *Herald* on Wednesday, 26 August, a mariner known only as 'D.P.' wrote:

I begin by denying the assertion, often made, that Sydney Heads are safe to enter in any weather; still, let it be understood that I speak of night-work only. With the wind off the land, smooth water, moon, stars, and all other assistances of that kind, it may be well enough, but even then it is fit to shake the nerves of a man coming off a long voyage, when he gets fairly in the entrance – for the light is then lost – and sees nothing but the towers of black rock in one unbroken line frowning defiance at him. If such be the coast when a weather-shore, what must it be when a lee one. The harbour is well enough to *make,* no-one can contradict that, but with a strong wind blowing on the land, the ship scudding, and thick sudden showers of rain, the characteristic of our east winds, making the darkness impenetrable; there perhaps is not another port in the world more terribly confusing to a seaman to *enter* than the loudly lauded one of Sydney. In most other ports, or estuaries, many mistakes may be made, and yet with little or no loss of life; here there only can be one made, but that is the final and the fatal one. An error of a little half-mile [1 kilometre], as in the case of the poor *Dunbar*, and all is lost; a single look from the most inexperienced eye reads on that rampart of cliffs nothing but rude and mangled death. If I have said anything to shake the general belief that Sydney is such a safe port to enter, let us now see what may be done to make it safer, and to prevent, if possible, by human means, the recurrence of two such shipwrecks [the *Dunbar* and *Edward Lombe*] as have slain their hundreds before our eyes. Although with only an interval of some twenty-three years between them methinks we have had time to think over the matter, and now to move ourselves . . .

My own convictions, borne out by the judgement of others of great experience, goes against the North Head *only* being lighted; and if only one light should be added, that there is another situation preferable. Because every seaman knows that a light on a high cliff in thick rain squalls, which is the weather we have here to dread, is not so easily seen as a light placed a moderate distance above the water's edge.

Therefore, if one light only should be added, that light should be placed where the turning point of the entrance takes place – in this case the *low point* of the South Reef – a red light visible eight miles. And perhaps it would not be at all amiss to say, in the Sailing Directions for the Port of Sydney, that unless such leading light is seen, no sailing vessel with an east wind at night (coasters excluded) should attempt the entrance without a pilot, as long as she can keep to sea.

Meanwhile, in a remarkable about-face, the *Herald*'s editorial of Thursday, 27 August, changed its vituperative tune of the previous Tuesday:

The verdict of the Coroner's jury, given on Monday, was perfectly consistent with their functions. It was not their business, upon conjecture, either to blame or exculpate the dead. It was their duty to confine themselves to the evidence, and to leave undecided whatever the facts before them were insufficient to determine. It was indeed scarcely possible for jurors to escape the influence of current opinion, and we believe that it was the wish of some to stigmatise the navigation of the ship with great severity. We are happy to learn that a more correct impression of the duty of a jury prevailed. It is improbable that any new light will be thrown upon the fate of the *Dunbar*, and when we find nautical men expressing very opposite opinions, it would not be advisable for persons having but slender pretensions to professional knowledge to pronounce, under an official form, a definite censure on the unfortunate deceased. With the Press the case is different; it is the pulsation of the day; it expresses the feelings of the general mind under the present aspect of affairs; it is open to contradiction and correction; it can affix no stigma if exaggerated or passionate which a few days will not remove. The public mind, surveying with more calmness events which have somewhat receded by the lapse of time, will probably embrace at last a sound conclusion. It was, therefore, right to leave the conduct of the unfortunate

Captain uncensured. Public sentiment will be ultimately just to his memory, and we shall not repine if the final judgement of the nautical profession should be a reversal of our own.

Exit the *Herald*, tail between its legs, until the next shipwreck. Yet the *Herald*, the *Dunbar* Inquest and the Light and Navigation Board were still to answer the fundamental question: Why was the *Dunbar* lost? How could the experienced captain of a vessel square away from the wind and point it almost straight at a large lighthouse atop a line of 100-metre cliffs. How could he not see them, even on a dark and stormy night, until it was too late?

What makes the loss of the *Dunbar* even harder to understand is the fact that only an hour before, in what could be presumed to be similar conditions, the *Nora Creina* had passed the *Dunbar*, seen the Heads and safely made port. Her skipper felt Captain Green was perfectly reasonable to attempt the entrance. How could conditions have changed in such a short time?

D.P. touched upon the answer with his comment that 'a light on a high cliff in thick rain squalls, which is the weather we have here to dread, is not so easily seen as a light placed a moderate distance above the water's edge.' And there are clues to the weather conditions the *Dunbar* may have experienced scattered throughout the accounts of the wreck. For example, in Parliament the day she was wrecked, Colonial-Secretary Parker had said that owing to the 'thickness of the weather the signals at South Head could not be distinctly understood.' On the Monday, a funeral vehicle had been badly damaged trying to negotiate the road to the cemetery. However the best indication of the weather conditions on the night of Thursday, 20 August 1857, comes from well inland, from the Hawkesbury region, some 50 kilometres west of Sydney.

A *Herald* report dated 21 August [a typographical error says 21 July] reported: 'Woe upon woe. Another inundation has visited our unhappy district, which promises to be more fearful and of greater magnitude than the former. The rain commenced yesterday morning (Thursday) – mild at first, but gradually increasing in violence until, during last night, it drifted alarmingly and fell in torrents . . . This morning when we rose [the river] was bank high, but by eleven o'clock it had passed over, and a great portion of Cornwallis was flooded. The waters were then rising at the rate of about two feet [60 centimetres] per hour, and the torrent was bearing everything before it.' By Saturday the floodwater had risen 11 metres.

So to say it was raining the night the *Dunbar* was lost is an understatement. All the indications are that Captain Green may have been overtaken by an extreme weather event – not just a rainstorm, but a deluge. Could rain alone completely obscure the lighthouse and the cliffs? According to D.P., the possibility was recognised by local mariners. The day after the wreck, in daylight, the Signal Station couldn't be seen clearly from the city. Johnson's account says the *Dunbar* saw the light intermittently on the port bow, then that when they saw the breakers it was almost directly above them. If they'd seen the light all the way in, Captain Green would surely have steered a course to keep a distance north of it.

It appears likely that when he gave the order to square away, Green could see the Macquarie Light, and possibly even the Heads. As he got nearer though, he was overtaken by a massive rain squall and lost sight of the light and the land. In his evidence at the inquest, Johnson maintained that initially the third mate was in the forecastle with two of the crew, trying to see ahead. As the vessel continued towards the Heads, the second mate was sent there as well, signalling Captain Green's increasing concern at his inability to see. He then called out: 'Do you see anything of the North Head?' The answer was no. The evidence makes it clear he was coming in blind. Moments later the breakers were seen and only then did the poorly positioned Macquarie Light loom out of the murk, almost directly above. But by

then it was too late. The *Dunbar* was about to become one of the few
shipwrecks caused by rain.

Two weeks after the *Dunbar* was wrecked, Parker's Government lost
another vote in the Legislative Assembly and fell. Parliament didn't sit
again before elections were called and the people of New South Wales
(which at the time included Melbourne) voted Parker out of office.
Cowper formed a new government, but Parliament hadn't resumed
when Sydney was rocked by yet another shipwreck at the Heads.

On the night of 24 October, only nine weeks after the *Dunbar* was
lost, the clipper *Catherine Adamson* managed to pick up a pilot and
get through the Heads, but struggled to reach safety in a strong
south-westerly wind. She started to make for the North Harbour,
however gear failure left her drifting towards North Head. Two
anchors were dropped, which held, and lights and rockets were
burned to attract help. The *Williams*, a steamer entering the harbour
on a voyage from Newcastle, came to the *Catherine Adamson*'s aid,
but a rope passed to the steamer for a tow snapped. It was passed
over again, but the wind blew the steamer sideways and she was
forced to drop the line and manoeuvre for her own safety. At 3 a.m.
the sea state changed, and heavy rollers coming in from the sea
swung the ship around and her stern started being battered against
submerged rocks.

The ship's boats were launched and some of the passengers and
crew got to the steamer. These included the skipper, who wanted the
steamer to manoeuvre closer to the ship. Shortly after, the *Catherine
Adamson*'s boats were swamped and the steamer tried to get in
closer, but was prevented by the breaking sea. She then went to the
pilot station to get help, but by the time she'd returned, the vessel

had begun to break up. Consequently twenty-one passengers and crew were lost.

Although the lighting of the harbour was not a factor in the *Catherine Adamson*'s loss, two shipwrecks in as many months fuelled the belief that Sydney Harbour was inherently unsafe. While pilot vessels were still plying the harbour picking up the corpses of shipwrecked voyagers, the former Treasurer Mr Donaldson rose in the new Parliament on Tuesday, 27 October, to demand some form of action to 'prevent the reputation of our magnificent harbour from falling into disgrace.'

So, after 29 had died on the *Edward Lombe* in 1834, 121 more on the *Dunbar* in August 1857 and 21 on the *Catherine Adamson* in October 1857, the thought that Sydney might become known as a port of shame finally brought some action. It was almost immediate. On 28 October the *Sydney Morning Herald* detailed a report from the Light Pilot and Navigation Board regarding the lighting of the entrance to the harbour. 'The light is to be placed on the Inner South Head, but not at the extreme point of the reef . . . The Colonial Architect reports that the spot offers a good foundation, and that the cost would be about £2732. The tower is to be 30 feet [9 metres] in height on a base 60 feet [18 metres] above high-water mark.'

The *Herald* article included the bitter information that: 'There is no need to send to England for a lantern, for it turns out that a first-class catoptric light, which cost £2700, has been lying in the Colonial Store ever since 1853. It is a pity it was not erected long ago instead of rusting in packing cases. Many lives and much property might have been saved.'

The Hornby Light was completed within a year and while it made the entrance to the harbour safer, the mayhem at the Heads wasn't quite over. On 12 September 1873, the Danish barque *Oscar* got into difficulties under North Head, in circumstances similar to the *Catherine Adamson*. She dropped anchor, but the chains snapped.

The vessel then grounded on the rocks and the crew abandoned ship. They took their boats around to Manly Cove, where they woke a local publican – who proceeded to abuse them for getting him up at such an hour, but eventually put them up for the night. While they slept the wind shifted and the ship was blown out of danger. At dawn it was sighted by a vessel coming in through the Heads. It was sailing backwards out to sea and was never seen again.

James Johnson's involvement with the sea wasn't over either. His brother, Henry, became the first keeper of the Hornby Light, which was completed in 1858. James worked for a while with the harbour pilots before becoming a lighthouse keeper at Newcastle's Nobby Head Light. Then in 1866, what became known as the Great Gale hit the New South Wales coast, wrecking and sinking many ships, among them the coastal steamer *Cawarra*, at Newcastle. There was only one survivor rescued from the sixty people on board. His name was Frederick Hedges. He was rescued by the sole survivor of the *Dunbar*, James Johnson, and another man, Henry Hannell.

These days, the entrance to Sydney Harbour is lit like a Christmas tree. There's a light on North Head, the Hornby Light on South Head, and the Macquarie Light remains (rebuilt in 1893 on the same site). Inside the Heads, the inner head of Grotto Point has a lighthouse, which can be aligned with another light deeper into Middle Harbour to enable ships to keep left or right as they enter Port Jackson. There are buoys lighting the east and west channels into the main harbour, including the two beautiful 'Wedding Cake' lights marking the inner ends of the channels. Then there are the lights of the city, which illuminate much of the shoreline.

If that isn't enough, even small vessels can navigate with the aid of global positioning systems, use depth sounders to ensure they haven't strayed into shallow water and employ radar to paint the approaching coast in exact detail. They can call the Volunteer Coast Guard on their radios for help, the squadron being located in the

Signal Station on the site first established back in 1790. In addition, all large vessels entering the harbour must do so with the aid of a harbour pilot picked up outside the Heads. But even today if the weather is so severe as to prevent pilots from boarding the vessel all of the modern navigational aids are rendered useless. Ships are still unable to make the safety of port.

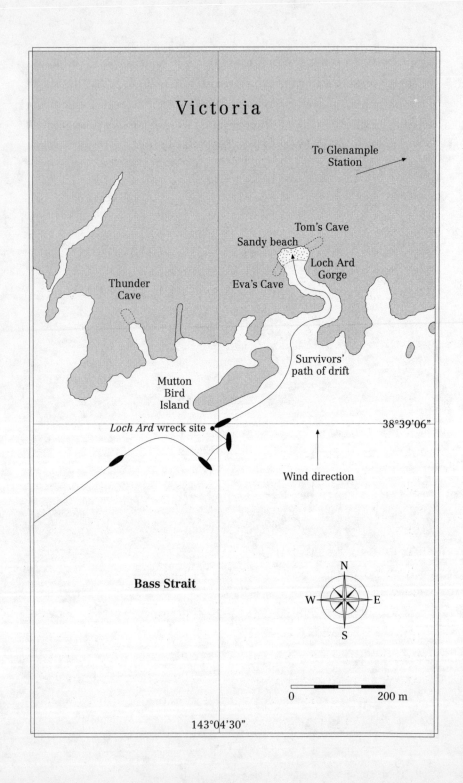

Victoria

To Glenample
Station

Tom's Cave

Sandy beach

Loch Ard
Gorge

Thunder
Cave

Eva's Cave

Survivors'
path of drift

Mutton
Bird
Island

Loch Ard wreck site

38°39'06"

Wind direction

Bass Strait

N

W   E

S

0   200 m

143°04'30"

The *Loch Ard*
(Flagstaff Hill Maritime Museum)

7. THE END OF THE AFFAIR: *LOCH ARD*, 1878

While Sydney was mourning the loss of the *Dunbar* (see previous chapter), it was also being replaced by Melbourne as the most populous city in Australia. Founded in the mid-1830s, by the mid-1850s, Melbourne's population of 53 000 (1854) was just passing that of Sydney. By 1861, thanks to the gold boom, Melbourne had twice Sydney's population.

Gold was fundamental to the population growth, but the reason it focussed on Melbourne rather than Sydney was the former's position as the first Australian port of call after the long voyage from England. Many Europeans, finding the climate resembled that which they'd left, chose it as their home and soon it had become the most European of all Australia's capitals.

The two cities had their differences, but none was starker than the reactions to their two most famous shipping disasters. For where Sydney had been shocked by the loss of the *Dunbar*, the loss of the iron clipper *Loch Ard* in 1878 gave Melbourne cause for celebration, glittering public occasions and an outpouring of joy. The reason was that survivors Tom Pearce and Eva Carmichael gave the people a real-life heroic romance that in its day equalled that of the Hollywood blockbuster *Titanic*.

The *Loch Ard* also embodied all the romance of the age of sail. Her long sleek lines and prodigious bowsprit proclaimed her speed through the water. The 1623-tonne, three-masted iron clipper could get up to 14 knots (26 kilometres/hour) in the right conditions.

Yet the glory days of sail were already numbered, due to developments in steam propulsion. In 1839, the English painter Turner foresaw the future with his famous painting of the legendary warhorse of the Battle of Trafalgar, 'The Fighting *Temeraire*', which showed her at sunset, being towed to the wrecking yard by an ugly smoking paddle-steamer. More than half a century later, the writer Joseph Conrad echoed Turner in his description of the clipper *Narcissus* putting to sea:

> Then the sheets were hauled home, the yards hoisted, and the ship became a high and lonely pyramid, gliding, all shining and white, through the sunlit mist. The tug turned short round and went away towards the land. Twenty-six pairs of eyes watched her low broad stern crawling languidly over the smooth swell between the two paddle-wheels that turned fast, beating the water with fierce hurry. She resembled an enormous and aquatic black beetle, surprised by the light, overwhelmed by the sunshine, trying to escape with ineffectual effort into the distant gloom of the land. She left a lingering smudge of smoke on the sky, and two vanishing trails of foam on the water. On the place where she had stopped a round black patch of soot remained, undulating on the swell – an unclean mark of the creature's rest.

However, in travel the race is almost inevitably won by the swift (few today would choose a sea-journey to England that takes weeks over an air-journey that takes hours) and while the clippers were capable of prodigious speeds, and cheaper since their fuel came free of charge, they still had disadvantages, compared to steamships. The most significant was that without the wind they were helpless.

Another issue was manoeuvrability, especially in enclosed waters. Steamships could more easily traverse the narrow channels of Torres Strait, for example. And in 1869, the opening of the Suez Canal, with its narrow approaches, further swung the advantage to the steamships, significantly shortening their voyages while the sail ships sought the speed of the roaring forties. All the clipper captains could do was drive their vessels harder. In May 1878, Captain George Gibb of the *Loch Ard* was nearing the end of his voyage, having done just that. He'd headed almost due south from England until the ship was as deep into the southern latitudes as he dared. As Brouwer had found 250 years before, the winds got stronger the further south one went, and the easting one had to do was greatly reduced. The *Loch Ard* may have reached as far as 55 degrees south (iceberg territory) before finally turning east.

Only after some eighty days at sea did she start heading north-east towards the Australian mainland, having skipped the stop at South Africa's Cape Town. The epic voyage was to end once she 'threaded the needle', the narrow passage into Bass Strait between Cape Otway's Shipwreck Coast and the treacherous west coast of King Island, which had claimed the *Cataraqui* 33 years before (see Chapter 5).

Tom Pearce was apprenticed on the *Loch Ard*, which was carrying general cargo, eighteen passengers and thirty-six crew. The nineteen-year-old (stepson of a ship's captain who had perished when the S.S. *Gothenburg* foundered off Queensland in 1875), detailed the events that followed at a subsequent Steam Navigation Board inquiry:

I know of my own knowledge that every opportunity was seized for taking azimuths [navigating by the sun instead of the compasses, which had been found to be inaccurate], but the weather for some time before the wreck had been rather thick and hazy. The last azimuth was taken the day before the wreck. From what I heard the officers say, the sights could not be depended upon.

There have been suggestions that the ship's cargo, which included a large amount of 'railway iron' may have been interfering with the compasses, although Pearce believed the compasses had always been a problem. Pearce testified that on Friday morning, 31 May, the vessel was steering east by north or east-north-east while nearing the southern Australian coast. In the afternoon, he recalled the second mate telling him the ship was some 240 kilometres south-west of Cape Otway. If so, and if the ship was headed on the course he supposed, the ship was headed for King Island, but it may have been that the young apprentice was mistaken on this point.

This was between 3 and 4 o'clock in the afternoon, when we were getting the anchors over the bows. I cannot say how far we were off the coast in a direct line as I only asked what distance we were from Cape Otway. The wind was about S.W., as it was on our starboard quarter. The weather was fine, with a moderate breeze, and we were carrying all plain sail. Between 6 and 8 o'clock that evening the wind freshened, and at the same time hauled more to the southward, so that we had to brace the yards forward.

During the evening the captain started to reduce sail in preparation for reaching port. Down below the passengers were celebrating the end of their voyage and their imminent arrival in the colony that was to be their new home. Of the eighteen passengers, eight belonged to one family – that of Doctor Carmichael, a general practitioner from Ireland who was planning to resettle in Australia. With him were his wife and six of his seven children. The seventh, William, estranged from his family, was believed to be in Australia, but unbeknownst to them he had taken ship to return home to them, while they were on the voyage out.

At midnight Captain Gibb hove the lead and found the ship in 53 fathoms (97 metres), with a sandy bottom, a clear indication that she was approaching land. This was fully expected, as the skipper was now on the lookout for the flash from the Cape Otway light-house, which went into operation in 1848, two years after the fearful wreck of the *Cataraqui*. As the ship progressed, Captain Gibb reduced sail even further. Pearce later reported:

> It was expected we should make the Cape Otway light about 3 o'clock on Saturday morning. Special orders had been given to the look-out man to keep a good look-out for both the land and the light, and dur-ing the middle watch a man was sent aloft about every quarter of an hour to see if he could make out the light.

Yet 3 a.m. came and went without any sign of the Cape Otway light. The weather, on the other hand was changing. A fog bank lay to the north of the ship, while it remained clear overhead and to the south. It should have been a clue as to what lay ahead. 'About three o'clock I noticed that the stars were shining brightly. It was just as the watch was being relieved at four o'clock that the land was seen. I think the Captain and the man at the wheel saw it simultaneously.'

What the crew saw must have terrified them. The *Loch Ard* was 45 kilometres out of her reckoning, to the north and west of Cape Otway, whose light was still well below the horizon. Instead, the Shipwreck Coast loomed out of the mist; a jagged line of high sheer cliffs stretched across the ship's course, less than a kilometre in front of them. It was the land that was causing the fog, which hid the ship's peril until it was too late.

Even so they still had a chance of escape, although the wind wasn't doing them any favours. Blowing from the south onto the stretch of coast extending from the north-west to the south-east, it cut off escape to sea unless the ship could turn south, then tack to starboard (she was already far too close to turn north-west and jibe to port). First, though, the crew had to hoist more sail to increase her speed enough to turn through the eye of the wind.

'Our watch was going below – some had gone – when I heard the order to hoist up the staysails, and at the same time the captain ran forward, calling all hands on deck,' Pearce recalled. 'We got sail on her as quickly as possible by hoisting the main and mizzen topsail, set the spanker, and hoisted the upper mizzen topsail.'

While this was being done the ship was gathering speed, but still heading straight for the cliffs. Captain Gibb waited as long as he dared before giving the order, 'All hands ready about.' It was a desperate roll of the dice, a roll with the lives of fifty-four people and an 80-metre ship at stake. The helmsman put the wheel hard down, turning the bows away from the cliffs till they could sniff at the open sea. As *Loch Ard* started coming up to the eye of the wind the sails luffed and started to flap. Now all she had to carry her round was her momentum, which decreased as she butted her head into the waves and the oncoming breeze. Would it be enough? There was enough time for the thirty-six crew to send up a prayer, while the elements decided their fate. Pearce reported: 'The ship just came up head to wind, and then commenced to fall off again, as there was not enough sail on her to bring her round.' Captain Gibb's gamble had failed, but he wasn't shipwrecked yet.

As soon as the captain saw she was beginning to fall off again, he ordered both anchors to be let go . . . I should say we were then about half a mile [one kilometre] from the shore . . . We were among the broken water . . . About 50 fathoms [90 metres] was given on each [anchor] cable. We could soon see that the anchors were not holding, for every time the ship lifted with the sea she brought the anchors home. We gave her a little more cable, but could not give her much, as we were afraid of a rock astern to which we had gone very close.

While the ship dragged dangerously close to the cliffs, the anchors did manage to bring *Loch Ard*'s head to the wind, which gave Gibb another chance to tack her out to sea.

. . . the Captain, finding that she was dragging, ordered the yards to be braced round on the port tack and the foretopmast staysail to be hoisted, keeping the sheet well to windward, so as to pay her head off. He then ordered the cables to be slipped [the anchors raised] and the topsails to be sheeted home, and while some of the men were slipping the cables, the rest of us were trying to get sail on her.

The manoeuvre worked. The ship fell away from the wind on the port tack as the crew worked feverishly to get the sails working and the ship moving out of danger. Yet, while she slowly gathered speed, she was still being pushed towards the cliffs.

At this time the mainsail was full, the wind being well abeam. We had no other sail on her, as there was no time. We were just about to hoist the mizzen topsail when she struck. Her starboard quarter appeared to strike a ledge of rock that was just awash. It was not far from the land and at every roll of the sea her yards would strike against the cliffs. The ship was just gathering way when she struck. I believe the rock made a great hole in her bottom, for she was bumping very heavily.

The vessel had been incredibly unlucky. She'd managed to hit Mutton Bird Island, which juts into the sea several hundred metres from the mainland. Had she managed to get a hundred metres to either side, she may well have had just enough sea-room to escape. But it was not to be. Like the *Dunbar* twenty years before, she was caught between the hammer of the ocean and the anvil of the cliffs.

Panic now took hold of the passengers and some of the crew, though Captain Gibb remained at his post on the poop deck. He gave orders for the lifeboats to be made ready. It was a complex operation made more difficult by the heavy seas that were now breaking over the ship. The masts were also being slammed against the cliffs overhead, showering the deck with broken spars and rock.

> The seas were coming over both sides, as the back wash from the cliffs was bringing the sea in over the lee side. If the lifeboat had been lowered, I believe she would have been thrown in-board by the back wash from the cliffs. When the order was given to clear away the boats, I and five others went to the lifeboats . . . There were six of us in the boat. I cut the after-gripe, and just then a sea came on board and washed us all away. I did not see any of the passengers on deck at the time. I saw the captain on the poop. The ship seemed to me to be gradually sinking by the stern. I saw several of the seamen clinging to a portion of the upper main-topsail yard which had been broken by striking against the cliffs. The spars were falling in every direction, so much so that some of the sailors got into the cabin with the passengers in order to save themselves. I believe some ladies had put on cork jackets, and were going on deck, when they were at once washed away.

One of those ladies was Eva Carmichael, the eighteen-year-old daughter of Dr Carmichael. Not only had she put on a life preserver, she'd heard Captain Gibbs last words: 'If you should be spared to see my dear wife, tell her that I stuck to the ship to the last, and went down with her like a sailor.' Pearce recalled how he escaped the wreck:

When the sea struck the lifeboat and knocked it overboard it capsized, and I was underneath it. I never saw any of the others who were with me. I was under the boat for some time. The bottom boards had fallen down and were lying along the thwarts. That is where I kept. The boat floated very high and there was plenty of air under her. I took out the plug [usually used for drainage] so as to get more fresh air.

Eva, meanwhile, was struggling in the water. As she was quoted in Richard Bennett's 1878 narrative of the wreck:

One of the strings attached to my life-belt broke, and the belt shifting up and down forced my head under the water several times, which almost cost me my life. Seeing a hencoop I swam towards it. God taught me to swim in my blessed plight; for I never swam before. I suc- ceeded in getting hold of the hencoop, and so did Arthur Mitchell [another passenger]. This hencoop had been an object of ridicule among the passengers on board; but I felt thankful for it in the water. By this time the *Loch Ard* had disappeared under the waves. Seeing a spar, I let go of the hencoop and made for it. In a few minutes Mitchell and Jones [another of the passengers] were clinging to the spar also. Mitchell began to shiver frightfully, and to despair of ever reaching the shore. He had a lifebelt; but poor Jones kindly took off the life-buoy that was around himself and put it round Mitchell.

Exposed to the icy waters of the Southern Ocean in the depths of winter, hypothermia was a greater danger than drowning for the three desperate survivors. Meanwhile, Tom Pearce was in much better condition, in the upturned hull of the lifeboat.

I suppose I was under the boat about three quarters of an hour, but it seemed much more. The backwash, together with the ebb tide must have taken the boat out to sea. When I came from under the boat

I could see nothing of the ship, nothing but a lot of floating wreckage.
I could not see anybody else floating. I went under the boat again, and
the flood tide must then have drifted me in shore again, as the first
thing I was aware of was the boat striking against a rock at the
entrance of an inlet. This righted the boat but as she was floating in
I still kept to her; but when about half-way up the inlet she struck
against the side of the cliffs and threw me out. I then struck out for the
beach, which I reached, and found it covered with wreckage.

Pearce had drifted into the only landing place for several kilometres
in either direction, up a flooded gorge that sliced deeply into the cliffs.
It was on the mainland, at the far end of Mutton Bird Island from
where the *Loch Ard* had struck. It was pure luck that he'd been carried there, along with an increasing amount of floating wreckage from
the ship. It was fortunate too that the surge hadn't battered him to
death on the rocks along the sides of the gorge. But if anyone else was
to survive, this was the only place where they'd have any hope at all.
Eva and her companions had their own problems.

Mitchell asked me to give him some of my clothing to keep the wind from
piercing him: I tried to do so, but I could not divest myself of my jacket,
having to hold on to the spar with one hand. Poor Jones and Mitchell
soon let go the spar, and, after swimming some little distance, they disappeared, and I saw them no more. I was now left alone, and could see
nothing but the waves rolling and a rock at a little distance. I let go the
spar and made for it. The waves dashed me against the rock, and then
sent me spinning round its point. I went down under the waves three or
four times, and began to despair of life. In a few minutes after turning
the point of rock, I saw Tom Pearce standing on the beach.

By then Tom Pearce had been on the beach for more than an hour,
taken a chance to rest and found a cave in which to shelter. He hadn't

Batavia timbers from the port-side stern, uncovered intact after more than 350 years on the sea bed. *(Photo: Patrick Baker, Western Australian Maritime Museum)*

The remains of a victim of the *Batavia* mutineers, with the ship's preserved timbers and a replica of the portico she was carrying to Batavia Castle in Java on display at the Western Australian Maritime Museum. The portico itself is in the Geraldton Maritime Museum. *(Photo: Patrick Baker, Western Australian Maritime Museum)*

Aerial view of the *Sydney Cove* wreck site in Bass Strait. Rum Island is in the foreground, Preservation Island behind, with Cape Barren Island in the background. In 1797 the survivors camped among the rocks of Preservation Island closest to Rum Island. The wreck site is off the small beach to the right. *(Photo: Mark Staniforth, Australian National Maritime Museum)*

Diver and archaeologist Cosmos Coroneos with one of two delicate porcelain vases recovered two centuries after the *Sydney Cove* was wrecked. *(Photo: Mark Staniforth, Australian National Maritime Museum)*

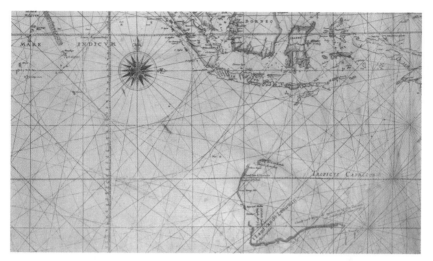

Detail of a Dutch map by Colom, circa 1633. Trial Rocks are south of Java, in the false position given by the *Trial*'s captain, John Brookes, in 1622. Their true position was finally established in the 1930s in the blank section of Australian coast well to their east. *(Map: Mitchell Library, State Library of New South Wales)*

Trial wreck site. Maritime archaeologist Mack McCarthy with an iron cannon damaged by a looter dynamiting the site to expose relics. *(Photo: Patrick Baker, Western Australian Maritime Museum)*

Batavia's Graveyard. This illustration accompanied the 1647 edition of Jan Jansz's *Ongeluckige Voyagie* and encapsulated many of the atrocities committed after the Dutch ship *Batavia* was wrecked off Western Australia in 1629. *(Image: Australian National Maritime Museum)*

The executions and hand amputations of *Batavia* mutineers on Seals Island as portrayed in *Ongeluckige Voyagie*. *(Image: Australian National Maritime Museum)*

Mrs Eliza Fraser, a survivor of the wreck of the merchant ship *Stirling Castle* in 1836. *(From John Curtis's* Shipwreck of the *Stirling Castle. Image: Mitchell Library, State Library of New South Wales)*

Captain Fraser being speared, also from John Curtis's account. Fraser took several days to die from his wounds. *(Image: Mitchell Library, State Library of New South Wales)*

Imminent Danger, a recent watercolour by Barry Collis of King Island, showing the emigrant ship *Cataraqui*, which was wrecked on the island in 1845. *(Courtesy Barry Collis, King Island)*

The view looking south from the *Cataraqui* wreck site. These rocks were strewn with the bodies of the worst civilian disaster in Australia's history. *(Photo: Barry Collis, King Island)*

The clipper ship *Dunbar*, hand-coloured wood engraving, *Illustrated London News*, 24 December 1853. When she was launched, she was one of the fastest vessels afloat. *(Image: Australian National Maritime Museum)*

Samuel Thomas Gill's *The Wreck of the Dunbar*, watercolour, circa 1857. The clipper ship went to pieces at the base of 80-metre cliffs below the Macquarie Lighthouse, near the entrance to Sydney Harbour. *(Image: Mitchell Library, State Library of New South Wales)*

Illustrations from a narrative of the *Dunbar* wreck published soon after it occurred in 1857, near Sydney's South Head, featuring its sole survivor, James Johnson. *(Image: Australian National Maritime Museum)*

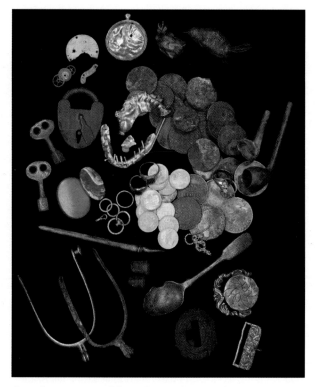

A selection of artefacts recovered from the *Dunbar* wreck site, mostly personal effects of the victims. *(Photo: Australian National Maritime Museum)*

The *Loch Ard's* last moments before breaking up on Victoria's Shipwreck Coast in 1878. *(Image: Australian National Maritime Museum)*

Eva Carmichael, the only passenger to survive the wreck of the *Loch Ard*. *(Photo: Flagstaff Hill Maritime Museum)*

Tom Pearce, Eva's rescuer and the only crewman from the *Loch Ard* to survive. *(Photo: Flagstaff Hill Maritime Museum)*

The RMS *Quetta* at anchor in Brisbane. Awnings can be seen over most of the ship's decks. These trapped many of the victims when the ship suddenly went down near Thursday Island in 1890. *(Photo: Townsville Maritime Museum)*

A contemporary illustration of the *Quetta* sinking. *(Image: Mitchell Library, State Library of New South Wales)*

Pearling luggers at the Goode Island pearling station. Every vessel in this photo-graph was subsequently sunk or wrecked in Princess Charlotte Bay in 1899, by Cyclone Mahina. *(From the memorial booklet, published 1899. Photo: John Oxley Library)*

All that remained of the lugger *Zanoni* after Cyclone Mahina.
(Photo: John Oxley Library)

The monument erected in 1899 to the memory of the victims of the cyclone. More than 300 non-whites who lost their lives were reduced to a footnote.
(Photo: Evan Ives)

The German raider *Kormoran*, which succeeded in taking HMAS *Sydney* by surprise and sinking her in an engagement off Western Australia in 1941. *(Photo: Australian War Memorial – AWM 053867)*

The Dutch merchant ship *Straat Malakka* that *Kormoran* had been disguised to resemble. *(Photo: Australian War Memorial – AWM 128097)*

Two motor vehicles that just managed to stop after the bulk carrier *Lake Illawarra* struck Hobart's Tasman Bridge in 1975, causing several spans to collapse. Four other vehicles weren't so lucky. *(Photo: Hobart Mercury)*

The remains of the Tasman Bridge seen from Hobart's eastern shore, looking towards the city. *(Photo: Hobart Mercury)*

In the days after the ship wrecked the bridge, thousands of Hobart commuters experienced its consequences first-hand. *(Photo: Hobart Mercury)*

In the Southern Ocean in 1997, Tony Bullimore emerged at the stern of his keel-less *Exide Challenger* after Royal Australian Navy rescuers (left) had pounded on the upturned hull. *(Photo: AAP)*

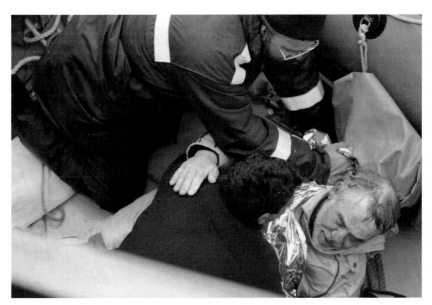

Rescuers tend to the slightly hypothermic Bullimore before his transfer to the rescue ship HMAS *Adelaide*. *(Photo: AAP)*

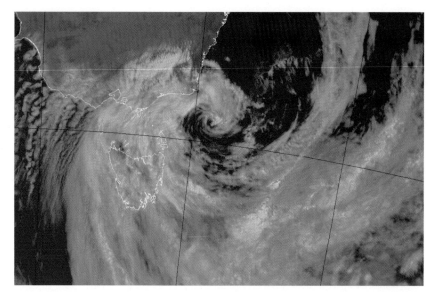

Satellite view of Bass Strait at approximately 2.30 p.m. on 27 December 1998.
The extreme weather event that swept the Sydney to Hobart Yacht Race fleet had all
the appearances of a cyclone, with wind and waves to match. *(GMS Image: Bureau of
Meteorology from the Japanese Meteorological Agency)*

The yacht *Midnight Special* foundered on the morning of 28 December 1998.
Moments after the *South Care* and *Polair 1* choppers had rescued the crew, the
yacht went down. *(Photo: AAP)*

yet tried to go for help because his beach was completely enclosed by cliffs. In the darkness he could find no way out.

> I went to look among the wreckage for something to eat. I then heard someone calling out and at first thought that it was somebody on the cliffs above me, but I could not see anybody. I heard a second cry, and then looked out to sea and saw a lady clinging to a spar. I saw it was one of the passengers, but could not tell who it was at first. I afterwards found that it was Miss Eva Carmichael.

Eva told how she 'shouted to him, whereupon he walked into the water and swam towards me. Tom had a desperate struggle to bring me ashore; and from the time I shouted to him to the time we were safe on the beach about an hour must have elapsed.'

The nineteen-year-old apprentice sailor and the eighteen-year-old doctor's daughter were the only survivors. But they were still a long way from safety. Numbed with cold, and barely coherent, Eva had been hardly able to help herself when Tom got to her.

> He took me into a wild-looking cave, a few hundred feet from the beach, and finding a case of brandy which was washed ashore, broke the neck of one of the bottles and made me swallow almost all its contents, after which he swallowed a drop himself. Cold and exhausted – for we must have been in the water about five hours – we lay down on the ground. I soon fell into a state of insensibility, and must have been unconscious for hours.

In 1878, the effects of hypothermia were little understood. Nevertheless, Eva was describing some of its symptoms. In her time, consuming strong spirits was considered a way of warming a person from within, whereas it actually does the opposite by increasing the flow of blood to the skin (which is why it flushes red and feels warm) consequently increasing the loss of body heat. Some accounts suggest that when Tom woke, around midday, he tried to rouse Eva, but was unable to do so.

Tom knew he had to find help, so once more confronted the cliffs. These days, there is a ladder down to the beach, and one end of the gorge has fallen in providing easier access than there was in 1878. Tom searched for a spot where the cliffs were not so high and started to climb. It took several attempts and a few close calls before he was able to get out of what is now known as Loch Ard Gorge.

What he found at the summit was far from promising. Low scrub stretched away in all directions with no sign of human habitation. He decided to head west, following the line of cliffs and hoping to find some sign of life. As luck would have it, he hadn't gone far before he came to a fence line and a rough track, which he started following. It had to lead somewhere. About an hour later he heard what sounded like sheep, and even better, voices.

William Till and George Ford were two young farmhands mustering on Glenample Station, whose homestead was east of Loch Ard Gorge. Coincidentally, Ford was also the son of the lighthouse-keeper at Cape Otway. The two men were more than a little surprised to see a bedraggled sailor stagger out of the scrub, smelling of spirits. Then they were shocked when he told them what had happened, of the wreck of the *Loch Ard* and the girl left on the beach. The men knew the spot Tom was talking about and set off immediately to bring help from the homestead, about two kilometres away, while Tom doggedly returned to the gorge.

It was nearing sunset when Ford and Till found Glenample Station owner Hugh Gibson yarding sheep near the homestead.

I was inclined not to believe it but when he [Ford] told me about the young lady I told them to go on and and get the sheep in whilst I went to Lavinia [his wife] and told her to get some food and drink ready, but not to tell a soul. I then, after instructing George and the boy Willie, who was with him, to follow me, and bring a blanket apiece . . . rode off and never pulled rein until I had got above Caves Gorge. It was then so dark that I could not tell that there was wreckage beneath although there was a barrier of at least eight feet [2.4 metres] from one side of the beach to the other. I cooeyed several times but got no answer and was uncertain if Tom had described the place properly or whether he had succeeded in finding the place again.

Down in the gorge, Eva had recovered consciousness.

When I awoke, Tom was not to be seen. Cold, weak and terrified, with the wild waves before me, and caves and steep cliffs around me, I hoped God would send someone to deliver me. After what seemed to me a very long time, I heard a strange noise. I imagined it to have been the war-cry of the Aborigines.

Eva's greatest fear in coming to Australia was the infamous hostility of the native population. It was a fear that may have been nurtured by the lurid tales of the fates of shipwreck survivors such as Eliza Fraser and the crew of the *Stirling Castle* (see Chapter 4). And the war cries were getting closer. As Gibson later told:

I went down and whilst fairly at the bottom I cooeyed again, and got an answer from Tom to the effect that he was fast in the scrub, he was bare-footed and in a nasty place. I got him out and we at once went to the cave where Eva had been left – saw the grass bed he had made for her but no Eva. Tom and I went round the cave again and again, then over to the other, still no sign of her. I then commenced to try and track her, but could only see Tom's tracks up . . .

Eva had disappeared.

'This must have taken an hour when George and Willie arrived, and finding some candles, we made lanterns with bottles and commenced the search over again,' Gibson wrote later. 'We then began to think she had gone into the sea again. I then determined . . . to get all hands so as not to leave a stone unturned.'

William Till was sent back to the homestead to recruit everyone for the search. Gibson later wrote:

> While the boy was away Ford and I sat down regularly puzzled, so I made Tom lie down and he went to sleep. After waiting what appeared to us two hours we began to think the people would not find the place as it was pitch dark, so I told Ford to go up and light a fire on the top to guide them.

Eva's recollections reflect her state of mind: 'I was afraid to answer and remained silent for a while, when I heard someone say "Yes." I thanked God when I heard that English word.'

Gibson resumes the story:

> When halfway up he [Ford] heard the voice – 'I'm dying' – when we sprung into where she was at once. She was in a regular hole covered with scrub, and must have crawled in. She had no recollection of leaving the cave but I am convinced that she must actually have walked in Tom's footprints prompted by some instinct or other. When I first saw her I certainly thought she was insane. She had only half a stocking on one leg and very little clothing although sufficient to screen her person.

Eva was extremely disoriented and barely coherent, both symptoms of severe hypothermia. As Eva described it: 'Mr Gibson took off his shoes and stockings and put them on me, wrapping me in blankets.'

At first it had the desired effect, as Gibson wrote: 'I . . . let her lie thinking she would get warm, but after a while she complained of being chilled, so I got a rousing fire made of wreck timber to which we took her.'

'A fire was soon lighted, coffee made, and brandy procured,' recalled Eva. 'I felt my strength somewhat recruited; but for all that, felt feeble and helpless, and sore with the bruises which I had received from the collision with the rocks and floating wreckage.'

Modern rescue personnel would find it remarkable Eva survived the checklist of 'Don'ts' that she detailed. Exposing the patient to fire, and administering coffee and alcohol are expressly warned against. For the same reason it was important to avoid handling her roughly, had her rescuers only known. The danger was that with her body temperature dangerously low, she could suffer a heart attack without warning. (For more details: http://www.hypothermia.org)

At least Eva was incapable of 'rescuing herself', which would also have been extremely dangerous.

In the darkness . . ., the young men, William Robertson (of Port Campbell), and William Shields, under the superintendence of Mr Gibson, conveyed me up a steep and lofty precipice. I cannot understand how they succeeded in bringing me to the top. It must have been a work of great difficulty and danger. Mr Gibson put me into his buggy, and drove on to his house, arriving there after 1 o'clock on Sunday morning.

Although at risk from every jolt on the way, Eva survived the journey along the rough bush track to the homestead.

News of the wreck and Tom Pearce's heroic rescue of Eva Carmichael caused a sensation in Melbourne. The age of sail and the romance that went with it may have been ending, but here was a tale that proved it wasn't over yet. Within a day of the news reaching the city, a media swarm had descended on Glenample Station, where the two survivors were recovering.

Tom was able to travel soon after his ordeal, but for Eva it was some weeks before she was able to leave the care of the Gibsons. While they were together, however, Eva is reported to have hugged Tom on at least one occasion and praised him as 'my saviour.' However, the public wanted more. As in the modern version of *Titanic*, they hoped that love would conquer all.

However, the reality was more in keeping with the times. Tom was a seaman and Eva was the daughter of a doctor. The stocky 5-foot-6-inch (168-centimetre) sailor and the willowy 5-foot-9-inch (175-centimetre) lady went their separate ways. Not that the facts stopped some media reporting the fairytale ending. One account had the couple married and living happily ever after in Melbourne; another had Tom shipwrecked off the coast of Scotland, and nursed back to health by none other than Eva, after which they tied the knot.

What is true is that Tom was treated as a hero in Melbourne. He was showered with gifts, navigational equipment and collections of money. While he tried to shun the limelight, he was the main attraction at a special function organised in the city, as *The Age* describes:

On the evening of the 20th [June] the further honour was conferred on him of a gold medal from the Humane Society of Victoria. The presentation was made in the Melbourne Town Hall . . . The announcement that Pearce would be present caused so much excitement that long before the hour for opening the doors, the neighbourhood of the building was thronged with eager seekers for admission. When the proceedings commenced it is said over five thousand persons had gained entrance to the hall, and as soon as the 'observed of all observers' appeared on the platform, the enthusiasm of the spectators found relief in cheering which lasted five minutes.

Tom also gave evidence at a marine board of inquiry, which made no recorded finding on the incident. The matter of the faulty compasses was discussed, and the poor sighting, but no explanation was given as to how the ship could be so far out of its expected position.

Tom Pearce returned to the sea, and married the sister of his best friend, Robert Strasenburg, who was lost on the *Loch Ard*. Tom's sons went to sea where one was lost when the *Loch Vennachar* disappeared off Kangaroo Island, South Australia, in 1905. Another son perished when his ship was bombed near Malta in World War II. Tom succumbed to an incurable disease in 1908.

Eva decided to return to Ireland, where she went to live with her grandmother. She eventually married and had three sons. Late in her life she wrote to one of Tom's sons, expressing the hope that they might meet and talk over old times. The letter eventually found Chief Officer Robert S. Pearce, but she died in 1934, aged 74, before his reply could reach her.

When Eva left Melbourne, Tom was among the crowd on the dock to see her off. Her passage was on the vessel *Tanjore*. It was a steamship. Eva had been insistent that she would not make the return journey in a sailing vessel.

And the *Loch Ard*? The fascination with the wreck has endured to the present day. The Shipwreck Coast is a major tourist attraction, reached by the spectacular Great Ocean Road. Many of the artefacts recovered from the wreck site by divers are on display at Glenample Homestead and Flagstaff Hill Maritime Museum, Warrnambool. But a last glimpse comes from Hugh Gibson. The day after he'd recovered Eva and Tom from Loch Ard Gorge, he returned to the site to see if he could find anything of the wreck. All that he found of the once-proud icon of the age of sail was part of a spar at the base of the cliff and a piece of sail, floating beneath the waves.

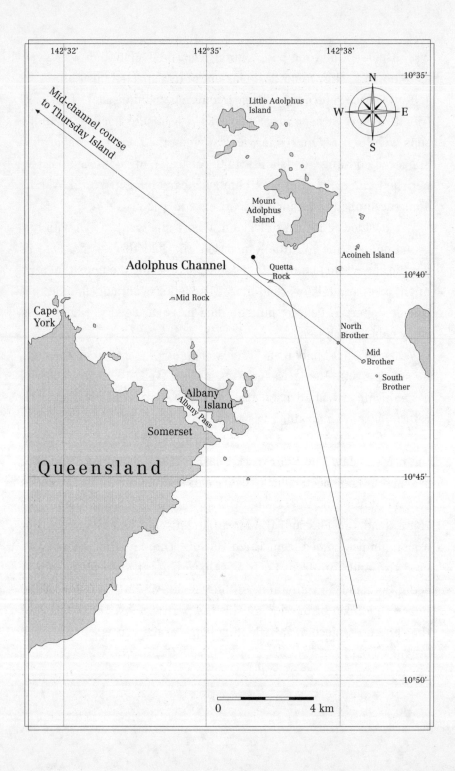

142°32' 142°35' 142°38'

10°35'

N
W   E
S

Little Adolphus
Island

Mount
Adolphus
Island

Acoineh Island

Adolphus Channel

Quetta
Rock

10°40'

Mid-channel course
to Thursday Island

Mid Rock

Cape
York

North
Brother

Mid
Brother

South
Brother

Albany
Island

Albany Pass

Somerset

Queensland

10°45'

10°50'

0   4 km

RMS *Quetta*
(Townsville Maritime Museum)

8. LABYRINTH: *QUETTA*, 1890

There may well have been a moment during the night of Friday, 28 February 1890, when Captain Frederick Sanders, master of the Queensland Royal Mail Steamer *Quetta*, thought to himself, 'I didn't do anything wrong.' Perhaps it was during the descent from shipboard discipline and order into absolute chaos. Perhaps it was as his ship was sliding rapidly beneath the surface of the gently lapping sea. Perhaps it was while hundreds of his stricken passengers and crew were left thrashing frantically in the water.

It all happened in less than five minutes. Sanders had been standing on the bridge of his proud three-decked iron steamship. The *Quetta* was a sleek vessel, 116 metres long, plying the route from Brisbane to London via the Torres Strait carrying mail, passengers and general freight. She was well maintained; her crew was experienced, well trained and well disciplined. She carried more than enough life-jackets and boats for all the passengers and crew.

At age forty-one, Sanders had been at sea for most of his life; a ship's master for the previous twelve years. Also on board, and directing the vessel's course, was Torres Strait pilot Eldred Pottinger Keatinge. He knew the *Quetta* extremely well, having previously been her chief officer for five years. His experience in the waters the *Quetta* was navigating was also first-rate, having logged four full years as a licensed Moreton Bay and Queensland coast pilot.

Just after nine o'clock on that Friday night, in balmy tropical weather, he had the *Quetta* positioned almost in the centre of the Adolphus Channel, the safer of two busy shipping routes that skirt Cape York on the approach to the tiny Torres Strait community of Thursday Island, at the northernmost tip of Queensland.

Keatinge, with Sanders by his side, was absolutely sure he was in safe water. Hundreds of ships before him had made their passage through the exact same place. Numerous surveys had been carried out since Torres Strait was successfully navigated by the Spaniard Luis Vaez de Torres in 1606, followed by Cook, Bligh, Flinders and countless others. Indeed, since the European settlement of Australia, navigation of the entire island continent's extensive coastline had become considerably safer as knowledge of hazards grew, beacons and lighthouses became more widespread, and navigation became more of a science than an art. The vessels themselves were safer as well, steamships being able to steer exactly where they wanted, unlike the sailing vessels they were rapidly replacing, which were at the mercy of the elements to a far greater degree, as the *Loch Ard* tragically demonstrated (see Chapter 7).

Steamships still had their moments, though. In 1886, the *Lyee-Moon*, en route from Melbourne to Sydney, was clipping headlands to get a quick passage when she was driven straight onto Green

Cape, right under its lighthouse, in good weather, killing seventy-one people. The third mate blamed the disaster on the captain, the captain blamed the third mate, and the marine board of inquiry, not wanting to punish an innocent man, refused to blame anyone.

Yet steamship navigators were far from complacent as they passed through Torres Strait. The whole area had a formidable reputation for treacherous currents, hidden reefs and shoals that had claimed countless vessels. The great navigator, James Cook, succinctly encapsulated the dangers when, rather than chart the innumerable obstacles that almost destroyed him during his nerve-wracking passage through the area in 1770, he wrote just one word on his map: 'Labyrinth.'

Cook's reference resonates even today. The labyrinth of Greek mythology was built for the Minoan king Minos and was so intricate that escape was impossible without external help. But the labyrinth wasn't a trap, it was a cage, built to contain the dreaded Minotaur – a monstrous creature with the body of a man and the head of a bull. In Cook's labyrinth, the Great Barrier Reef, the terror lurked beneath the surface, in the rocks and coral reefs that had gored and almost sunk his ship.

There were alternatives to the Torres Strait route, but they had even greater drawbacks. As modern-day Torres Strait pilot, Captain John Foley, wrote in his book on the *Quetta*:

> On the [longer] New Guinea route, which straddled the equator, light winds provided scant motive force for sailing ships. Across the Bight the exact opposite was the case; gale force westerly winds bit square in the teeth of westbound ships and stunned them to a standstill . . . Even in modern times huge bulk carriers bound from Port Kembla (NSW) to Port Hedland (WA) to load iron ore take the Torres Strait route in preference to the Bight, despite a 600-odd mile [960 kilometre] distance penalty. The choice is made on economic grounds it should be

added – overall despatch and less weather damage – and not for the comfort of those on board.

The violence of the roaring forties is highlighted by the fate of the *Singa See,* a 16 000-tonne bulk carrier, which was headed west from Bunbury, Western Australia, in 1988, when she struck a storm 300 nautical miles (555 kilometres) off the coast. She hit three giant waves, snapped in half and went down so fast the crew had no time to send a distress call. A month later six of the crew were found in a liferaft; nineteen others had died. And of course, the fates of the *Sydney Cove, Cataraqui* and *Loch Ard* have shown that travelling eastward in the roaring forties is no picnic either.

Aboard the *Quetta*, the terrors of the labyrinth were far from most minds. Dinner was over and an idyllic tropical evening was taking the edge off the fierce heat of the day. The ship's motion was creating enough breeze to lure many passengers onto the decks. Their children had been put to bed, and most of the ship's portholes were open to freshen the air inside their cabins.

The thirty-three saloon passengers, many of them representing the cream of Queensland society picked up from ports from Brisbane to the previous morning's stop at Cooktown, were getting to know one another. The sixty-seven steerage passengers were doing likewise. On the after deck, seventy-one Javanese men, women and children were sleeping rough, but looking forward to getting home after three years of backbreaking work in the Queensland cane fields. In their pockets were all their savings, enough to set them up for life upon their homecoming. Even the twenty-eight European crew and ninety-two lascars had relaxed into the rhythm of shipboard life.

Alice Nicklin, nineteen-year-old daughter of prominent Brisbane church leaders and saddlery owners, Reubin and Jane Nicklin, described the activities of herself and her fellow passengers:

Mrs Lord [wife of Brisbane accountant James Lord, travelling with her son] and the youngest Miss Lacy [thirteen-year-old sister of seventeen-year-old Emily (known as 'Bunnie'), both travelling from their parents' property near Townsville, with their uncle, the Reverend Tom Hall, to an English 'finishing' school] and my mother were in their cabins. Captain Whish [former British army officer and popular Queensland Inspector of Roads, travelling with his wife, Ann] and Miss Waugh were in the saloon writing letters. Mrs Lord just before retiring to her cabin was writing to her husband, and had cut off a lock of her hair and plaited it to send to him. Upon some one saying, 'Anyone would think it was a sweetheart you were sending your hair to,' she replied that he was far dearer to her than a sweetheart. She then retired to her cabin. I then met Miss Prentice [travelling to London with her grandfather, George, a retired marble merchant and former mayor of Sandgate], who asked me to join her in a stroll on deck.

Bunnie Lacy also recalled, 'Shortly after 9 p.m. on Friday, 28th February, I was sitting in the saloon writing a letter to my mother.' Henry Corser, a Rockhampton solicitor, was travelling to England with his wife and five-year-old son: 'At about 9.20 I was on the saloon deck with the other passengers. Some were playing and singing, others talking.' Henry Wrathall, a well-known cricketer from Townsville travelling in steerage, was enjoying a respite from the tropical heat, sitting on the front hatch with his wife and babe-in-arms. Also taking their ease were the Brisbane manager of the Bank of New South Wales, Alexander 'Sandy' Archer, and his wife, Mary ('Minnie'); successful printing business proprietor John Watson; the ship's doctor and prominent Brisbane resident, Dr Poland, and his wife, Emily; and wealthy fruiterer William Blackford.

Up on the bridge, the scene was entirely different. While the passengers chatted, played music and wrote letters for the last Australian mail drop at Thursday Island the next morning, pilot Keatinge was a picture of quiet concentration. Piloting vessels through the labyrinth required it. Unlike the open ocean, where a ship can establish a rough estimate of its position and set its course accordingly, navigating narrow channels requires a totally different set of skills. Keatinge had to position the *Quetta* with great accuracy and keep her on course at all times. To this end, compass bearings were frequently being taken to every prominent landmark available – recognisable islands, reefs, protruding rocks. Sometimes the course was maintained by keeping two visible objects aligned (following leads) until the compass bearing to another landmark indicated a turn to port or starboard to stay in the sinuously twisting channel.

Such navigation can be an entertaining challenge when you're at the helm of a small vessel with a forgivingly shallow draft, working through relatively harmless sand shoals or mudbanks with rescue services just a radio or mobile phone call away. It's an entirely different story when it's a steamship drawing 5.8 metres of water at the bow and 6.9 metres at the stern, carrying 292 souls (all those mentioned, plus one possible stowaway), and the hazards are rocky outcrops and coral reefs. As for the radio, in 1890 Guglielmo Marconi was still five years from pioneering wireless telegraphy.

As Keatinge reported later, the *Quetta* had passed the entrance to the narrow Albany Pass, between the mainland and Albany Island, which was usually used for daylight passages, and was going round the outside of Albany Island to take the wider Adolphus Channel between Albany and Mount Adolphus Islands. Keatinge's earlier concern about a rain squall coming up behind the ship (that might obscure his landmarks and force him to anchor) had passed as it now drifted away from them. Although the night was dark, he had good visibility with the bulk of Mount Adolphus Island an easy landmark ahead, along with several smaller islands nearby.

At the south-eastern end of the Adolphus Channel, two small islands in particular, North Brother and Mid Brother, provide two natural leads for keeping in the centre of the channel and avoiding its only known hazard, Mid Rock, which lies 2.9 metres below the surface at low tide on the Albany Island side of the channel. With the Brothers in line astern, you track right down the centre of the channel, which Keatinge did shortly after 9 p.m., giving the order to turn to port onto a north-west heading. Once he was past Mid Rock, it was a virtually clear passage to Thursday Island, about 50 kilometres distant.

Unfortunately, the tidal current had slightly different ideas. As the *Quetta* pushed up the channel, the current pushed her towards the Mount Adolphus side of the channel. Astern, the Brothers, which had been 'closed', or perfectly in line, 'opened' again. The officer of the watch, third officer Tom Babb, reported this to Keatinge, who was sufficiently experienced to have been expecting it. As the Brothers opened further, he ordered the helmsman, quartermaster James Oates, to steer north-by-west-a-half-west. He was not particularly concerned about his drift as it was well known that there were no hazards on the Adolphus side of the channel. Keatinge was more concerned about overreacting and steering the ship back across the channel towards Mid Rock.

It was at this point that Captain Sanders also joined the watch on the bridge; he'd been socialising with the passengers. Babb reported to him that the Brothers were still open, which Keatinge confirmed, ordering the helmsman to steer nor'-west-by-west to close them more quickly. The ship was now moving through the water at 11 knots (20 kilometres/hour), to which was added the tidal flow of some 3 knots (5.5 kilometres/hour). Astern the Brothers were almost closed again, the ship almost back to the very centre of the channel. It was two minutes later that, as Keatinge reported, he felt 'a slight shock.'

According to Alice Nicklin: 'The noise caused by the vessel in striking sounded like a tank going overboard, then there was a grating sound, and then a smell of the water from the engine room.' Steerage passenger William Gregory, who was on the upper deck, said the impact did not stop or jerk the vessel much. To Henry Corser it was 'a sort of grating sensation.'

Whatever the *Quetta* had hit, the order was immediately given to stop engines, which was obeyed promptly by the men in the engine room, fourth engineer Michael Cardock and eleven lascar firemen. Then Captain Sanders called to the ship's carpenter to 'sound the wells', to determine if the *Quetta* was taking water. Keatinge started taking bearings. If they'd hit an unknown obstacle, it was vital to ascertain its exact position, for future reference.

Sanders left the bridge to prepare the lifeboats in case they were needed. However, the ship's carpenter, Nigel Robertson, hadn't needed to sound the wells. He shouted from his position forward that the ship was filling fast.

Cricketer Henry Wrathall later reported, 'The captain called all hands aft; but the second steward said, 'It's alright – only the anchor dropped.'

'We almost immediately heard the captain cry out to all the ladies to go aft to save their lives,' recollected solicitor Henry Corser. 'I rushed down into the saloon and carried up my little boy, aged five, who was in bed. I handed him to his mother, and led them aft. I said I had better go and fetch his cap. She said, "Never mind."'

'I ran down to mother, who returned with me on deck,' Alice Nicklin recalled. 'I then heard the captain say, "All who want to be saved go aft."'

Bunnie Lacy interrupted her letter writing.

I at once rushed on deck, and saw all the passengers in a great state of commotion. I rushed downstairs, and dragged my sister May out of bed. She came on deck in her nightdress. I then went to my uncle and said, 'Is there any danger?' and he said, 'A little, but you both stick by me.'

Sanders' well-drilled crew responded immediately, reporting to their emergency stations, preparing boats for launching. Down below, chief engineer McMurchie was seen rushing to his station in the engine room. Whether he succeeded in getting there will never be known, for when the *Quetta* struck, Michael Cardock and the others in the engine room must have seen the hull literally tear open beneath their feet, and seawater come pouring in. Even so, Cardock managed to obey the telegraphed order to stop engines. Doing so may have bought the *Quetta* precious time as she slowed to a halt, rather than drive beneath the waves. The men in the engine room remained at their stations, even when the water reached the fires, quenching them in a burst of steam that exploded up the funnel with a mighty roar. Then, as the water swirled around the boilers, they ruptured, filling the engine room with boiling water and steam. Everyone there was almost instantly cooked alive.

Up on deck, pilot Keatinge, still on the bridge, looked up from taking his bearings to the horror of seeing the deck forward already awash. The cry went up, 'She's sinking.' 'Terrible confusion ensued, especially amongst the women,' Henry Wrathall noted. 'The coloured men were particularly noisy and unmanageable. The forward hatch was blown several feet into the air by the pressure from below.'

His duties as pilot abruptly ended, Keatinge stayed at his post.

I remained on the bridge with the third officer throwing spare lifebelts used for the emigrants on the outward voyage, and which were kept in a box on the bridge, to the passengers. After the engines had been stopped for about one minute and a half the water was up to the bridge.

Passengers at the front of the ship were trying to get to the stern, but found themselves crammed at the foot of two small ladders that led to the upper deck. When the rising water reached them, some leapt over the side, but most were trapped by an awning spread over that part of the ship to provide shade during the day. In the forward steerage compartments, trapped women and children were already drowning.

The saloon passengers and Javanese flocking to the stern fared a little better. 'We then went aft, and it was like going uphill; the ship was so high above the water where we were going,' recounted Bunnie Lacy. 'On my way I heard Mrs Whish say to Captain Whish, "Claude, will you take care of me?" They were such dear old people. Miss Nicklin was so kind, and offered to go down and get some shawls to wrap my sister in.'

By then it was too late for shawls. As Alice Nicklin recalled: 'Mother asked father to go down and help Mrs Lord up. He went down, and we never saw him more. I saw Dr Poland give his wife a plank before the vessel sank, and I advised her to take off her dress.'

'We went over the side,' Keatinge would later recall, 'and by that time the stern of the ship was standing high out of the water, and the propeller and a large part of the keel were visible. The *Quetta* appeared to hang in that position for half a minute.'

There was a faint hope that the *Quetta* might have just enough buoyancy for part of her to stay afloat. Her bow had already driven into the bottom, 20 metres below the surface, supporting much of her weight. Even a few minutes would give more time to get the lifeboats launched. The tide, meanwhile, was still pushing at the *Quetta*, causing her to pivot on her bow.

According to Henry Wrathall: 'One lifeboat was lowered to the water's edge as the vessel was sinking, but it was rushed by the Javanese, causing it to swamp.'

By then Henry Corser was with his wife and little boy just above the officer's cabin.

My wife said, "Let us go down together," and we stayed together. The water was rising up to our feet, the steam was coming up around us and the vessel then lay with her forepart under water, the afterpart being raised high above the surface. She then turned over to our left and went right over.

As the *Quetta* heeled to port, Captain Sanders scrambled up into the rigging above the awnings. Alice Nicklin and her mother had both made it to the stern.

We just had time to get upon the railing over the stern so as to avoid the awning. The ship seemed not to sink, but the waters seemed to rise around us. The vessel went down suddenly at the last moment, leaving 200 people all huddled together in the water treading upon each other.

From the moment she'd struck until she went down, as little as three minutes had elapsed, certainly no more than five. That's as long as it takes to read a couple of pages of this volume, nowhere near enough time to launch the lifeboats and save the lives of 292 people. The *Quetta* sank to the bottom of the Adolphus Channel. Her hull was torn open from just behind the starboard bow for 53 metres along her 116-metre length. In places the rent was 2 metres wide. No ship could survive such a wound. It was as though a horn of the Minotaur had thrust up from the depths of the labyrinth to deal her a mortal blow.

As the vessel went down, the suction created dragged many under with it. Pilot Keatinge was one of them. 'I was sucked down with her, and remember nothing after that till I was lying on the water on a bit of wreckage.'

'When the vessel went down I lost mother, but know not how,' Alice Nicklin recalled, 'I sank twice, and then floated for a while, as I could swim.'

Henry Corser's ordeal was even more terrifying: 'All I remember then is that I was under the water and felt myself kept down by the rigging, awning and ropes. After struggling for a while I shot up and found myself among a lot of sheep and Javanese.'

Henry Wrathall had watched his wife jump into the sea before the ship went down, then followed her, with his child clutched in his arms. 'I never saw my wife afterwards. When in the water I was held by a coloured man, and in the struggle lost my child, which was drowned.'

Passenger William Gregory recalled that, 'The cries of the women when the vessel was sinking were heartrending.'

Bunnie Lacy was also dragged under, separated from her uncle and sister.

I found myself going down, and as I was drinking in the salt water I thought I was going to be drowned, but I came up again, and was surrounded by Cingalese [sic] and sheep. I felt myself being pressed down by them. It was terrible.

Then I saw a raft a short distance out. I swam for it and was dragged on to it by the purser, who was so kind to me. We were attached to a bigger raft crowded with Cingalese. When we got away some distance, as the Cingalese became very noisy, we cut our raft adrift and I remained on her with the purser a long time – till we were about, as I thought, 2 miles [3 kilometres] from shore, and as he told me he could not swim I left him and swam for the shore. I could not reach it, however, as it was so far away.

I went on swimming towards the land, and saw another raft, on which were two Cingalese, and to which I made my way and got on to it, but as they were very red and excited, and I thought they might be drunk, I left it and took to swimming again. It seemed so long.

Henry Corser was having better luck.

I then swam out some distance and caught hold of a grating, but finding this useless I let it go. Then I saw what appeared to be a boat laden with people. I struck out for it and found it to be a boat [the *Quetta*'s cutter], bottom up, swarming with some eighty or ninety Javanese. I held on to this, and after a time the weight of those above turned the boat over. One man ripped off the cover, and everyone was trying to get into her at once. She filled and went under. We tried to bail her out, and many of us jumped overboard and held on while others bailed.

Another passenger, H. Ashford, also got to the boat: 'They got the boat righted and bailed out. A second steerage steward named G.P. Stallard then came up, and threw a child he had picked up in the water into the boat. The child was apparently dead, but was carefully attended to, and is now safe. The steward left the boat and swam to the cowshed, followed by Morphy.'

Stallard and Morphy, a steerage passenger from Port Douglas, had left the boat 'owing to the number of coloured men and their quarrelsome attitude.' While they were clinging to the cowshed: 'Dr Poland came up, and Morphy got him up several times, but he was too weak to hold on, and fell off. He was never seen again by Morphy.'

When the *Quetta* went down, Captain Sanders had just had time to climb into the rigging and leap into the water as his ship heeled over. He stripped off his clothes in the water and after swimming for half an hour, found another lifeboat. Despite having been badly damaged and, consequently, full of water, it was crammed with people.

Others, like Alice Nicklin, didn't fare as well:

I then caught hold of a grating, to which the purser and two or three
Javanese were also clinging. Another Javanese came and tried to get
on the grating. This frightened me so that I let go. I floated a little
longer, and then caught a dead sheep, which I clung to until I got hold
of a plank. I was alone.

Yet she could hear the boats, and other people, all around her.

I called out to the boats, the people on which could hear but not see
me, as the moon had gone down. When screaming for the boat I heard
Miss Lacy, who asked if it was I, and telling me to hold on and I would
most likely be washed ashore; but I never saw her. All through the
night I could hear people calling out for help, and I could also hear
the boats. I tried to swim and paddle away to the shore, but became
too weak to work any longer. I then waited for daylight, and fell partially asleep several times, lying upon the plank.

Fortunately for those struggling in the water, hypothermia was
a distant threat, given the warm tropical climate and almost tepid
waters. Yet those immersed in the sea were starting to feel its effects.

During the night, Captain Sanders and Pilot Keatinge, who both
survived the sinking, met in the shattered lifeboat. Sanders asked if
it was Mid Rock they'd struck. Keatinge was adamant they were
nearly two kilometres from it. It was more confirmation that Sanders
had not done anything wrong. Yet his ship lay at the bottom of
Adolphus Channel and he was sure the loss of life would be immense.
He was at a loss to understand what had happened, unless it was
an uncharted rock.

Meanwhile, Henry Corser and the crowd in the cutter were on the
move. They started for the nearest land, Mount Adolphus Island.

However, the tide carried them on to one of a small group of islands called Little Adolphus. 'On our way we passed another boat [Sanders' lifeboat] full of water and people clinging to it. We called out and told them to hold on and we would rescue them as soon as we had landed our crowd.'

When the cutter returned, it took some of the people on board to lighten the lifeboat, and towing Sanders, Keatinge and the others, it headed back to the island. Then Sanders organised a crew of able-bodied men to return to the scene of the wreck and search for more survivors. When it returned, at about 3 a.m., the total number of people on the beach had risen to 98, but that left nearly 194 unaccounted for.

Among them were Bunnie Lacy and Alice Nicklin. Bunnie was still trying to swim to shore. Alice had been drifting, clinging to her plank all night. 'At daylight I swam towards the shore,' Alice recalled, 'still holding the plank, and reached the land in about three hours' time. When I got into shallow water an Indian cabin boy, who was the only person on the island [treeless, waterless Acoineh Island, near Mount Adolphus Island], helped me ashore, as I was too weak to walk.'

Also at first light, the cutter departed Little Adolphus with Keatinge, Sanders and a fresh crew, first to search for more survivors, then to make for the nearest outpost of civilisation for help. At around 10.30 in the morning, the cutter had covered the 16 kilometres to Somerset, the failed seat of local government overlooking the Albany channel that was now the home of pearl sheller and salvage expert, Frank Jardine, son of the area's first settler.

Jardine had seen the cutter approaching and gone to meet it. He was confronted by a half-naked man, haggard and near exhaustion, at the head of a group of men who were in similar condition. The man was Captain Fred Sanders. The story he had to tell both shocked the long-time resident and spurred him to action.

He gave orders for his Aboriginal stock supervisor to saddle up to ride to the nearest telegraph station, at Paterson, 25 kilometres distant. His Samoan wife, Sana, was soon organising food and drink for the exhausted men. Jardine's head boatman, a Torres Strait Islander, was organising a crew for the cutter to go and search for more survivors. Jardine started ransacking his house for every bit of clothing he could find.

At two o'clock on Saturday afternoon, the telegraph station at Thursday Island received the following message, addressed to John Douglas, the Government representative:

Quetta struck an unknown rock nine last night. Filled and sank within three minutes. About 100 souls rescued on Mount Adolphus. Anticipate appalling loss of life amongst European passengers. Islands in vicinity should be thoroughly searched for crew and passengers. Will endeavour to stop [steamer] *Victoria* to take food and water to North Adolphus Island. Send [government steamer] *Albatross* here to bring us on in case *Victoria* fails to have made arrangements. Sanders.

Half an hour later, the message was relayed to the office of the *Quetta*'s owners in Brisbane with the additional comment: '*Albatross* leaves immediately. Hope arrange [local steamer] *Merrie England* leave in a few hours.'

The message having passed through telegraph stations all the way down the Queensland coast, from where many of the European passengers had embarked, the shocking news rapidly spread and telegraph offices were soon besieged by frantic relatives and friends desperate for news.

At Thursday Island, the tiny community reacted in a similar manner to Frank Jardine and the handful of people at Somerset. The *Albatross*, essentially the local workhorse vessel that had been waiting to assist when the *Quetta* arrived, left as soon as the order was given. The *Merrie England*, a small steamer that normally plied between

Thursday Island and New Guinea, left an hour later, after loading supplies hastily gathered by the entire population of some 500 people.

A visiting missionary, Rev. Albert McLaren, went aboard the *Albatross* with the local doctor, Dr Salter, to render assistance.

> About three hours later the *Albatross* came alongside the SS *Victoria*, and took on board Captain Sanders, the pilot, and some lascars, and at once proceeded on her way to Mount Adolphus Island [actually Little Adolphus], where nearly 100 shipwrecked people anxiously awaited her arrival, among them being the second and third officers of the *Quetta*, as well as the quartermaster.

Among the survivors was the tiny child who'd been thrown, half-dead, into the cutter. As McLaren reported:

> Many of us were very much touched when we saw and heard of the attachment of a Javanese to a little white child about three years of age. He had rescued her from the deep and had tended her with the greatest care. The poor little child was crying for mamma, and he told us she had been crying out all day for her. We gave her milk and other nourishment, and wrapped her in some pyjamas till other clothing arrived on board the steamer *Merrie England*.

The *Albatross* did what she could with the little food and clothing she had until the *Merrie England* arrived shortly after laden with the clothing, food and water that the Thursday Islanders had gathered with incredible speed. Also on board was a Miss Brown who had volunteered to act as a stewardess for any ladies that might be rescued.

One of those was Alice Nicklin, who was still on Acoineh Island with the Indian cabin boy, and a number of other crew and deck passengers who struggled there during the day. Without shade, and having stripped off most of their clothing while in the water, the

fierce tropical sun severely burned many of them. They also spent
the day without water, and had tried vainly to signal several passing
steamships that were still oblivious to the fate of the *Quetta*. Then at
four o'clock, as the *Albatross* and *Merrie England* were closing in on
Little Adolphus, the cutter crew from Somerset found them. The
crowded boat was forced to leave most of the people on the island,
but shuttled Alice to the increasingly busy homestead at Somerset,
where she arrived at 11.30 on Saturday night. There, Alice recalled:
'We could not have been treated with greater kindness.'

The two steamers anchored in darkness, then set off at first light,
splitting up to widen their search of all the islands, reefs and shoals
that might hold more survivors. Four men were found on Mount
Adolphus Island, plus the fifteen on Acoineh Island, where the cutter had left them the night before. The *Albatross* then steamed
towards the Brothers, as Rev. McLaren recalled:

> When Captain Reid, whose marked and worthy efforts to save life are
> beyond praise, and who never left the bridge for an instant, but with
> glass in hand scanned the sea in every direction, suddenly saw some-
> thing not much larger than a cocoanut – floating out to sea. He at once
> steamed towards it, and as we drew nearer he saw that it was a per-
> son swimming. Just once a hand was lifted up, but before this a boat
> was sent out and a poor young lady was lifted in. One of the sailors
> took off his flannel shirt and wrapped her in it, but she had in the
> meantime fainted. I at once recognised her to be Miss May [actually
> Emily] Lacy, sixteen years of age, the eldest daughter of Mr Dyson Lacy,
> of St Helen's Station, Mackay.

Bunnie had been in the water for nearly thirty-six hours and for
much of that time she had been swimming. She had left the raft with
the purser some time during Saturday afternoon and was picked up
at 8.10 a.m. the next day. When they'd got her into the boat, severely

sunburned, she'd continued trying to swim, her arms sweeping in front of her until she passed out. She later told Rev. McLaren that:

> I remember nothing till I saw your ship, which I took to be the *Quetta*. When the boat came along I didn't want to get into it, as I thought it was not going to take me to your ship. I thought you were the steward when you waved your hat to me on board when I was in the water, but I knew you, as well as Dr Salter, when I came on board. I thought I had been staying in a large hotel under the water, and I think I must have been unconscious from time to time.

Bunnie Lacy's survival is one of the most remarkable in Australian maritime history, and she was the last person to be taken from the water alive. Her sister was never found. As Rev. McLaren reported: 'All hope of her little sister's safety is at an end, as she must have gone to her eternal rest clinging to her uncle.'

At Malalog Island the *Albatross* recovered another man who had been rescued by a passing fishing boat, the *Black Fish*, whose owner had also joined the search. Next the *Albatross* found the *Quetta*'s mail boat (a small rowboat used to collect and drop mail from ship to shore) floating upside down. It was in mint condition, 'perfectly lashed', suggesting it had broken free of the wreck after any survivor who might have made use of it had been swept away.

At Albany Island, the *Albatross* intercepted a cutter, belonging to Frank Jardine, that had left Somerset the previous Thursday to go turtling under the command of 'Cockroach' Abinghi. She was returning when she started encountering wreckage from the *Quetta*. As McLaren reported: 'She stopped to search it, with the result that she picked up ten persons, including the chief officer, Gray, and had put him on board our dinghy earlier in the day.'

At Somerset, all those rescued, with the exception of Bunnie Lacy, who was in a serious condition and being tended by Dr Salter, were put aboard the *Merrie England*, which carried them to Thursday Island that evening, where the population increased significantly and the tiny town was stretched to its limits to care for the stricken passengers and crew. It was now becoming possible to account for those lost and saved, though the communications at the time meant that it was some time before the tallies were complete.

Out of 292 on board, 158 survived and 134 were lost, making the *Quetta* one of Queensland's worst shipping disasters. Most of the bodies were buried on the islands where they were found; only a few were buried at Thursday Island. It was soon realised that most of the dead were the European passengers. Out of a total of a hundred European passengers, all but fifteen had died. There were accusations about the Javanese rushing the boats, and being unruly, which cost extra lives. However, most of the passengers who died were women, unable to swim and burdened by their heavy Victorian-era clothing, and their children. Many were in their cabins, in steerage, which was at the front of the ship and went under almost immediately after the ship struck.

As for the Javanese, their emotional state may have been due in part to the realisation that they were about to lose three years' wages from their grindingly hard labour, many being forced to jettison their money in the water or risk being dragged under by the weight of the coins.

What made the loss even harder to bear was that most of the victims were well known. As the *Brisbane Courier* put it on the Tuesday after the wreck:

No such fatality has ever befallen Queensland; the *Dunbar* wreck in August 1857, inflicted a similar sorrow on New South Wales, and is the only record of the kind which can compare in point of domestic and local sorrow with the present one. Greater loss of life, numerically speaking, has occurred on the Australian coast in some shipwrecks, but the lives have been those of immigrants and strangers, and did not enter into our hearts as the present misfortune has done, a national calamity worthy of a memorial tablet in our leading church.

The people of Queensland ended up going considerably further. Within a few years, they'd raised the money to build the *Quetta* Memorial Cathedral on Thursday Island, in which were placed several relics salvaged from the wreck. And in the days after the wreck, extraordinarily generous subscriptions were sent to Thursday Island, where they were distributed somewhat unevenly between Europeans and non-Europeans.

However, in the days after the wreck two items remained unaccounted for. The first was the fate of the tiny child thrown into the *Quetta*'s cutter by the steward, G.B. Stallard. The problem was that no-one among the survivors either claimed her or knew who she was. Even her exact age wasn't known, but she was certainly too young to say who her parents were. A thorough investigation yielded no clues, which left her an orphan. However, the generosity of the Thursday Islanders ensured she was well cared for. When no relatives came forward to claim her, she was eventually adopted by a childless Thursday Island couple, Captain Edmund and Marjorie Brown. The Browns gave her the name Cecil, or 'Cissy' for short. But the name the locals gave her, and which followed her to her death, in 1949, was *Quetta* Brown.

The other item on a lot of people's minds was: what exactly did the *Quetta* hit? Even during the search for survivors, as vessels crisscrossed the Adolphus Channel, they were alert to finding some evidence of an 'unknown rock', especially as they were guided by the bearings taken by pilot Keatinge immediately after hitting something on that fateful night.

However, as the days passed and nothing was found, the doubts grew. The ship was found and assessed for salvage operations, with evidence of her calamitous impact amply evident. Frank Jardine, who knew the waters at his doorstep extremely well, suggested that perhaps there was no rock, that perhaps one of the *Quetta*'s boilers had exploded. However, this theory didn't tally with the accounts of the numerous survivors. Meanwhile, for Captain Sanders, the thought 'I didn't do anything wrong' must have become a mantra.

Finally, nearly two weeks after the *Quetta* struck, the labyrinth yielded its secret. As the *Brisbane Courier* reported:

> Thursday Island, March 13. The *Albatross* has just returned. Captain Reid found a rock with the lead line showing 14½ feet [4.4 metres, though at the lowest tide it's only 3 metres] of water. This rock is fully half a mile [800 metres] away from the wreck of the *Quetta*, showing that the vessel must have passed over that distance after striking it . . . The rock, which is considered to be very small, has not yet been examined by divers. The water being clear, a black rock was seen, with a large white patch, leading to the belief that the *Quetta* broke off portions of the rock.

It has been known ever since as *Quetta* Rock. At the subsequent marine inquiry it was found to be the cause of the loss of the *Quetta*, no blame being attached to either Sanders or Keatinge. Indeed much of the evidence given by other pilots and ships' masters indicated they all must have passed terribly close to *Quetta* Rock on numerous occasions.

Naturally, the loss of the *Quetta* raised questions about how many other horns of stone still lay in Australian shipping channels, waiting to be discovered. For years after, ships actively surveyed the entire region, so that today's charts are highly detailed and there are few nasty surprises. The last was in 1970, when the cargo vessel *Oceanic Grandeur* ran aground on an uncharted rock in Torres Strait, eighty years after the *Quetta* met her fate, with serious environmental consequences. Ships still run aground, pushed off course by currents or strong winds, or while manoeuvring past other vessels in the tight channels. For this reason, and because of the potential for a disaster to the Great Barrier Reef's tourism industry, fully-laden oil tankers take the longer outer route. And to this day, even with the most modern navigational aids, the skills of the Torres Strait pilots remain crucial for every one of the many giant vessels that dare to enter the labyrinth.

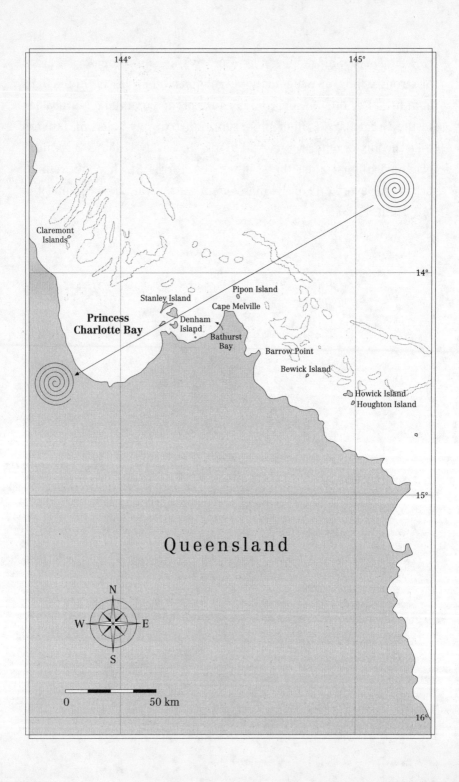

144°   145°

Claremont
Islands

14°

Pipon Island

Stanley Island
Cape Melville

**Princess
Charlotte Bay**   Denham
Island
                         Bathurst
                         Bay
                                      Barrow Point

                         Bewick Island

                                   Howick Island
                                   Houghton Island

15°

Queensland

N

W   E

S

0   50 km

16°

Luggers wrecked after a cyclone, Broome,
WA. Scene was similar after Mahina
swept far-north Queensland.
(J.S. Battye Library – 25101P/000645D)

9. THE TAHITIAN GIRL: CYCLONE MAHINA, 1899

The first sign that the weather report for the coast of Queensland for Saturday, 4 March 1899, might not be entirely accurate was when all telegraphic communication between Cooktown and Thursday Island was lost.

'Conditions are again becoming suspicious between the Louisiades and the north of New Caledonia,' was the somewhat specu- lative outlook by meteorologist Clement Wragge, published in the *Brisbane Courier* on 3 March. It continued: 'And although no danger yet threatens the Queensland Coast, we must needs keep a bright lookout.'

The view was very different from Thursday Island, where it was obvious something truly terrible was approaching the coast to the south of Cape York. As Thursday Island postmaster H.P. Beach recalled:

> I remember the nights of 2nd and 3rd March very well. They were uncommonly hot and generally oppressive. The eastern part of the horizon was terribly lit up with distant lightning which disclosed a black, leaden, fierce-looking sky. The lightning was singularly severe and an almost continual electrical discharge, although not the slightest sound of thunder reached the ear.

The next night was the same, and on the morning of 5 March came the telegraph message from nearby Cape York, 'No communication south of the Coen.'

The tiny township of Coen is some 450 kilometres south of Cape York, 50 kilometres inland from the northern end of Princess Charlotte Bay. There may have been any number of reasons for the telegraph's breakdown, but at Thursday Island one look at the sky was enough to raise concern among a large part of the population. Everyone knew several of the Thursday Island-based pearling fleets were operating in the vicinity of Princess Charlotte Bay. If a cyclone had smashed through the area, many of the relatives and friends of people at Thursday Island may have been in its path.

Among all of the maritime endeavours around Australia's coastline, the pearling industry was the realm of the bravest and most adventurous. Throughout the industry men died when their primitive diving equipment failed, when they ascended from the depths too fast and suffered the bends, when they were attacked by sharks.

The industry had grown rapidly since 1860, when explorer Francis

Thomas Gregory and his crew in the *Dolphin* first collected pearl near Broome, Western Australia. By 1874, there were eighty boats working from Broome, and in 1883 it was around 400, making the town the world's leading pearling centre. In 1883 pearling was also established at Thursday Island and soon over 200 vessels were working the waters of the Cape York Peninsula. Eventually the industry extended right across the north of Australia, from Broome to Darwin, across the Gulf of Carpentaria to Cape York, then down the Queensland coast.

In its early days the industry was primarily interested in pearl shell, rather than pearls. The shell was the raw material for the manufacture of buttons and ornaments. And the shell beds were plundered, rather than fished. Speculators seeking good returns cared little for the long term, exhausting the supply in one area, then moving on to the next. They also exploited their workers, bringing in cheap labour from wherever they could find it. Thus most fleets consisted of a few white managers and a mixture of Pacific and Torres Strait Islanders, Malays, Japanese, Indians and others.

It was hard and dangerous work, especially during cyclone season. In his book *Port of Pearls*, Hugh Edwards detailed the loss of life in the Broome pearl fishery. On Christmas Eve 1875, 59 died in the Exmouth Gulf; April 1887, 140 were lost at Eighty Mile Beach. In January 1894, 50 died at Cossack; later, another 50 died; in April 1908, 50 died, plus 50 more in December. In 1910, 40 died. In 1935, 141 lives were lost.

The problem for the pearling fleets was that the science of cyclone prediction, indeed of weather forecasting, was still in its infancy. In the 1890s, Australia may have developed to the point where it was on the brink of nationhood, yet the understanding of the weather systems that affected large parts of the nation-continent was still being developed.

Prediction often relied on intermittent reports from isolated stations, but where cyclones were concerned the stations were often battered into silence shortly after the weather struck. As for the ability to photograph cyclones from satellites in space, and accurately predict the direction and speed that they were moving, that was still nearly a century away. It wasn't even possible to issue warnings to vessels that might be in the path of a cyclone. Marconi had tested his wireless telegraph in 1895, but it would not be until 1901 that the first message was transmitted across the Atlantic. It would be many years more before a pearling schooner could tune in its wireless for a weather report, accurate or not. Instead, masters relied on their ability to 'read' the local weather for signs of an approaching cyclone and, if possible, manoeuvre to avoid it.

There are two sides to every cyclone. On one side the hurricane force wind is 'accompanied by torrents of rain, vivid lightning, reverberating thunder, which could scarcely be heard against the noise of the wind, the swish of the spray, the dashing of the waves against the doomed vessels, the groaning of the planks, and the straining of the cordage and spars.' On the other side it's much worse.

The reason is that the winds of a cyclone don't just rotate around a fixed centre at up to 300 kilometres per hour (clockwise in the southern hemisphere and anti-clockwise in the northern, due to the Coriolis effect). The whole system is also moving forward, which means that the winds blowing in the direction the cyclone is travelling are much faster than those blowing towards where it's been. If a southern-hemisphere cyclone is moving west at between 8 and 24 kilometres per hour, for example, the winds on the southern side of the cyclone's path will be between 16 and 48 kilometres per hour faster than those on the northern side. It's a big difference. It's even bigger when the wind increase is from, say, 160 kilometres per hour to 200 kilometres per hour, because the force of the wind doesn't increase in direct proportion to its speed, it increases by the speed of the wind squared.

The cyclone can be further divided into quadrants. In the case of a cyclone moving west, the two quadrants to the north of the cyclone's path are preferred, because the wind and waves aren't as fierce and they tend to push vessels away from the cyclone's path. The trailing quadrant on the southern side, while accompanied by much stronger winds, still tends to push vessels away from the track. But the winds in the leading quadrant on the southern side tend to blow a vessel towards the centre of the storm, where the conditions are worst and the full fury of the cyclone lasts the longest. It's the place no vessel ever wants to be.

So with all this in mind, one can run from a cyclone, if you know it is coming and where it's coming from. Essentially, if it's moving west (as they tend to do on Australia's east coast), try to get to its north. If it's moving east (as is usual on the west coast), try to get to the south.

Unfortunately, while there may have been ominous signs at Thursday Island prior to 4 March, around Princess Charlotte Bay there was no concern at all. Saturday evening was a time for relaxation after a hard week's work. Most of the pearling luggers, solidly built workboats usually with crews of six, had returned to their mother ships, the schooners with crews of a dozen or more, to unload their pearl shell and resupply for the coming week. Many of the crews were relaxing, looking forward to a water-sports carnival among the pearling fleets that was planned for the next day.

At around 4 p.m., the 143-tonne schooner *Meg Merrilees* was at anchor on the north-west side of Princess Charlotte Bay, near Pelican Island, with her fourteen diving luggers and swimming boats (smaller luggers without diving apparatus). As evening approached other fleets anchored as well. Near the *Meg Merrilees* were the 102-tonne schooner *Aladdin* with fifteen luggers, the 92-tonne *Olive* with sixteen luggers, the 124-tonne *Tarawa* with eighteen luggers and the tender vessel *Wai Weir*.

Anchored 40 kilometres to the south-east, in Bathurst Bay and off Cape Melville, were many more pearling vessels. The 104-tonne *Silvery Wave* was anchored with her fleet of fifteen luggers, the 84-tonne *Sagitta* with nine luggers, and the 112-tonne *Crest of the Wave* with thirteen luggers. They were accompanied by up to twenty smaller vessels. The 25-tonne schooner *Admiral* had also arrived from the south that day to work as a tender. Not far away, anchored to the north-west of Cape Melville, was the *Channel Rock Lightship*. With a crew of four it was in a more exposed position in the main shipping channel, but it was purpose-built to withstand whatever the elements threw at it.

South of Cape Melville, the lugger *North Wales*, on its way from Thursday Island to Cooktown, was off Barrow Point. Nearby in the Howick Group were the cutters *Spray*, *Jamaica*, *Caledonia*, *La France*, *Dackle*, *Yunyo* and *Rattler*, plus other unknown Japanese vessels. The estimates of the number of people on the water were between 620 and 1000.

Making camp south of Cape Melville, at Barrow Point, was Constable J.M. Kenny. He and four native troopers were searching for a South Sea Islander who'd deserted from the pearling fleet and was lost somewhere in the bush. 'I reached Barrow Point on Saturday, 4th March,' Kenny reported, 'and camped about 6 p.m. on a ridge fully 40 feet [12 metres] above sea level, and about half a mile [1 kilometre] from the beach, with scrub and a high sand ridge between the camp and the beach. On Saturday afternoon a light south-east breeze prevailed, with drizzling rain.'

At 7 p.m., the *Meg Merrilees*, 'Bingo' Thompson master, was riding safely at anchor in a moderate breeze from the east. It had started to rain there as well, threatening to put a dampener on the festivities of the following day. Then the wind started to increase in strength. As the night darkened, it started to blow harder and harder.

By 9 p.m. the first vessels started getting into trouble. South of Cape Melville, Captain Hanson of the cutter *Spray* was anchored at Stapleton Island, in the Howick group, 'in company with a Japanese cutter, when the wind started to blow strong from the south-east, and about midnight changed to east. About 9 p.m. the Jap boat broke adrift, and went on to the reefs of the island, after which she was not seen again, evidently breaking up.'

To the north, near the Claremont Group, H. Vidgen on the schooner *Olive* watched the barometer drop from 29.6 inches to 29.1 – the rapid drop in pressure heralding the approaching tempest. The wind was blowing strongly from the south-east, but then it turned to the south-west and came on harder, picking up to hurricane force. Cyclone Mahina had arrived.

A detached observer might note the wind direction meant Vidgen was on Mahina's gentler northern side, if she had one. But no-one in the fleet off the Claremonts was in a position to be detached. The *Olive* started dragging her anchors, 'the sea was running mountains high.' Her crew saw the schooner *Aladdin* drifting as well. She slipped her anchor, missed an island, and dropped another anchor. It didn't hold. She continued to drag, beyond the help of vessels hard-pressed to save themselves. She was last seen drifting towards D reef, 'flying distress signals, dismantled, bulwarks gone.' Around the schooners, the luggers were dragging anchors and snapping anchor chains, their crews desperately bailing as the waves pounded them to pieces.

In Bathurst Bay, Captain William Porter of the schooner *Crest of the Wave* watched the glass fall to 27 inches (the central pressure has been estimated at 91.4 kilopascals or 26.9 inches). He was in the most intense cyclone that has ever crossed the Australian coast, a Category 5 cyclone with winds in excess of 280 kilometres per hour.

It was also his first, and on board the *Crest of the Wave* were his wife and baby daughter. Porter observed: 'the wind being strong off the land [south-east] and the vessel dragged in consequence. The cyclone cut away the masts, and the schooner sprang a leak.' The wind direction put *Crest of the Wave* and the other vessels in Bathurst Bay in the worst possible place, the leading quadrant of the worst cyclone in Australian history. As the vessel dragged, it was heading further into the maelstrom of seas and wind.

Mrs Porter was below with the child, but witnessed the mayhem on board and all around them: 'After the storm burst on them the position of the *Sagitta* was dangerous to the *Silvery Wave*, as the anchors were dragging. Guns were fired by the vessels at intervals to warn each other of their positions.'

A memorial booklet published in 1899 observed of Captain Porter:

He not only kept up his own courage, and would not give up hope or relax his endeavours to keep the vessel afloat, even when he told his wife that they were sinking fast, but he infused his own brave spirit into his coloured crew, and would not let them give way to despondency.

The *Crest of the Wave*'s crew desperately sought the leak. While some of the crew manned the pump, others frantically bailed. Finally, the leak was found, near the rudder. The crew stuffed anything they could find – blankets, sacks of flour – around it to staunch the flow. Then they returned to the pumps and buckets. At least Mahina's ill winds blew *Crest of the Wave* some good. As she dragged she got into deeper water where the waves weren't so steep.

Down at the Howicks, the strain on the cutter *Spray*'s anchor-chains finally took its toll. At 11 p.m. she broke adrift, at the mercy of the screaming wind and huge waves. She was washed towards Stapleton Island, pounding against the muddy bottom as she was driven ashore. Pushed into a stand of mangroves, she battered her way forward through the trees, smashing to matchwood those the storm hadn't torn apart.

With the storm raging all around him, Captain Porter of the *Crest of the Wave* still managed to glimpse the *Channel Rock Lightship*. At 11 p.m. she was still at her anchorage a couple of kilometres away. But Mahina was only getting started.

Back on shore, Constable Kenny was caught in the open:

About 11.30 p.m. it came on to blow very stiff from the south-south-east, increasing every minute. At 12 p.m. the troopers' tent was carried away, and they came into my own tent; and about ten minutes after this it too was demolished by a limb falling across it, and smashing through my hammock. Luckily I had left the hammock, as the rain was pouring on it, caused by a tent-peg pulling up.

When the tent collapsed, all hands made for the biggest open space near, guided by very vivid lightning which occurred at intervals. Here it was necessary to cover up face and hands in a blanket to keep off the pelting rain, which seemed to hit as hard as hail.

All around the *Crest of the Wave*, luggers were snapping chains and sinking. The 1899 memorial booklet recorded:

Albert and Moses were natives of Ware Island in the South Seas, and although two strong fellows, had a hard struggle for their lives. They have fine physiques, and most exceptional powers of endurance. Their boat, the *Little Bill*, was wrecked about midnight; they swam from Boulder Rocks, and in attempting to reach the mainland were driven by wind and sea to Pipon Island [off Cape Melville].

Some luggers were blown into the night, never to be seen again. Other crews bailed their vessels constantly, trying to stay afloat, all the time in peril of being smashed to pieces on a reef or in a collision with the other vessels being flung before the waves. Some people dived into the sea hoping to reach the safety of the shore. Some were driven mad by fear, the constant screech of the wind and the agony of the driving rain. In the water, the pouring rain, lashing spray and breaking waves blurred the margin between air and water. Fighting for air, some men drowned with their heads above the sea.

Meanwhile, the *Meg Merrilees*, in the Claremonts, was being overwhelmed. At about 3 a.m. she was struck by several tremendous waves, which smashed away her whaleboat. Then, as Captain William Thompson recalled, things got worse.

One of my luggers which was anchored alongside of me for provisions before the gale came on was driven on the reef and smashed to pieces: there were six of a crew (four Manila men and two Cingalese), two of whom were saved two days afterwards on a reef after being in the water one day. Another of my luggers which was lying close to her had her masts blown out, and after dragging about six miles [10 kilometres] her anchors held and she weathered the gale. I had five more luggers alongside; these were blown miles away, but came off with slight damage. At No. 1 Claremont Island had three other boats; one dragged quarter-mile and broke to pieces, five men drowned (coloured). The other two boats dragged on to the same reef, being only slightly damaged, [they eventually broke up before they could be refloated]. I had also fourteen diving luggers, four of which were lost; and nine coloured lives. During the gale the *Meg Merrilees* dragged her anchors ten miles [16 kilometres], and brought up on a reef north-east from the position she left. When in four fathoms of water I cut away the mast to try and save the vessel, but she still dragged as if she had no anchors down, until 6 a.m., when she grounded on a high reef, and filled with water.

Also around 3 a.m. the schooner *Tarawa*'s cables snapped and she was promptly blown onto Pelican Island. There she lay being battered by the surf, barely managing to hold together. Down in the Howicks, the *Rattler*, with Douglas Pitt Jnr in command, was being wrecked on the Howicks. He and his crew abandoned her and took to the water. Pitt was a 'West Indian negro' whose father and two brothers were somewhere out in the storm as well. Pitt's wife was with him, as was another crewman and his wife. In the darkness they tried to swim to Noble Island. The women may have been the two who also had children with them, the *Brisbane Courier* reporting that: 'Two coloured women swam for ten hours with children on their backs, but the children were dead when landed.'

It was around this time that Mahina finally showed the few vessels still fighting to survive in Bathurst Bay her full fury. At 4.30 a.m., the eye of the cyclone passed over Bathurst Bay. Still bailing desperately in the brief calm, one Japanese diver noticed dead seabirds strewn about the lugger *Estelle*'s deck. The wind had stripped every feather from their bodies. Then the wind that had been blowing off the land from the south-east turned to the north-east, pinning the boats against the shore with enormous waves that had built up as they were blown across the main channel.

'Between the hours of 3 to 5 a.m. a tidal wave swept along the coast, in many instances completing the ruin the hurricane had begun,' the memorial booklet recorded. 'It was during this warring of the elements that hundreds of lives were lost and bereavement brought home to thousands.'

All of the *Sagitta*'s luggers – the *Nellie*, *Kathleen*, *Estelle*, *Sybil*, *Zephyr*, *Zanoni* (10 tonne), *Sea Breeze*, *Zoe* (10 tonne) and *Here's Luck* – were sunk or smashed on the shore. All of the *Silvery Wave*'s luggers – *Enterprise*, *Kirkham* (12 tonne), *Jessamine* (9 tonne), *Ehime*, *Daisy*, *Flora*, *Vailele* (11 tonne), *Boomerang*, *Endeavour*, *Clara Merriman* (15 tonne), *Gipsy*, *Johnny*, *Lily*, *Narellan* and *Pearl King* – were sunk or smashed on the shore. All of the *Crest of the Wave*'s luggers – *Vera*, *Kata*, *G.P.*, *North Star*, *Leopold*, *Carrie*,

Vision, Pert, Pearl Queen, Endymion, Little Bill, Maggie and *Gitana* –
were sunk or smashed on the shore. In all forty-five vessels were lost
in Bathurst Bay. Many that were wrecked were found to have their
masts snapped off at the deck. It appeared that the waves had rolled
them over and over as they were driven through the shallows. To be
caught in such a surge of wreckage was certain death.

From the mainland Constable Kenny observed:

> At 5 a.m. [the wind] shifted to the north-east and, if possible, blew
> harder than ever, with torrents of rain. Shortly after . . . an immense
> tidal wave swept in shore, and reached waist deep on the ridge with
> the camp on it, completing the misery of myself and troopers. Here the
> wave stretched between two and three miles [three to five kilometres]
> inland.

There are reports that at Cape Melville, a group of Aboriginal
people was trying to help shipwrecked men ashore when the tidal
wave struck. The backwash may have swept them into the sea,
drowning as many as a hundred.

Out in Bathurst Bay, the *Silvery Wave* was one of the few vessels still
afloat. She may have been hit and fatally damaged when the *Sagitta*
dragged her anchors and was blown into the night, never to be seen
again (the only trace of her was a lifebuoy later recovered 160 kilometres down the coast). She may have been battered to pieces by
the waves breaking all around her. In any event, now she was sinking.
Captain Jefferson and Messrs Nicholas and Atthow had previously gone
off in a dinghy, but were immediately swamped and seen no more.

Two survivors are thought to have escaped the *Silvery Wave*. One
was a diver who got hold of a plank just before the schooner went
down. The other may have been an islander woman named Maura
who was thrown into the sea when the *Sagitta* and *Silvery Wave* col-
lided. While she was trying to swim to shore, she found two white

men in the water, close to exhaustion. She is reputed to have helped both stay afloat and swam, supporting them, towards the coast. At one point they were almost struck by a half-sunk lugger careering wildly before the wind and waves. After rescuing the men, she was awarded a medal from the Royal Humane Society.

There was no sunrise over Bathurst Bay on 5 March. There was no dawn. At around 10 a.m., as Mahina's ferocious winds started to ease, it started to grow light. At Barrow Point Constable Kenny found 'whole areas of scrub were blown flat, huge trees uprooted, and all those standing were stripped of bark and leaves. It was estimated the wind gusts attained a velocity of 120 miles per hour [200 kilometres per hour, but they were probably much stronger]. Huge areas of mangroves along the coast disappeared.'

Out in Bathurst Bay, only one vessel remained afloat. The *Crest of the Wave*, dismasted, her boats all gone, was holding at anchor in the deeper water near Channel Rock. The *Channel Rock Lightship*, with all hands (master C.D. Fuhrman, mate Douglas Lee, H. Karr and D. Crowley) was gone. Near shore there was, according to accounts in the *Brisbane Courier*, 'quite a forest of mastheads and floating wreckage. There are tons of dead fish, fowl and reptiles of all descriptions, and the place presents the appearance of a large cemetery. Stones were embedded in the trees to a depth of 6 inches [15 centimetres] and rocks weighing tons were thrown up. At Flinders Island thirteen porpoises were found 15 feet [4.6 metres] up the cliffs.'

At 7 p.m. that day the steamer *Duke of Norfolk* picked up Mrs Porter and the baby from the *Crest of the Wave*, and proceeded north to Thursday Island through rafts of wreckage and floating bodies. Mrs Porter's impressions were recorded in the memorial booklet.

The days that followed were sad ones. Thirty men were picked up off the beach; these had saved their lives by swimming. Thirty-two bodies were buried, and others were found floating in the sea. In all about 80

bodies were accounted for out of 280 men drowned [in Bathurst Bay]
. . . Numbers of other cases are known where men were in the water
from the time their boats sank, between midnight Saturday and daylight Sunday morning, till Sunday night, floating about on pieces of
wreckage. Of the sufferings of the poor fellows who floated about for
hours, but were not rescued, nothing will ever be known.

On Noble Island the 'West Indian' Douglas Pitt of the *Rattler* and
his wife, the other crewman and his wife, headed back into the
water when the seas died down and swam from island to island, reef
to reef, back to the mainland. From the island where they'd sunk to
the shore was 18 kilometres. Then they walked north to Cape
Melville, passing dead bodies all the way.

The two South Sea islanders, known only as Albert and Moses,
who were cast on Pipon Island, waited until the following Tuesday
for the seas to abate. They lived on plum pudding, a case of which
was cast on the beach. They buried the dead as they washed ashore.
Some of the bodies were of men they knew, such as two divers from
Manila who had been with the *Crest of the Wave* fleet.

On Wednesday, 8 March, the AUSN steamer *Warrego* passed
through the area on her way south. She found several vessels ashore
on Pelican Island, and learned some of the details of what had happened. Continuing south, between 6 p.m. and 7 p.m. she passed
'a number of dead bodies floating in the water'. The *Warrego*
reached Cooktown the following day, and the news finally started to
reach Brisbane and cities to the south.

The *Warrego* was immediately placed at the disposal of the government and ordered to recoal and return to the scene to search for
survivors. By then the *Duke of Norfolk* had arrived at Thursday
Island with Mrs Porter. What she had to tell did nothing to calm the
growing fears among the tiny community. The government representative there sent the steamer *White Star* south to assist.

On 10 March, the telegraph was repaired and it was reported from Thursday Island that: 'The reports received here have created much consternation here, as the friends and relations of the men who were working in the pearling boats are unable to ascertain their fate. The loss of so much life and property affects Thursday Island to an enormous extent, and it will take a long time to recover.'

Meanwhile, in Bathurst Bay, the *Warrego* met the *White Star* at Flinders Island, where thirty pearling boats had mustered. Pearling-boat operator George Smith reported that on No. 2 Howick the lugger *Rosa* was a total wreck. The *William* was high ashore. On Pelican Island the *Gavarra Peres*, *Two Brothers*, *Yomoto* and *Jenny* were total wrecks. The *Rotomuh* and *Martha* were damaged. Of 265 employees, he thought only 28 were still alive.

The *Warrego* reported finding several vessels on its journey. By an account from the *Warrego*'s purser:

Two small cutters were seen anchored between the Lizards and Newt Island. The steamer was brought to anchor, and a boat sent off to the cutters which proved to be the *Jamaica*, in charge of a West Indian negro named Douglas Pitt, Senior, and the *Loafer*, No. A260, in charge of Charlie Lifu, a French negro. While anchored at the Lizards the wind blew with hurricane force from the east, and he [Pitt] lost both his anchors, and was blown between the Lizards and Newt Island, and made fast alongside the *Loafer*. On Sunday morning the wind blew with terrific force, and shifted to north-east. He had three sons in the fleet and was very anxious as to their safety. It was afterwards found that two of these had been drowned, and the third, young Douglas Pitt, on hearing a report that his father was drowned, attempted to take his life on Flinders Island.

Pitt also reported seeing the cutters *Caledonia* and *La France* with French skippers, six native crew and one Bengali at No. 8 Howicks

before the cyclone. He believed theirs were the bodies first seen by
the *Warrego*.

In their search the vessels found twenty-seven bodies at Cape
Melville, where the local Aborigines had buried another thirty-seven.
Many of the bodies looked like they had been mutilated by sharks,
but it was the result of the tempestuous seas and wreckage. One of
the *Olive*'s employees reported seeing a portion of the *Channel Rock
Lightship* on Pipon Island. At Barrow Point, Vidgen, from the *Olive*,
found the beach 'strewn with dead gulls, birds, snakes and fish – so
much so that in parts the stench was unbearable.'

The loss of life was horrendous. The final estimate of those lost at
sea was 307. Those who perished on shore was put at 100. Other
cyclones have caused great loss of life, notably when the *Koombana*
was sunk off Broome in 1912, killing all 150 on board. In 1875 the
steamship *Gothenburg* (skippered by the stepfather of the *Loch Ard*'s
Tom Pearce), went down with 102 on board. But at 407 lives,
Mahina was the most terrible of them all.

Among the vessels lost were the *Silvery Wave* and her entire fleet
of fifteen, the *Sagitta* and her entire fleet of nine luggers, the
schooner *Admiral*, and all thirteen of the *Crest of the Wave* luggers.
The *Meg Merrilees* was wrecked with four luggers; the tender *Wai
Weir* was sunk. The *Tarawa* was later refloated. The *Aladdin* was
eventually found, battered but intact. The crew of the *Spray* took two
days to cut their way out of the mangroves on Stapleton Island. Her
skipper reported that: 'A previous gale had left shell on the island, but
after the gale it was found to be covered with huge boulders, as if
a volcanic eruption had taken place.' Elsewhere the rough seas gen-
erated by Mahina sank several luggers – the *Xarifa*, *Rosa* and *Two
Brothers* near Thursday Island, the *Kavite* and *Jenny* in Torres Strait.

Only eight of the 400 dead were white and, while the devastation
caused was widely reported, in the southern states it had far less
impact than other tragedies in Australian shipwreck history. In part

this was due to the fact that, as mentioned by the *Brisbane Courier*
in relation to the *Quetta* disaster, people care more when those lost
are people they know. The owners of the pearl fleets were interviewed, and in the true spirit of speculators, one of them, James
Clarke, said that it was 'a most unusual thing for such storms to be
experienced so far North. So free from storms are the grounds
usually worked by the pearl shell boats that Mr Clarke's company
have not insured their fleets for years.'

At Thursday Island, population around 1500, up to a fifth of its
people may have been lost. The consequences rated just one paragraph in the *Brisbane Courier* of 16 March:

> On the receipt of news here yesterday definitely stating the loss of life
> in the recent disaster, a most distressing scene occurred, especially on
> the part of the coloured women whose husbands it became known
> were gone. The various business houses closed, flags were flying half-
> mast, and today business is suspended. The craft in the harbour are
> also flying flags half-mast.

Clement Wragge, the meteorologist, got more space for his colourful explanation of the name he'd given the cyclone, too late to do
anyone any good.

> March 6. A new tropical disturbance which we have named Mahina, is
> about 350 miles [560 kilometres] south-east of Sudest [Papua New
> Guinea], and as it is not improbable that it will make south-westing,
> shipping along our coast will do well to be on the alert.
>   Now Mahina is a girl's name culled from fair Tahiti with its coral
> strand, waving palm groves and mountain peaks; the loveliest of the
> lovely islands of the wide Pacific, and mothers will agree that no infant
> daughter can bear a softer or prettier name.

At the time he didn't know about the many mothers who would soon be mourning the sons the Tahitian girl had killed. Eventually a plaque was made up to honour all those lost. It was placed in the *Quetta* Memorial Cathedral, built in 1893 on Thursday Island. Another monument was erected at Cape Melville, to the eight white men lost in Mahina. It carries a footnote mentioning the loss of more than 300 'coloured' men but makes no mention of the 100 Aborigines lost on the coast while assisting sailors.

Mahina's reputation has endured to the present day and, while the understanding and prediction of Australia's weather has become much more accurate, it was almost exactly a hundred years later, in the Sydney to Hobart Yacht Race of 1998, that the weather showed it still had tragic lessons to teach (see Chapter 13). Meanwhile, science is still learning from Mahina. In 2000 Jonathan Nott from James Cook University, Cairns, and Matthew Hayne from the Australian Geological Survey Organisation, Canberra, visited the area at Barrow Point where Constable Kenny was camped, seeking evidence of a tidal wave 13 or more metres high that swept kilometres inland. One of their motivations was that if such a thing were true, a repeat occurrence would have disastrous consequences for the growing populations on the coast of Far North Queensland and the rest of Australia's tropical north.

By analysing marine deposits above the highest tide levels, the scientists concluded that such an enormous tidal wave was unlikely. It was more probable the surge was closer to 3 to 5 metres above the highest normal tide level. In the mayhem of the cyclone, Constable Kenny may have become disoriented and confused about his exact height above sea level, yet a 3- to 5-metre surge is still immense, especially if it's combined with massive waves and local flooding from the deluge. Kenny may well have found himself up to his waist in water, while camped on the ridge.

It's not good news for the large coastal communities of the

present day – the 110 000 residents of Cairns, the 90 000 residents of Townsville, the 80 000 people of Darwin, and the numerous other towns and communities in Australia's tropical north. They've all experienced the fury of cyclones, but they never want to meet a Tahitian girl like Mahina.

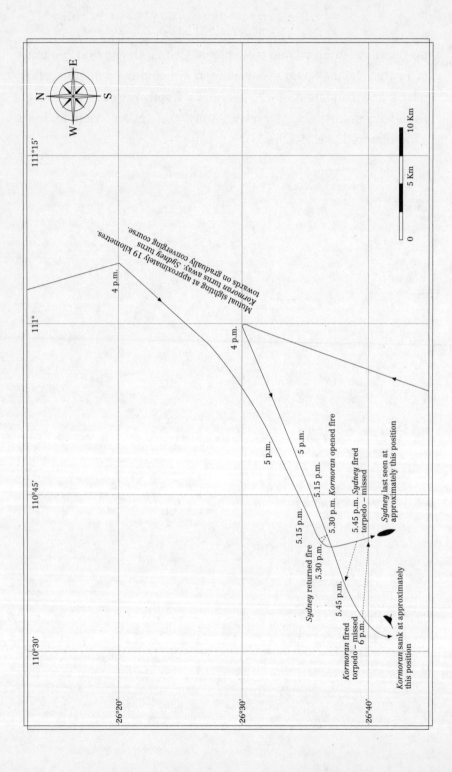

Mutual sighting at approximately 19 kilometres.
Kormoran turns away; Sydney turns
towards on gradually converging course.

4 p.m.

4 p.m.

5 p.m.

5 p.m.

5 p.m.

5.15 p.m.

5.15 p.m. Kormoran opened fire

5.15 p.m.
5.30 p.m.

5.30 p.m.

5.45 p.m. Sydney fired
torpedo – missed

Sydney last seen at
approximately this position

Sydney returned fire

5.45 p.m.

Kormoran fired
torpedo – missed
6 p.m.

Kormoran sank at approximately
this position

HMAS *Sydney*
(Australian War Memorial – AWM 301407)

10. MISSING IN ACTION: HMAS *SYDNEY*, 1941

Perhaps the greatest mystery surrounding the loss of HMAS *Sydney* is why no-one believes the 315 eye-witnesses. Yet when she disappeared late in 1941, taking with her every one of her 645 crew, it was inevitable that she would leave behind far more questions than anyone could ever answer. Not that it has stopped them trying.

As early as 1945, that much was already well understood. Referring to the famous mystery ship *Marie Celeste*, which was found adrift in good condition but without a trace of her crew, Lieutenant Commander Gill, later the official naval war historian, advised at the end of World War II: 'in many minds there will never be any finality in this matter, and I imagine that *Sydney* will take her place with *Marie Celeste* . . . whatever is written.'

Gill's comment was included in a recommendation not to publish
one of the earliest of many accounts of HMAS *Sydney*'s end. Yet over
the ensuing years, numerous articles, several books and forums,
a parliamentary inquiry, and continuing public interest have made
the *Sydney* a matter of controversy, passionate argument and often
acrimony. The source of much of the frustration is that little progress
is possible when attempting to answer the unanswerable: what
really happened and why?

Compared to her activities earlier in the war, November 1941 was
shaping up as a dull month for HMAS *Sydney*. The previous year,
operating in the Mediterranean, the 7000-tonne modified Leander-
class cruiser (originally laid down as HMS *Phaeton*, but launched as
HMAS *Sydney* on 22 September 1934) had been involved in a number of actions against the enemy, including the Italian cruisers
Bartolomeo Colleoni and *Giovanni delle Bande Nere*. The former
was sunk, the latter badly damaged, while HMAS *Sydney*, under the
command of Captain John Collins, suffered almost no damage. At
a time of almost constant defeats and reverses for Britain and her
allies, it was a victory that heartened the Australian people, many of
whom came to consider the ship invincible. When she returned to
her namesake port in 1941, she was given a hero's welcome. Her
crew marched the streets in triumph.

Soon, however, she was back at sea, under her new commander,
Captain John Burnett, patrolling the Australian coast and escorting
convoys. War has been described as long periods of boredom punc-
tuated by moments of sheer terror, but escort duty off the coast of
Western Australia consisted almost entirely of boredom. A long way
from Germany, submarine attacks were highly unlikely. And most

German warships were busily engaged with the British convoys in the North Sea, the Atlantic and the Mediterranean. There was only an outside chance of meeting one of the small (and dwindling) fleet of long-range raiders. Early in the war several ships had been sunk near Australian and New Zealand ports, but increased patrols and variations to routes had forced the raiders into the open ocean where they were reduced to picking off the few stray vessels that happened along.

In November 1941, HMAS *Sydney* had been babysitting for nearly three solid weeks without incident. Early in the month she had escorted the vessels *Duntroon* and *Talabot*. On 4 November she met the troopship *Zealandia* in the Great Australian Bight and escorted her to Fremantle. On 12 November both vessels left Fremantle for Singapore, where *Zealandia* was to land 1000 troops of the Australian 8ᵗʰ Division. Once they left port both vessels maintained strict radio silence as they voyaged up the coast, past the Abrolhos where the *Batavia* was wrecked, past the Trial Rocks where the *Trial* went down. Despite maintaining her own radio silence, *Sydney* received a number of signals. On 14 November one was addressed to Leading Seaman Stanley Roy Davis: 'Son born both well.'

On 17 November the two ships rendezvoused with HMS *Durban* in the Sunda Strait, where *Sydney* handed over her babysitting duties before turning for home. The next two days were more like a tropical cruise than a dangerous military undertaking. The weather was fine, the crew lulled by the heat and shipboard routine.

The only relief from the monotony came late on the afternoon of 19 November when a plume of smoke on the horizon indicated the presence of another ship. Less than a day's voyage from well-defended and patrolled Fremantle, and just 160 kilometres west of the Western Australian coast, it was probably just a local freighter, but *Sydney* knew the procedure for such encounters. At approximately 4.05 p.m. she turned towards the ship to investigate.

Then things got interesting.

The other vessel had been on a course of 025 (north-east), but now it turned to 250 (to west-south-west) and increased its smoke. It was almost as if she was trying to lay a smokescreen and escape into the setting sun. However, she was only doing 14 knots (compared to *Sydney*'s maximum of 30). Even a freighter should be able to put on a better spurt than that.

Nevertheless, Captain Burnett called his crew to action stations. As *Sydney* bore down on the freighter her forward turrets, A and B, each with two 6-inch (15-centimetre) guns, turned to train on a spot just ahead of the ship. The after-turrets, X and Y, also with twin 6-inch guns, swivelled to be ready if they, too, could be aimed at the ship. *Sydney*'s amphibious aircraft was fuelled ready for launch. Anti-aircraft batteries were loaded, aimed and secured for action.

To a casual observer the ship going to action stations may have appeared to be a scene of absolute chaos. The reality was that *Sydney*'s crew was one of the best drilled and most efficient bodies of fighting men afloat. The previous year, according to the report of the Commander-in-Chief of the Mediterranean Fleet, Admiral Sir Andrew Cunningham, they 'had the unique opportunity of firing 2200 main armament rounds in action in six weeks.'

On the bridge, Captain Burnett and his executive officers represented a body of experience enviable in any warship. All had decades of experience and training as officers with both the Australian and British navies. Burnett had been in the Australian Navy almost since its inception, having joined at age fourteen in 1913. He'd served in the North Sea on HMAS *Australia* and the destroyer HMS *Tower* during World War I, later on the battleship HMS *Royal Oak* as Executive Officer in the Spanish Civil War. Before taking command of HMAS *Sydney*, he'd been Deputy Chief of Naval Staff.

Burnett knew the procedure for approaching suspicious vessels: keep your distance, stay ahead to avoid a submarine that might be lurking in the ship's wake, position yourself so the enemy can't fire torpedoes. The vessel was then to be asked for its four international signal letters. Then the Admiralty code book would be consulted for the vessel's secret call sign, another four letters. The warship would signal the two inner letters, the ship would signal the two outer letters. If the ship didn't do so, it was to be ordered to stop and a boarding party would check the ship's identity. If it refused to stop, the warship would fire a shot across the bows. If it still defied the order, the warship would 'fire for effect.' In its recent patrols *Sydney* had challenged numerous freighters in this way, without incident, often finding that some didn't know their call sign or how and when to display it.

'What ship?' HMAS *Sydney* signalled.

The vessel hoisted flags that couldn't be made out clearly, so *Sydney* demanded her identity again.

'*Straat Malakka*,' eventually came the reply. *Sydney* could now check the vessel's outline in the code books to determine whether she was who she said she was. The vessel definitely looked like the Dutch freighter that plied between Australian ports and Batavia (now Jakarta), under the Dutch flag.

'Where bound?'

'Batavia.'

It was the right answer. The problem was that after sighting *Sydney*, *Straat Malakka* had turned and was headed in the completely wrong direction.

While this exchange was going on, the distance between the two vessels was rapidly shrinking. *Sydney* already had the vessel in range of her guns (approximately 14 000 yards or 12.8 kilometres). At some point, around 5 p.m., when *Sydney* was between 9000 and 13 000 yards (8 to 12 kilometres) distant, the ship sent a radio signal 'QQQ *Straat Malakka* 115-1-26S.' Giving her identity, longitude (it was 111°15', so the 1 may be a corrupted longitude) and latitude may have been intended to make *Sydney* leave her alone, but the warship continued to close in.

Sydney was now rapidly overtaking the freighter. Throughout her approach, her crew reranged her guns as they'd done countless times before, in the midst of battle and as part of routine encounters like this one with a rusty old steamer. Most of the men were able to do their jobs by instinct, which freed them for idle thoughts about Fremantle shore leave the next day, savouring that first taste of a beer in one of Freo's many lively pubs.

Sydney now signalled, 'Have you suffered damage from cyclone, typhoon or tempest?' That was the meaning of the two-letter signal 'IK' in the international code book. But it was also the middle two letters of *Straat Malakka*'s secret code. While the *Sydney* waited for the response, which with some vessels could take several minutes while the skipper rummaged through his papers to find it, the distance between the two vessels closed to less than two kilometres.

At this point Burnett broke the rules for engagement with suspicious vessels. He came almost abeam on a parallel course. It was a far more exposed position, but it also meant he could train all his formidable firepower on the cargo ship. Eight 6-inch guns and four torpedo tubes now threatened *Straat Malakka*. Resistance was less than useless.

Nevertheless, instead of replying with the outer two letters of her four-letter secret code, at 5.30 p.m. *Straat Malakka* took down her Dutch flag and raised the German ensign. She dropped the camouflage screens on six 5.4-inch (13-centimetre) guns, several anti-aircraft guns and her starboard-side torpedo tubes.

The initial reaction on the bridge of HMAS *Sydney* may have been incredulous. In a matter of seconds the innocuous *Straat Malakka* had transformed into the heavily armed German raider HSK *Kormoran*. And she was preparing to fight.

Sydney had barely any time to react. Burnett may have considered putting a shot across the ship's bows; he may have realised his ship was horribly exposed to a broadside should the raider fire. Then there was only horror as the raider opened up at close range.

Sydney did manage to fire back. The first salvo, however, passed over the raider. *Kormoran's* first salvo was devastating. Shells exploded in *Sydney's* bridge, gunnery control tower and A and B turrets. The refuelled amphibious aircraft was hit and erupted in a ball of flame, pouring burning fuel amidships. The first torpedo struck near the *Sydney's* bow and exploded with such force that the bow was almost completely swamped. A and B turrets were so badly damaged they were unable to fire another shot. While the forward turrets had ceased firing, X and Y turrets were able to continue operating, presumably under local control as the command and control systems were already destroyed. Meanwhile, the raider continued pouring shells and anti-aircraft fire into *Sydney*.

While the raider held her course, *Sydney* now veered to port, towards *Kormoran*, as if to ram. She only barely missed the raider's stern, gaining a momentary respite from the raider's deadly fire as most of her guns couldn't be brought to bear. *Sydney* meanwhile brought her X and Y turrets round and fired several salvos that struck their mark. The raider's bridge was hit, as was the engine room, starting massive fires and destroying the extinguisher system. *Sydney* fired a pattern of four torpedoes, but the raider successfully manoeuvred to avoid them.

The raider's skipper then turned to bring all his guns to bear and continued to fire on the vessel. Not long after, the raider's engines failed completely and she lay dead in the water, burning fiercely. Yet she continued to fire at the slowly escaping *Sydney*. Fifteen minutes after the engagement began, *Sydney's* guns fell silent, though she continued steering to the south at low speed. The raider continued to fire for the next 45 minutes while her fires raged and the range between the two vessels increased. Finally, at around 6.25 p.m., her captain gave the order to cease fire.

His own vessel was doomed. With the fires unable to be brought under control, and 300 mines on board, orders were given to prepare to scuttle the vessel. The crew were mustered and embarked on lifeboats and rafts. At around 11.30 p.m. the raider *Kormoran* exploded and sank.

And *Sydney*? She continued to limp away to the south, enveloped in fire from bow to stern.

HMAS *Sydney* was due to arrive in Fremantle on 20 November. When she failed to appear, there was little initial concern. The next day, Friday, 21 November, the District Naval Officer in Western Australia signalled the naval office in Melbourne: 'HMAS *Sydney* has not yet arrived.'

The signal was sent early in the morning and there was still no alarm as *Sydney* might be delayed for any number of reasons. However, that Sunday there was still no sign and a radio signal was sent out requesting HMAS *Sydney* to break radio silence and report her whereabouts. Ominously, there was no reply.

The same day the former liner *Aquitania*, now a troopship, discovered a raft carrying twenty-six German survivors of the *Sydney–Kormoran* encounter, 160 kilometres west of Carnarvon. The men were picked up but *Aquitania*'s captain, fearing other raiders might be lurking nearby, maintained radio silence while continuing his voyage to Sydney.

On Monday, 24 November, the Naval Chief of Staff informed the Minister for the Navy that the pride of the Australian fleet, HMAS *Sydney*, was missing. Around Australia communications stations commenced calling *Sydney* continuously while an air and sea search was mounted off the coast of Western Australia. All that day, survivors turned up on sea and land. The merchant vessel *Trocas* picked up twenty-five Germans in a rubber raft some 200 kilometres north-west of Carnarvon. Another forty-six Germans reached the coast north of Carnarvon, where they surrendered without a struggle. However, none of the survivors were from the *Sydney*.

It was the same story the next day, 25 November, with the liner *Centaur* taking sixty German men in a lifeboat in tow, including Captain Theodor Detmers. During the tow to Carnarvon, the lifeboat started to sink, but the *Centaur*'s skipper, fearing the Germans might attempt to seize his vessel, deployed two of his lifeboats for the Germans to continue their journey. He remarked that should they sink, he'd leave the men to swim to shore. (The *Centaur* was later sunk, while operating as a hospital ship, in an infamous attack by a Japanese submarine off the coast of Queensland.)

By 25 November hopes of finding HMAS *Sydney* had faded. The following message was passed to the Prime Minister, John Curtin, by the Secretary of the Department of Defence Coordination and Secretary to the War Cabinet: 'The admiral has just spoken to me on the secraphone. A raft has just been picked up carrying some German sailors from a raider, which they said was sunk by a cruiser. The admiral fears that *Sydney* was also sunk by the raider.'

By the time the War Cabinet met the next day, Wednesday, 26 November, there were still no survivors from HMAS *Sydney*, but details of the encounter were being reconstructed from the German survivors. Rumours of *Sydney*'s loss were also being censored in the media. The Chief of Naval Staff, Admiral Sir Guy Royle, read the cabinet an account of the engagement, which may have been based on the report of the *Trocas*'s Captain Dechaineux based on what he had learned from the survivors he picked up:

> . . . the *Sydney* altered course to the westward, closed rapidly, challenging with daylight lamp. Raider made no reply but opened fire when cruiser was within comparatively short range. Estimated range varies from about 1 to 5 or 6 miles [2 to 8 or 10 kilometres]. One

survivor stated that he could see men on deck of cruiser. First shot from raider hit cruiser's bridge and started fire. Cruiser altered course to port. Survivors stated that it appeared that he intended to ram. Passed close around stern of raider and proceeded on parallel course, gradually drawing ahead on port side of the raider. Cruiser was now heavily on fire in bridge and midships section. Raider also badly damaged and on fire in engine-room area. Hit in engine room, put electrical controls out of action. Literally all electrical equipment, including fire-fighting inoperative. Action commenced at about 1730 and lasted for about one hour. Raider abandoned ship at about 1900, her reason that fire could not be put out, and it was certain that fire would reach ammunition stowage. Survivors stated that captain and officers were on board when they abandoned ship at about 1900. At this time, cruiser was seen still heavily on fire and shortly afterwards disappeared. No violent explosion was seen or heard. They believe she [was] torpedoed.

Notes of the War Cabinet discussion, released in 1994, include shorthand details of the discussion that went on while the Navy outlined what it thought had happened:

if Syd sunk only if took unwise approach . . . every cruiser captn know certain things – keep ahead – because may be trailed by submarine – inconceivable that this cd have happened . . . condition cruiser not known . . . when last seen cruiser was on fire . . . Cruiser vanished, burning – believed sunk . . . at [?] 7 miles cruiser (Syd) cd have sunk her she has 3-inch armour – but at ½ mile or mile point blank range not so good not effective ag[ainst] raider with 6-inch guns.

Finally, the Prime Minister cut across the discussion to say it was entirely conjecture. The conclusion was: *Sydney* was gone. In the midst of war, that was all the speculation Cabinet had time for. It promptly moved on to a decision about what immediate action to take about the loss. There was a body of opinion that no information should be made known until it was clear the enemy knew it anyway. Prime Minister Curtin was of a different view, wanting to tell relatives as soon as possible. The compromise was to tell them that the *Sydney*'s crew was missing, while keeping media restrictions in place.

The same day the following telegram was sent: 'With deep regret I have to inform you that your [relationship and name] is missing as a result of enemy action. Minister for Navy and Naval Board desire to express to you their sincere sympathy.'

What action? Where? How many of the crew were missing? Was there a chance of survivors? The telegram gave nothing away. Turning to the media for some news of what had happened to their husbands, fathers, sons and brothers, the relatives found nothing but silence. During four days without any further news, the belief that there was a cover-up had plenty of time to grow.

Meanwhile, the search continued, as did the interrogations of the prisoners. It was a haphazard affair. The navy was trained to operate warships, not extract information from unwilling subjects. Initially the prisoners were able to mingle, which certainly influenced their version of events.

Some prisoners were more cooperative than others. Many told stories that were slightly or significantly inconsistent with those told by others. Some made statements about things they could only have heard about, rather than seen from where they were positioned on the *Kormoran*. Some said they saw *Sydney* explode. Most said she disappeared quickly over the horizon, giving rise to the suspicion that they'd actually seen her sink.

One of the most thorough descriptions was given by Sub Lieutenant Willhelm Bunjies, who was rescued by HMAS *Yandra*, along with 70 others, on 27 November:

She starts signalling with helio lamps. We do not answer but maintain our speed and course 250 degrees. Steadily nearer comes our doom and we distinctly recognise the vessel as an Australian cruiser of the *Sydney* class. Fight is out of the question, but maybe we can deceive her somehow. Our ship with a wooden gun covered with brass and mounted on the stern, strikingly resembles the Dutch steamer, *Straat Malakka*. At 1635 hrs. Engine No. 4 starts working again, but it is too late now. The cruiser keeps on asking us for our name. She is so close that it is impossible to overlook her helio signals. We answer *Straat Malakka* and hoist the Dutch ensign astern. All [sailors] disappear from deck, but behind the camouflage flag shutters everyone stands in feverish excitement and holds his breath. We can distinguish every single man on board; the bridge is full of officers. She is now travelling parallel to us on our starboard side at the same speed as ours. She wants to know more and asks for our destination and cargo. We are flag-signalling the answers. The tension is reaching boiling-point; what will she do now? We observe that the engine of her plane which has been running is stopped, and the aircraft replaced under cover. Her eight 6-inch guns, however, still point threateningly at us . . .

Of the engagement he stated:

Splinters cause several dead and wounded on our bridge. Another hit on our third gun pierces the armour, causes some casualties but explodes in the water behind us. All our guns are firing rapidly. The enemy answers with No. 3 [X turret] and No. 4 [Y turret] but the remaining two turrets are silent. We are hit by several shells. The deck where the officer's quarters are situated is ablaze and the engine room is also hit.

During the battle the *Kormoran* fired about 600 [5.9]-inch shells and three torpedoes and sank a more powerful opponent, of whose crew of 645 not one was rescued.

His account in large part expanded on the more circumspect information given by the captain of the *Kormoran*, Theodor Detmers.

One key piece of information that was obtained was the approximate location of the action. This was vital for focussing the area of the search effort, though it wasn't helped by the fact that it hadn't started until four days after the engagement and was slow in gaining momentum. One cabinet minister commented that Catalina flying boats could have been brought into the search earlier.

During the search, pieces of timber and oil slicks were observed. On 28 November a large Carley life float was found by the *Heros*. It was the most substantial piece of wreckage thought to have come from *Sydney*, and had clearly been badly damaged by shellfire. The *Wyrallah* also picked up two lifebelts thought to have come from the *Kormoran*, plus two small Carley floats with the body of one German.

Not one survivor of HMAS *Sydney* was ever found. The ship itself had disappeared with almost no trace, and without a single person who could say definitely what had become of her, let alone what she had been doing on the fateful afternoon when she engaged the heavily armed German raider *Kormoran*.

On Sunday, 30 November, the loss of HMAS *Sydney* was announced to the media by the Prime Minister. Publication was embargoed until the next day. Two days later, Curtin released the few details the government had ascertained regarding the engagement and commented: 'In the absence of any information from the *Sydney*, one side only is given from direct evidence. Certain of the aspects on board the *Sydney* must remain a matter of surmise as to details. The broad canvas can, however, be taken as giving an accurate picture.'

Relatives of the crew also received a second telegram, from the Secretary of the Department of the Navy:

The Naval Board direct me to inform you that an intensive search by sea and air has failed to find HMAS *Sydney* or any survivors from her

gallant Ship's Company. The Naval Board, therefore, announce that all
are considered to have lost their lives in action, and, with the Minister
for the Navy, they tender to you again their heartfelt sympathy.

However, amid the rumours that were already circulating about
the *Sydney*, by 4 December, the public controversy was already off
and running. The *Sydney Morning Herald* headlines told the story
on 5 December:

> SYDNEY'S FATE. CONFLICTING STORIES. RAIDER'S FLAG. Melbourne, Thursday. –
> Prisoners from the German raider *Kormoran*, which was sunk by
> HMAS *Sydney* before the *Sydney* herself disappeared, will be further
> interrogated in an effort to discover whether she fired on the *Sydney*
> under the protection of a neutral flag, or hoisted the Nazi swastika
> before beginning the action. This was stated to-night by the Minister
> for the Navy, Mr. Makin.

The report added a denial of a rumour that had sprung up since
the discovery of the Carley float: 'There is no known basis for any
report that personnel of the *Sydney* could have been machine-
gunned while in boats.' But further it was said, 'The Government's
investigation of this, as of many other aspects of the battle between
the *Sydney* and the *Kormoran*, is hampered by the fact that the only
source of information are the survivors of the *Kormoran*, and there
can be no certainty that their account of the action is accurate.'

In other words, no-one believed the 315 eye-witnesses. Australians
couldn't believe that there were absolutely no survivors among the
645 aboard *Sydney*. They didn't believe that *Kormoran* alone could
sink *Sydney*. They couldn't believe that Burnett would put his ship at
risk in the way he appeared to have done.

The Government and the armed forces, meanwhile, had more
pressing problems. December 1941 was one of the darkest months

of the war. Shortly after announcing the loss of the *Sydney*, the government announced the loss of the destroyer HMAS *Parramatta* with only 20 survivors from a crew of 161. Just days later, on 7 December 1941, the Japanese launched their surprise attack on Pearl Harbor. Three days later, the British battleship *Prince of Wales* was sunk near Singapore, along with the battle cruiser *Repulse*.

Suddenly, not only was Australia facing the German threat, she was at war with Japan, and the massive defensive protection afforded by the USA and Britain, of which HMAS *Sydney* was a small part, had all but evaporated.

Soon the nation was fighting for its very survival and was little able to afford the luxury of a thorough investigation into the loss of HMAS *Sydney*. The desperate situation may explain why when a body, thought to be that of a crewman from the *Sydney*, washed up on Christmas Island, it was buried in an unmarked grave that has defied subsequent attempts to find it.

However, the Government's Advisory War Council did receive a report into the loss on 18 March 1942. In response to a question from the Prime Minister about a Naval Court of Enquiry, the Chief of Naval Staff replied that a full inquiry had been conducted. No records of such an inquiry have been located, though the lack may be due as much to imprecision in language as a cover-up, as the handwritten minutes of the meeting suggest. In any case, the Naval Chief summarised the findings:

> The *Sydney* had worked into a position approximately 1500 yards from the raider. The raider opened fire and launched two torpedoes, one of which hit the *Sydney*. The raider had given a wrong name and was not on the daily list. The Captain of the *Sydney* was 24 hours late in arriving at his rendezvous and had taken a risk in getting so close to the raider. In doing so he had not followed his orders.

Further, the Gunnery Officer of the *Sydney* was not ready. He should have been able to fire first and get in two salvoes before the raider attacked.

After the war, there were many who didn't believe that 'the broad canvas' could be taken as giving an accurate picture. As more documents relating to the two vessels were gradually released, they only raised more questions. The publication of the relevant volume of the official war history (*The Royal Australian Navy 1939–1942*, Volume 1), purporting to be the definitive account, was little help.

Rumours abounded. One said the ship was sunk with the help of a Japanese submarine, prior to Japan's declaration of war. Another that some survivors were taken prisoner by the Japanese submarine. Or some were machine-gunned by the sub. A destroyer was seen by fishermen off the Western Australian coast the day after the engagement, on fire and heading south at high speed. A message was sent from *Sydney* during her engagement with *Kormoran*, but it was missed because radio operators were having a smoko. A pilot heard a distress call that could have initiated a search. There was a cover-up by the Navy to hide its failings in the matter.

Assuming for a moment that the *Kormoran* survivors were telling the truth, it is conceivable that the raider was able to sink the *Sydney* with all hands. From their accounts, *Sydney* was subjected to continuous heavy fire for up to an hour, much of it at close range, from weapons ranging from anti-aircraft guns to 13-centimetre guns. She was hit by at least one torpedo. When last seen, she was on fire from end to end.

Under the circumstances, why she didn't sink sooner is a mystery in itself. Her crew's efforts to keep her afloat may have been heroic in the extreme, especially as it was noted by some survivors that they didn't see any of *Sydney*'s crew abandon ship.

A summary of warships lost in World War II also reveals that the loss of large vessels with all, or almost all hands, was tragically common. These include HMS *Hood* which blew up in 1941 killing 1418 of her crew (3 survivors); *Bismarck* in 1941 sank with the loss of 2097 (115 survivors); the raider *Komet* blew up in 1942 killing 351 (no survivors); the troop carrier MV *Donizetti* was sunk in 1943 taking 1800 down (no survivors); the battleship *Scharnhorst* was sunk in 1943 killing 1933 (36 survivors). In 1944 the troop carrier *Yoshida Maru* went down, taking with it an entire regiment of 3000 (no survivors); the battleships *Fuso* and *Yamashiro* were both lost with 1400 hands each (no survivors and 10 survivors respectively). In 1945 the carrier *Awa Maru* blew up killing 2003 (1 survivor).

It should also be noted that on 1 July 1942, the *Montevideo Maru* was accidentally sunk in the Philippines by the US submarine *Sturgeon*. On board were, among others, 1035 Australian POWs, including 845 members of 2/22 Battalion, 8th Division (Lark Force). There were no Australian survivors, making this Australia's worst maritime disaster in terms of Australian lives lost.

In *Sydney*'s case, the slow search response would have added to the losses. As for lifeboats, Captain Detmers suggested that the amount of fire that had been directed at *Sydney* would have destroyed every boat on deck. Those below deck would have been sunk with the vessel. The lack of any signs of survivors suggests that when *Sydney* went down, she took all hands with her. Perhaps by that time there was no-one left to give the order to abandon ship. Perhaps none of the crew would abandon their injured mates.

As for the suggestion that a submarine was involved, the genesis of the theory is in the fact that some of the *Kormoran*'s crew suggested that HMAS *Sydney*'s sudden disappearance may have been due to her being torpedoed. If so, who by?

It's already been noted that *Sydney* was beyond the normal range of German subs, unless they were resupplied during their voyage to give them longer range. The more common suggestion is that the attack came from a Japanese submarine, even though at the time Japan had not declared war on Australia, her allies, or America. So was it a surprise attack, like Pearl Harbor? To believe such a theory one has to accept that the Japanese Navy, just three weeks before confronting massive US and British fleets in carefully planned and highly secret operations whose outcome would affect the future of the entire Asia–Pacific theatre of war, decided to pre-empt them with an attack on a light cruiser from a country that was at the very end of its list of objectives (geographically and strategically).

As it happens, no evidence has yet been found to establish the presence of Japanese or German submarines in Australian waters at the time *Sydney* was sunk. Meticulous research has instead tended to show that every submarine capable of launching an attack was elsewhere at the time.

Nevertheless, in the early 1980s, a package was washed up on a Western Australian beach that appeared to prove that a submarine was involved. Found by an amateur naval historian it contained a number of items that appeared to be from HMAS *Sydney* (a typed casualty list, service manuals, a life preserver, and Captain Burnett's cap badge). It also included a Letter of Proceedings, typed after the action with the *Kormoran*, then thrown overboard. Written by Sub-Lieutenant B.A. Elder R.A.N. and signed with an X, it stated that a fire earlier in the day had knocked out *Sydney*'s radio equipment. Then a submarine was sighted. '1459: Bridge confirmed the sighting as an "I" Class Japanese ocean-going submarine headed S.S.W. and diving.' During her fight with the *Kormoran*, at 1718: 'The raider broke out a large white flag about the size of a table cloth from her triadic stay halyards and hove to on our port beam.' Then, while HMAS *Sydney* was launching a boat to board *Kormoran*, she opened fire with guns and torpedoes. At that point:

> The raider ran up the Nazi Battle Ensign at 1751, to her fore-top and
> then struck the Dutch flag and White Flag in that exact order. Nobody
> can respect their piratical behaviour and arrant cowardice in opening
> fire wearing false colours after they had already surrendered.

It was damning stuff, if it was true. However, Navy experts, histo-
rians and Australian War Memorial personnel who have subjected
the find to elaborate scrutiny have concluded it is almost certainly
fake. Among many doubts is the fact that the bag containing all these
items appears to have been washed at some point, before being
immersed in salt water. The washing powder used included bright-
eners not in use until the 1980s.

The accusation that *Sydney* survivors were machine-gunned in
the water has also found no basis in fact. Flatly denied by the Minister for the Navy in 1941, the shot-up Carley float, now held at the
Australian War Memorial, Canberra, was cited as evidence of an
atrocity until subjected to forensic analysis in 1993. It was found to
have been hit by at least one high-explosive shell and not by any
small-arms fire, which was consistent with it being hit during the
exchange with *Kormoran*, not after.

Yet the continuing controversy and accusations of navy cover-
ups eventually led to a parliamentary inquiry in 1997, which
largely disappointed the conspiracy theorists. Rather than finding
a cover-up, it found that the National Archives now contain some
21.6 shelf-kilometres of material relating to HMAS *Sydney*. However, in its 1999 report, the inquiry recommended that a search
for *Sydney* and *Kormoran* be conducted, after research to define
the area to be explored. Further, if the wrecks were found, they
should be declared historic shipwrecks with an appropriate zone of
protection.

To date the Federal Government has not acted on the recommendation, part of the problem being that both wrecks are likely to be in deep water beyond the continental shelf, making a search both costly and likely fruitless. It is possible that the discovery of either or both wrecks would shed light on what really happened on 19 November 1941. However, what is more certain is that no depth of water or declaration will protect them from the ravages of souvenir hunters. As matters stand, the wrecks of *Sydney* and *Kormoran* are the final resting places of many men who died in the service of their countries, so any search for answers also has to respect their right to rest in peace.

For many years there have been hopes that some of the *Kormoran* survivors would relent and finally tell the truth about their engagement with the *Sydney*. At least one, it was thought, would attempt to clear a guilty conscience with a death-bed confession. None of them have and many, including Captain Detmers, who was awarded the Knight's Cross of the Iron Cross while a POW, have already passed away.

During his interment, Detmers was fearful of being tried as a war criminal, as there was sufficient suspicion after the action for charges to be considered. Whatever means he used to lure the *Sydney* close, and there's little doubt that *Sydney* erred in this respect, Detmers' decision to fight was also questionable. Faced with a clearly superior opponent, surrender may have been ignominious, but the alternative was suicide.

As the Australian Navy observed after the engagement, *Sydney* should have been able to hit *Kormoran* with two salvoes before she fired one. A commander aware of this fact could at best have hoped for certain death for most of his crew while inflicting limited damage on the enemy. Perhaps the greatest element of surprise that Detmers had was his willingness to fight like a fanatic, to the death, taking all his men with him. At the beginning of what later became the most barbaric war of all time, such an irresponsible attitude to the welfare of the people under his command may have been completely unexpected. As it turned out, Detmers succeeded in sinking *Sydney* while managing to avoid complete annihilation himself. However, he still lost his ship, with 78 dead, and his remaining 314 crew were all taken prisoner.

Strategically, the loss of *Sydney* was a blow to Australian morale at the beginning of a period during World War II where Australia feared for its very survival. However, the loss of *Kormoran* was another vital nail in the coffin of Germany's sparse raider fleet. In the end they were seen as more expensive and more vulnerable than submarines and aircraft, which were far more effective in sinking enemy vessels. After the sinking of the *Kormoran*, the threat from German raiders was substantially eliminated.

Since 1941, the Australian Navy has done little to honour the bravery of the crew of HMAS *Sydney*. Indeed, it has been slow to recognise the courage of any of its personnel, having not awarded a single VC during World War II. However, on 18 November 2001, a memorial to HMAS *Sydney* was dedicated on Mount Scott, in Geraldton, Western Australia. It comprises a dome formed by 645 interlocking seabirds, one for each member of *Sydney*'s complement. The memorial dominates the Geraldton skyline and has sweeping views of the Indian Ocean, where the ship remains hidden, wrapped in questions. What happened? Truth is often described as the first casualty of war, but the truth about HMAS *Sydney* is different. Like her crew, it's still missing in action.

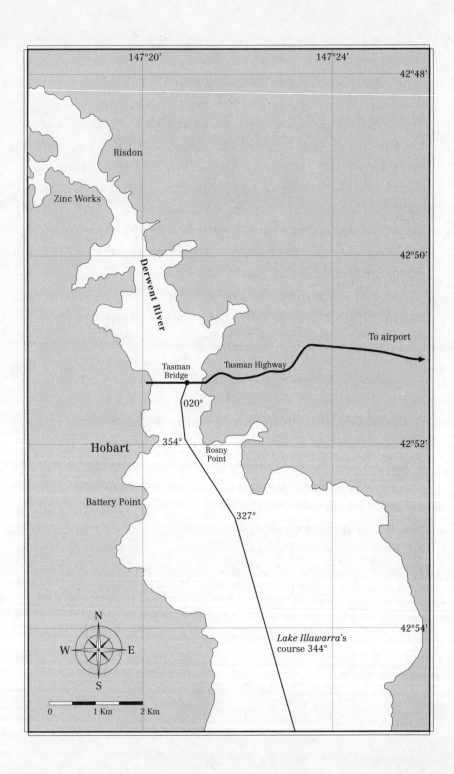

147°20'   147°24'

42°48'

Risdon

Zinc Works

Derwent River

42°50'

To airport

Tasman
Bridge   Tasman Highway

020°

354°   42°52'
          Rosny
          Point

Hobart

Battery Point

327°

N

W   E   42°54'

S   *Lake Illawarra*'s
          course 344°

0   1 Km   2 Km

Lake Illawarra
(Archives Office of Tasmania)

11. THE SHIP THAT WRECKED A CITY: *LAKE ILLAWARRA*, 1975

Nestled on the shores along both sides of a drowned valley, the city of Hobart, capital of Tasmania and Australia's second oldest settlement, has a close association with the sea that reaches back to its origins. It was a shipwreck, the storm-wracked *Sydney Cove* (Chapter 3), that led to the investigation of Bass Strait, the strategic importance of which prompted Hobart's settlement in 1804. Since 1945 it's been the destination of Australia's famous blue-water sailing event, the sometimes ill-fated Sydney to Hobart Yacht Race (Chapter 13). But it was a shipwreck that occurred in Hobart's sheltered, charted waters, in calm conditions and involving a well-manned vessel with all the necessary navigational aids, that literally tore the place in half.

Like most of Australia, Hobart had wound down for the annual summer holidays on the evening of 5 January 1975. Christmas, New Year and the celebrations to mark the arrival of the 1974 Sydney to Hobart yachts were over, although the festivities had been somewhat overshadowed by news of the devastation of another Australian city, Darwin, at the hands of Cyclone Tracy over Christmas. In Hobart, though, the perils of the tropical north were about as remote as it was possible to get.

At nine o'clock on that Sunday evening, those who hadn't left Hobart for one of the holiday destinations that abound in Tasmania were taking it easy before work the next day. There had been a little light rain earlier in the evening, but it had cleared and a light breeze had blown away a slight haze that had gathered on the water.

On the eastern shore, overlooking the Derwent River, the Read family had gathered at their parents' house and were in the midst of dinner. On the western shore, Frank Manley was starting for home with his wife Sylvia and sixteen-year-old daughter, Sharon. And on the water, brothers Ian and Lyndon Pidgeon were enjoying a spot of fishing from a dinghy anchored just off shore, some 300 metres upstream from the Tasman Bridge, whose graceful 1025-metre sweep rises nearly 50 metres above the water to allow the passage of ocean-going ships.

Some 10 kilometres downstream, one of those ships, the 136-metre, 10 800-tonne Australian National Line Lake-class bulk carrier *Lake Illawarra*, Captain B.J. Pelc master, had crossed Storm Bay and was entering the river mouth at the end of a short, storm-tossed voyage from Port Pirie, South Australia. After passing the Iron Pot, the beacon at the headland of the Derwent's Cape Direction, she'd set a course of 344 degrees, to take her up the river to her eventual destination, the Electrolytic Zinc Company's works at Risdon, just north of the city, where she'd unload her cargo of zinc concentrate.

As she made her way up the river, the ship's course was being determined by Captain Pelc, rather than a pilot. Before the voyage he'd checked with Hobart's Marine Board regarding the need for a pilot and was informed that an earlier exemption still applied. Yet, since he hadn't brought a ship into Port Hobart since March 1972, three years earlier, technically, his exemption had lapsed.

Nearing the city, the river's main channel kinks slightly to the left, then to the right, before passing under the main navigation arch of the Tasman Bridge. So after passing the John Garrow Shoal, Pelc ordered a course change to port: 'Steer 327 degrees.'

The helmsman, Robert Banks, responded promptly and settled the ship on the new course. At this time Pelc was expecting that there would be no tidal flow to contend with. According to the tide tables on the ship, low tide was at 9.12 p.m. on 5 January, but in reality low water was two hours later. So instead of slack water, the tide was going out at between two to three knots (4 to 6 kilometres/hour).

'Steer 354,' Pelc ordered. The ship now had Rosny Point abeam and was some 1200 metres from the Tasman Bridge. The course change to starboard turned the *Lake Illawarra* to take the right-hand kink in the channel and, more importantly, line it up with the channel leads that guided her through the main navigation arch of the bridge. At this point she was doing about 8 knots (15 kilometres/hour) through the water, though to Pelc, steering by landmarks around him, the speed appeared to be much lower. The difference was due to the tide.

It was only a matter of moments before Pelc noticed that the ship was still too far to the left of the main channel. He knew there was 'foul ground' there, so he ordered a major change of course to compensate.

'Steer 020!'

Helmsman Banks altered course immediately and the ship swung to starboard. Almost immediately Pelc realised he'd overcorrected. The bow came around much more quickly than he expected. 'Steer 015,' he ordered.

It was still too much and the bow kept coming round.

'Stop engines,' Pelc ordered. The bridge was now only 800 metres from the bow of the 136-metre ship, which had zigzagged from the left side to the right side of the main channel. The ship was losing speed rapidly, but it was still heading for the bridge pylons to the right of the main arch.

'Hard aport!'

It's one of the idiosyncracies of vessels of all kinds that the slower they're going, the harder they are to steer. It's counterintuitive to someone who has only ever driven a car, but well understood by mariners of everything from rowboats to 10 000-tonne ships. Eventually, if the vessel slows down too much, it won't steer at all. And now, as the *Lake Illawarra* continued to head for the unprotected pylons on the eastern side of the bridge, her bows refused to swing back to the left.

'Hard aport!' Pelc ordered again. This time the rudder indicator was checked to ensure the order had been obeyed.

'Hard aport!' Pelc gave the order three times but the massive ship remained true to her course. Pelc was now only one or two ships'-lengths from the bridge.

'Full astern! Double ring!' (That is, maximum revolutions without destroying the engines.)

All he could do now was try to stop the ship.

'Full astern! Triple ring!' The order meant that saving the engines was a lower priority than saving the ship, and the bridge.

'Drop anchors.' Up in the foc's'le, shipwright Graham Kemp obeyed immediately as the bridge loomed almost overhead. Within moments he'd managed to drop the port anchor.

From his small fishing boat, Ian Pidgeon had been watching the ship approach. Then in an appalled voice he said, *'Gee, he's going to hit the bridge.'*

The ship struck pier 18 first, by then moving forward at barely half a knot (1 kilometre/hour). But for an 11 000-tonne ship that was more than enough to demolish the pylon. The ship then swung and demolished a second pier, pier 19. The centre span fell, leaving two spans protruding into mid-air.

The *Lake Illawarra*'s chief officer, Eddie Condon, was off-duty when the ship struck. A veteran of the sea, in World War II he'd been on a vessel that was torpedoed and sunk, after which he'd become a POW. On the *Lake Illawarra* he only felt a slight bump, but decided to go on deck. There he met the radio officer who said, 'Eddie, put on your life-jacket.'

Condon headed for the bridge. There Captain Pelc told him: 'Eddie, that arch is going to fall on us.' Condon looked up. 'I couldn't see the piers,' he recalled, 'only the arch, unsupported at one end.'

Second officer Robert Choppin was also off duty when he felt a bump and thought it was the tug coming alongside to push the ship to its wharf. Feeling the engines going astern, he headed on deck: 'The first thing I saw was the lights go out on the bridge, and then this mass of concrete came down. Huge sparks flew off the front of the ship. The forecastle disappeared.'

'Down it came on the ship. I saw at least one car go over in the debris and dust,' reported an amazed Ian Pidgeon. 'Probably 30 seconds later I saw another car go over and somersault before hitting the water.'

On shore, the Read family heard the noise and looked out from their home to see the drama unfolding before them. 'I was drawn by a tremendous rumbling noise,' Jock Read said. His wife added, 'The worst part was seeing the cars coming down. It was a very emotional thing. The cars seemed to fall in slow motion. It was horrifying thinking there were people inside them.'

An unnamed crewman also saw one of the cars fall: 'It went straight out and then came down into the water backwards. It was bloody awful.'

Up on the bridge, homeward-bound Frank Manley was among the cars heading for the abyss:

I was driving up the bridge from the Hobart side and about three-quarters of the way up, all the overhead lights went off. I thought it was just a power failure, and kept driving. After we got over the brow of the bridge, I saw what I thought was a car broken down on the side of the bridge. I slowed down, and then all of a sudden, my wife screamed out: 'The bridge has gone.' I hit the brakes, but it was too late, and the car went over the edge. The centre of the car grounded and we just hung there. I had a bit of trouble getting out of the car because my door was partly over the edge.

Murray Ling, of Bellerive, was also heading home with his wife and two children when the lights went out: 'I knew something bad must have happened and I slowed down.' He'd stopped near the edge and got his family out when a car slammed into his and pushed the front over the edge. 'A bus and several other vehicles, approaching at normal speeds, were stopped before they reached the broken span.' Ling tried to wave down two vehicles that swerved around him and skidded off the bridge.

Down in the water, Ian and Lyndon Pidgeon rowed for shore, expecting to be hit by waves caused by the concrete falling on the ship. They'd almost got there when a 1.5-metre wave struck their small craft. They were immediately swamped. However, both the brothers were sensibly wearing life jackets for their night fishing and were eventually washed onto the rocks nearby.

Further downstream, the Reads acted quickly. Jock and his son Kevin put out in Jock's launch, *Merus*. Jock's son David was in his small boat. The *Merus* was the first private launch on the scene. 'We could hear chaps calling for help,' said Jock Read. 'We picked up one and got him on board when Kevin said the ship was going down. We were about 50 yards [45 metres] away. A great surge threw us into a pylon head on and we bounced off.'

'She didn't go quick – she went halfway and then stopped,' said

Able Seaman Ronald King. 'I thought her bows were on a mud bank. But we had 10 000 tons of ore in her and it was just a matter of settling. Most of us got in the lifeboat, but then that went too, so all the boys got in the water.'

Chief engineer Max Dalton recalled:

Someone yelled that we were going down so I scrambled forward to get on the deck but I was going the wrong way and I ran into a wall of water. I was swept aft along the corridor by the water and managed to clamber up to the deck. [He tried to lower a lifeboat] but it seemed to be stuck because of the angle of the ship and the lifeboat went down with the ship. I didn't have a life jacket so I grabbed hold of another bloke who had one and we jumped over the side together. We were about 50 yards away when she went down. She went down nose first and there was a sort of underwater blast when something exploded. The sea foamed up and there was stuff everywhere. We wouldn't have got out unless someone yelled the warning. I think it was the third officer, Royce Davies.

Dalton was saved by a fishing boat: 'They got there pretty quickly. The mast got caught in some wires that were hanging down from the bridge, but they managed to free her.'

Able seaman John Bush was suffering shock when he related his story: 'It is all very confused, but I remember standing on the rear deck and being washed into the sea with the others. I got to a pier of the bridge and hung on until I was picked up.'

Eddie Condon was sucked under when the ship went down. 'When I surfaced and the white water which accompanies a ship sinking cleared, I saw the lifeboat. I swam to it and climbed aboard.'

After failing to free a lifebuoy, Robert Choppin got his life jacket and dived overboard:

I was not making much progress and I rolled over on my back and tried to kick to see if I could go faster that way. I was on my back when the ship went down. As the ship went down there were two terrific explosions as the boilers exploded. Then a wall of water came at me. It pushed me under and I came up for air and went down again. When I came up the second time, Mr Campbell [a crew member] was beside me. I thought he was still alive and tried to help him. He was already dead. His life jacket was in his hand.

The *Merus*, meanwhile, was recovering from its collision with the bridge-pier. Jock Read: 'We saw this man in the water. Kevin took the dinghy off and man-handled this big bloke into it. How he did it I don't know. He must have been at least 15 stone [95 kilograms] of dead weight.' They eventually rigged a halyard to haul the man into the launch. David, meanwhile, was picking up half-a-dozen men from a life raft. Soon ambulances had gathered on the shore to ferry the survivors to hospital.

From a crew of 42, 35 were rescued, including an injured and shaken Captain Pelc. Seven of those aboard *Lake Illawarra* were lost, including Graham Kemp, who remained at his station in the foc's'le as thousands of tonnes of concrete fell on it. He later received a posthumous commendation for bravery. Five motorists lost their lives in four vehicles, three of which went off the western end of the bridge, one from the eastern end.

The shattered *Lake Illawarra* lay on the bottom in 30 metres of water just south of the bridge she'd failed to negotiate. Had she struck the heavily reinforced bases around the main navigation span's pylons, constructed as insurance against navigational mishaps, all may have been well. Instead, she'd hit the unprotected outer pylons on the eastern side of the channel. The result immediately changed the landscape of Hobart. It became a city divided.

Before the collision, the bridge was carrying up to 22 000 vehicles a day. The city's business district lay on the western side of the Derwent; the city's airport and such suburbs as Lindisfarne and Bellerive on the eastern side. The car journey to the city now involved an additional 40-kilometre trip, up the river on badly potholed minor roads to Bridgewater, then back down the river.

The morning after the disaster was a Monday. Although the number of commuters was slightly down due to the January holiday season, nevertheless, it was bedlam. Ferry services were hastily upgraded, but the services were jammed with people. Motorists trying to drive the long way round to the city found the roads so hazardous that several vehicles lost control and ran into ditches. Meanwhile, helicopter services were established to carry critical medical cases from the eastern shore to the city's hospital.

It was soon discovered that the bridge had more problems than at first appeared. It was found that one of the surviving pylons had shifted as well, and was swaying. Then it was discovered that the only things supporting a surviving 1100-tonne span were eight bolts only four centimetres in diameter. Sightseers were quickly evacuated from the span while the divers below cautiously went about the task of recovering bodies and vehicles from the water.

Meanwhile, the loss of the city's vital piece of infrastructure had not daunted its bureaucracy. Private ferry operators were soon confronted with a restriction on the amount they could charge for operating their services. Led by ferry operator Robert Clifford, they argued that the price (20 cents for a one-way ticket) meant they couldn't recover their costs and amounted to restricting services to subsidised government services, which were still inadequate for the demand. Clifford's solution was to ask his passengers to make donations if they liked his service, and he gleefully reported his donation tins were soon stuffed with money.

What to do about the bridge presented its own problems. It was thought that simply reconstructing the ten-year-old structure might be exposing the city to more disaster and serious consideration was given to the construction of a suspension bridge that would open the entire width of the river to shipping. In the end it was decided to demolish the damaged sections of the bridge and reconstruct it; the work was expected to take two years. It was decided to leave the *Lake Illawarra* where she was, rather than risk further damage to the bridge while attempting to raise her.

The news caused a temporary slump in house prices on the eastern shore, and an 'atmosphere of gloom' among the residents. There is anecdotal evidence that the loss of the bridge and problems with commuting contributed to an increase in marital breakdown in Hobart, however any spike was largely masked by the national introduction of the 1975 *Marriage Act* that made divorce easier and led to a significant increase around the country at that time.

On 18 February, a Court of Marine Inquiry opened before the Chief Justice of the then Australian Industrial Court, Sir John Spicer, and Mr Justice Neasey of the Tasmanian Supreme Court. It heard evidence for nearly a month, during which Captain Pelc first suggested that his vessel had suffered steering failure, later conceding that he may have lost steerage. He also conceded that had he known the true state of the tides, which would make steering the vessel more difficult, he would have set a course to bring him into line with the navigation channel much earlier. Trying to line up with the navigation leads where he did was 'cutting it fine.'

Hobart pilot Captain Richard Williams, who had brought the *Lake Illawarra* into port several times, testified that he would normally approach the leads at 3 to 4 knots (5.5–7.5 kilometres/hour), then increase speed to 6 knots (11 kilometres/hour) to pass under the bridge with good steerage. He said he would never stop engines as the Lake-class bulk carriers would lose steerage efficiency almost immediately. He also pointed out that the *Lake Illawarra* was 'a typical turbine ship – slow in going astern and needing plenty of astern to stop her.'

Pelc was found not to have handled the ship in a proper and sea-manlike manner and his master's certificate was suspended for six months. Set against the damage done – the destruction of a vital transport link, the loss of a ship and the deaths of a dozen people – Pelc got off lightly. However, the incident underlined the difficulty of navigating large vessels in enclosed waters, and most skippers of vessels large or small will admit they've lost steerage at some time or other and nudged a dock, a bridge, a navigation beacon or another vessel. Few have seen the consequences result in such death and de-struction and deliver such a heavy blow to an entire city.

Meanwhile, back on the Derwent, the Clifford family was making a small fortune out of their ferry service. Robert Clifford, the former fisherman turned innovative entrepreneur, eventually diversified from operating ferries and started building them instead. His innovative company constructed high-tech, wave-piercing catamarans for the high-speed, ocean-going, passenger-and-vehicle transport market. Ultimately, its vessels were plying the waters of North and South America, Asia, the English Channel and Mediterranean, and were in service with the navies of various countries. International Catama-rans Tasmania (also known as Incat) eventually grew until it was the single largest private employer in Tasmania, with a staff of 750. In recent years Incat has struggled in a tightening market and its future is shaky. However, while its growth may have been due to the energy of the Cliffords and Incat's work force, the thing that launched the company was a shipwreck.

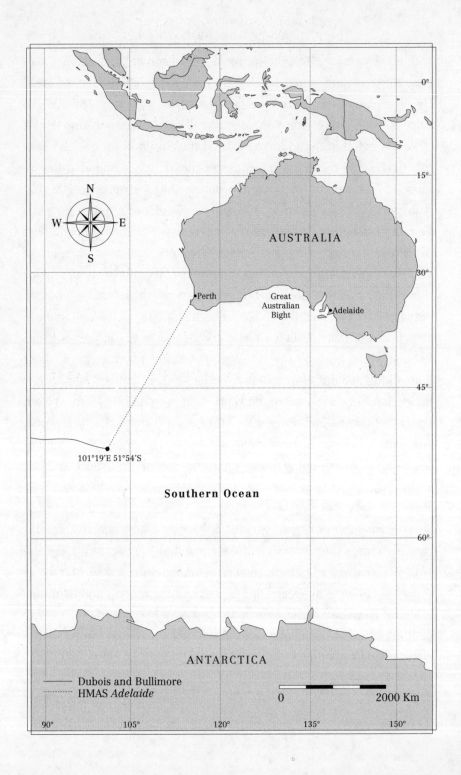

N

W   E

S

15°

AUSTRALIA

30°

•Perth

Great
Australian
Bight

•Adelaide

45°

101°19'E 51°54'S

Southern Ocean

60°

ANTARCTICA

——— Dubois and Bullimore
·········· HMAS *Adelaide*

0   2000 Km

90°   105°   120°   135°   150°

Tony Bullimore at the stern of
his upturned *Exide Challenger*
(AAP)

12. NEVER GIVE UP: TONY BULLIMORE AND THIERRY DUBOIS, 1997

The 19th century may have seen the eclipse of the great sailing clippers, but just as the days of sail appeared numbered, a new breed of mariner arose to keep the romance alive down to the present day.

In the 1890s, Joshua Slocum, a clipper captain displaced from his job by the competition from steamships, acquired the hulk of a small sailing vessel and set about making her seaworthy. He eventually set out in the *Spray* on a voyage, under sail, that was to become the first solo circumnavigation of the world.

It was a cruise that visited ports around the world, including Australia, where he found the sport of sailing thriving. Australia

has since produced some of the world's most famous solo circum-
navigators, such as Jon Sanders (first triple, non-stop, solo
circumnavigation), Kay Cottee (first solo, non-stop circumnavigation
by a woman) and Jesse Martin (youngest recognised solo, non-stop
circumnavigation).

As if the challenges of a solo circumnavigation were not enough,
the 1980s saw the emergence of solo-circumnavigation races. The
yachts involved are extraordinary pieces of state-of-the-art yachting
technology, at first glance as far removed from such vessels as the
Batavia (Chapter 2) and the *Loch Ard* (Chapter 7) as it is possible to
get. Yet in one respect they're identical. The yachts that compete in
the Vendee Globe race and the Around Alone race adopt the tactic
first introduced by Hendrik Brouwer in 1616 (see Chapter 1).

The yachts are designed to catch the roaring forties and fifties
and, with shallow displacement hulls, virtually surf their way around
the world at speeds approaching 20 knots (37 kilometres/hour).
Like the *Loch Ard*, they venture as far south as they dare, searching
for the winds that will give them an advantage over their rivals.
What they sometimes find is why old sailors believed that below
40 degrees south there is no law, and below 50 degrees there is no God.

On 4 January 1997, two satellites (TOPEX/Poseidon and ERS-2) were
tracking over the South Pole and peering down at the earth below.
Among their sensory capabilities, these altimetry satellites were able
to measure with great accuracy the wave heights in all the oceans
south of Australia, South Africa and South America. The mariners of
centuries previous would have regarded access to such information as
an absolute godsend. They would have loved the satellite-supported

global positioning systems (GPS) and emergency position indicating radio beacons (EPIRBs) as well.

In 1997, though, two mariners in the Vendee Globe solo, non-stop circumnavigation race didn't need the satellites to tell them about the state of the sea around them. Englishman Tony Bullimore aboard the yacht *Exide Challenger* and France's Thierry Dubois on *Amnesty International* were surfing the 12-metre waves the satellites were monitoring. As both 18-metre vessels hit speeds above 20 knots (37 kilometres/hour) they risked ploughing into a wave trough and either pitchpoling (somersaulting forward) or rolling. The problem then was that even if the vessel survived the capsize, it wouldn't right itself. For not only were the vessels in the 1996–97 Vendee Globe able to go as far south as they dared, they were of a type that was as stable upside-down as it was right-way-up.

Amnesty International was the first to go. She surfed at impossible speeds down a steep breaking wave, hit the bottom with the wave curling behind, and rolled. The mast went under, sails tearing under the strain, and then, with the massive weight of the spar acting effectively as the keel (that was still attached to the hull), the yacht stopped dead in the water. Fearing his yacht would sink, Thierry Dubois activated an emergency beacon on his yacht and swam outside to assess the damage.

Protected from the cold in an immersion suit, he clambered onto the hull of his yacht, where he clung to the keel and wondered who might come to rescue him. The closest land was Antarctica, a thousand kilometres to the south.

A few hours later, *Exide Challenger* suffered a similar fate. This time, though, there was a loud bang before the yacht rolled. Tony Bullimore's keel had snapped off. Without it, the boat was going only one way – it capsized. Fortunately, for Bullimore, the rolled boat was battened down when it went over, and he found himself in a sealed section of the hull, which remained buoyant. Shortly after the roll,

however, one of the perspex skylights smashed, partially submerging
the vessel. Then, too, Bullimore activated his emergency beacon.

Far above both yachts, more satellites were silently passing overhead. These were equipped with sensitive antennas designed to pick
up specific frequencies broadcast from below, then pinpoint their
positions with an accuracy of just a few kilometres. In this way, the
EPIRBs that were carried on *Amnesty International* and *Exide
Challenger* were able to signal their yachts' distress, even though
thousands of kilometres from the nearest human habitation.

When the signals were received, the satellites then relayed the
information to ground stations linked to a network of rescue services
around the world. On computer screens displaying a map of the
world, two small red dots soon lit up in an extremely remote section
of the world's oceans.

One of those screens was in a small office in Australia's capital,
Canberra, at the offices of the Federal Government's Marine Rescue
Coordination Centre (now known as Australian Search and Rescue or
AusSAR). Roughly 150 kilometres from the sea, Canberra is an
unlikely location for a marine rescue organisation.

However, the Canberra rescue centre's location is more a reflec-
tion of the size of its area of responsibility. Australia's jurisdiction for
maritime safety covers an area that encompasses one-tenth of the
world's oceans. It extends well into the Pacific and Indian Oceans,
across the north of Australia almost to the shores of Indonesia, and
all the way down to Antarctica.

One of the duty officers on the evening of 5 January was Senior
Search and Rescue Officer Mike Jackson-Calway: 'I was on the night-
shift, 11 p.m. to 7 a.m., and when I came on at 2245, the bloke who

was there said, "You're going to have a busy night. We've received a Mayday and we're awaiting further information."'

The positions of the two emergency beacons were well beyond the range of normal search-and-rescue services. The signals were more than 2000 kilometres south of Perth, Western Australia, only 1350 kilometres from Antarctica. The only good news was that both vessels were relatively close together. Jackson-Calway began his shift:

> I looked at what he had and said, 'I don't like the look of this', so I put out an XXX broadcast, an urgency broadcast. Basically you send it out to everyone you can think of. We put the RAAF's 92 Wing in Edinburgh, South Australia, and MHQ Aust on the list and they came back with what they had available. We spoke to the Navy and said, 'Have you got something that can go down there?' And they said, 'Yes. HMAS *Adelaide* is ready to go.'
>
> Someone may have said, 'Gee that's a bloody long way,' but everyone who got a signal did their homework, looked at it, rang who they had to ring. And once they found a warship that was capable of doing it, it was under way.

Dubois and Bullimore had just become the targets of what may be the longest-range rescue attempt in history.

The Royal Australian Air Force base at Edinburgh, South Australia, is home to P3 Orion aircraft designed to hunt submarines. However, they had both the range to get down to the yachts and back, and the ability to drop air sea rescue kits (ASRKs). Soon four aircraft were being readied and the first of them was on its way south on the long flight down into the icy Southern Ocean waters.

It required three hours' flying time to cover the immense distance to the source of the emergency beacons. The range of the aircraft allowed only four hours on scene before the three-hour return journey. That meant that with the ability to fly for eleven hours, there would always be one aircraft on the way to the scene, one actually there, and one on its way back.

In Fremantle, the frigate HMAS *Adelaide*, under captain (now Rear Admiral) Raydon Gates was prepared for immediate departure. The Australian Navy had never been into waters that far south, but her crew were hastily assembled and the boat readied for a dash into some of the most dangerous waters in the world.

During the afternoon of Monday, 6 January, the first Orion spotted *Amnesty International*. Dubois was sitting on the hull as the aircraft swept in. The conditions were terrible. The cloud cover was very low, the wind-lashed sea was a mass of spray and large breaking waves.

With the *Adelaide* only just making her way out of port, and still days away, the Orion that had spotted Dubois tried to help him the only way it could. As the aircraft came in low, they dropped an ASRK upwind of him. In the air it split into two parts on a long length of rope. The aim is for the first part to land one side of the target and the second part to land on the other side. Then it should drift down with the rope in between so it can be picked up. Each part contains a life raft with survival rations and equipment.

Dropping an ASRK requires pinpoint precision and as the Orion's crew watched, the first ASRK drifted past Dubois' upturned vessel. So, they dropped another. And then they watched.

Success. There was elation aboard the aircraft as they saw Dubois get hold of the rope and start pulling the life raft towards him. His chances of survival had just risen substantially. *Adelaide* now had a definite mission: the recovery of Dubois.

Meanwhile, the Orions shifted their attention to the search for Tony Bullimore's *Exide Challenger*. As the aircraft shuffled back and forth, just to make it more interesting, the immense low-pressure systems that had hit Dubois and Bullimore were so big they were sucking warm air south from the deserts of central Australia. The hotter air being thinner, when they were taking off the fully fuelled Orions had to accelerate using every metre of their 3500-metre runways to get enough lift to get airborne.

The distance also put limitations on *Adelaide*. If she travelled at full power she wouldn't have enough fuel to reach the yachts and return to Fremantle. The only way she would be able to increase speed was if the supply ship *Westralia* could get to sea as well, to refuel her.

In the early evening of Monday, an Orion finally sighted the *Exide Challenger*, but the situation at the partially sunken vessel looked ominous. There was no sign of Bullimore on or near it. There was no response to repeated calls on the radio. The aircraft tried to get a response by dropping devices that sent a loud ping through the water, while sonar buoys were dropped to listen for a response. There was none.

On Tuesday, 7 January, the Orions continued to monitor Thierry Dubois while trying to establish contact with Tony Bullimore. To no avail. If he was alive, he was surviving in the most difficult conditions imaginable. The water that far south was just above freezing. Even in a survival suit there are limits to the length of time a person can endure the ocean's sapping cold.

Meanwhile, *Adelaide* was still jogging south while the staff at the Marine Rescue Coordination Centre monitored a series of severe weather fronts advancing on the stricken yachtsmen and the frigate itself. 'It was typical southern ocean weather,' Jackson-Calway said.

'Bastard weather. It was not pleasant but down there it's always pretty bad.'

Then came the good news that the *Westralia* was going to be able to put to sea. As soon as it came through, *Adelaide* opened up. Her second engine was spun up to speed and she broke out of her trot. At speeds of up to 30 knots (55 kilometres/hour), the sprint was on. Even so it was going to take thirty-six hours to reach the rescue scene, some 2400 kilometres south-west of her home port.

Into Wednesday, the Orions continued flying mission after mission. Between them, four aircraft and six aircrew had logged over a hundred hours' flying time. They had maintained continuous coverage over Dubois. It was a resource-hungry exercise, but one that maintained the morale of the waiting sailor, while ensuring his exact position was constantly known.

There was still no sign of life from Bullimore's yacht, and speculation grew about his chances of surviving. The lack of any sign, of a signal of any kind, suggested the worst had happened. Perhaps he'd been lost overboard during the capsize. Or the mast may have hit him when it came down. But most likely of all was if he'd survived all that, exposure to the freezing water would have led to hypothermia, and he would eventually have lost consciousness and drowned within the hull.

'His boat was upside down. We were speculating about what could have happened. You could see the jagged scar where the keel had been,' reported Mike Jackson-Calway. 'We didn't even know if he was inside. He probably had a survival suit on, but if you were in the water down there, your survival would only be a couple of hours. We didn't know what to expect.'

By then the rescue attempt had become world news. Satellite TV links beamed the unfolding saga into lounge rooms from Sydney to the south of England, where Bullimore's wife, Lalel, still believed Tony would be all right, even as increasing numbers of armchair pundits concluded otherwise. Jackson-Calway:

I said to the media, when they asked 'Is he alive?', 'There's a good chance otherwise we wouldn't be going out there.' We hoped that he was still alive. To keep your mind focussed on the rescue, mine anyway, I always assumed there was going to be someone at the end of the line, otherwise you might slack off and say 'He's probably dead. Well, we'll put up an aircraft anyway, but you know . . . ' Someone else kept saying 'Negative thoughts get negative results.'

The rescuers, meanwhile, continued their efforts to save both men. As night fell on Wednesday, HMAS *Adelaide* was almost within striking distance of both yachts, and they started planning the details for rescuing both sailors. The warship would head for Bullimore. When the warship's chopper was in range of Dubois, it would take off to winch him from his raft. *Adelaide* would continue to the *Exide Challenger* to discover the fate of Tony Bullimore, one way or another.

At dawn on Thursday, 9 January *Adelaide*'s Sea King helicopter lifted off. The rescue of Thierry Dubois was virtually routine. For a man who had been floating in the freezing Southern Ocean for four days, he was in remarkably good condition.

The operation to determine the fate of Tony Bullimore was altogether different. First, they would deploy an inflatable rescue boat to try and find out if he was alive. If he wasn't, a Navy diver would have to enter the upturned vessel to search for his body. However, the doors were likely to be blocked by the pressure of the water pushing against them, in which case the rescuers would have to cut through the hull. The danger then was that there was a good chance the yacht might quickly sink, taking the rescue diver and Bullimore's body with it.

Jackson-Calway described the mood: 'We were expecting or hopeful of finding him, but nagging somewhere was the thought that it was going to need a miracle.'

As *Adelaide* closed on the *Exide Challenger*'s upturned hull, conditions were as good as could be hoped for in that part of the world. There was a grey sea mist and short choppy seas on a moderate swell. The ship had arrived during a gap in the fronts, but there were more on the way.

The ship put an inflatable rescue boat into the water but, as it closed in on the hull of *Exide Challenger*, there was still no sign of life. It appeared the task ahead was more likely to be the recovery of a body rather than a rescue. When the inflatable was alongside the upturned yacht, its crew started banging on the hull. Then they listened for a reaction. There was none. They tried again. Nothing.

Their worst fears seem to have been realised. All that was left was to go inside to find out if Tony Bullimore was there, dead or alive. A naval engineer prepared for the risky procedure of cutting a hole in the yacht's hull.

And then, a cry went up on board HMAS *Adelaide*. 'He's in the water! He's in the water!'

A head had suddenly bobbed up beside the yacht. Tony Bullimore was alive and still able to get himself out of the boat when he heard his rescuers. He was on the other side of the hull from the inflatable which quickly put its diver into the water. It then powered away from the vessel and sped around the stern. Diver and boat reached the swimming sailor together, as elation swept the crew of HMAS *Adelaide*.

Tony Bullimore had hung on inside the hull of his yacht, in total darkness and freezing water, for four days. He'd survived on water and chocolate. His only injuries were a severed finger, lost when the sea slammed a hatch on it, and mild hypothermia. All he'd been able to do was wait, holding on and hoping against hope that someone would find him. Despite the cold he'd tried to limit his activity to conserve the oxygen trapped inside the hull. He gave his rescuers: '10 out of 10 . . . It was an incredible rescue.'

Back at the rescue centre in Canberra, Mike Jackson-Calway was on duty. 'I took the phone call and just blurted it out, "He's alive!" It was a great outcome. I had a lump in the throat, and there was some moisture in quite a few eyes as well.'

The sense of elation soon swept the world, and messages of congratulations came pouring in from politicians, heads of state and the general public. Queen Elizabeth II was among the well-wishers:

> I would be grateful if you would pass on both my congratulations to all members of the Australian Defence Forces who have made possible the two dramatic rescues in the Southern Ocean over these recent days and, through HMAS *Adelaide*, my warm good wishes to Tony Bullimore on his extraordinary feat of survival.

At the Marine Rescue Coordination Centre in Canberra, there was just one more job to do. They picked up a phone, and yet another satellite connected Senior Search and Rescue Officer Mike Jackson-Calway to the home of Lalel Bullimore: 'Tony's wife had quite a few people there, as the rescue was imminent. I didn't speak to her initially, so I said, "We've just received confirmation that he is alive." And when I spoke to her I said, "Lalel, he's there, he's all right, he's been picked up."'

Interviewed after the rescue, the captain of HMAS *Adelaide*, Raydon Gates, was asked what lessons there were to be learned. He replied that you should never give up. He was talking about Tony Bullimore's survival, but it could have been the motto of his rescuers. And it was to be good advice less than two years later, when their resources were taxed to the limit once more, during the 1998 Sydney to Hobart Yacht Race (Chapter 13).

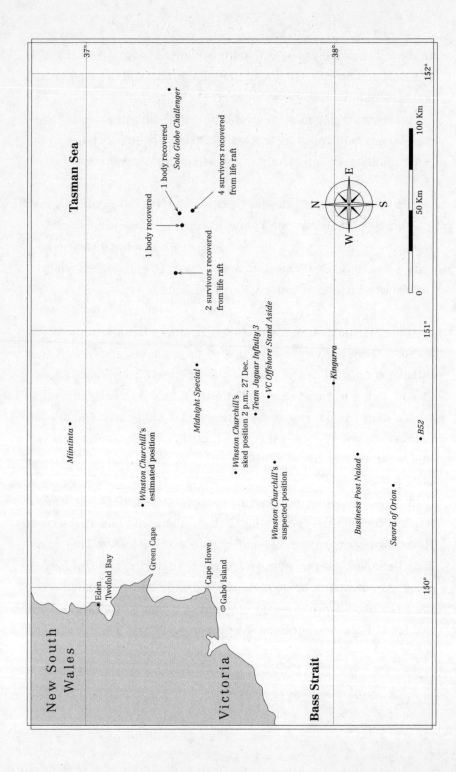

New South Wales

Eden
Twofold Bay

Green Cape

Cape Howe
Gabo Island

Victoria

Bass Strait

Miintinta •

Winston Churchill's • estimated position

Midnight Special •

Winston Churchill's • sked position 2 p.m., 27 Dec.

Team Jaguar Infinity 3 •

VC Offshore Stand Aside •

Winston Churchill's suspected position

Business Post Naiad •

Kingurra •

Sword of Orion •

• *B52*

Tasman Sea

• *Solo Globe Challenger*

1 body recovered →

← 1 body recovered

4 survivors recovered from life raft

2 survivors recovered ← from life raft

37°

38°

150°   151°   152°

N
W — E
S

0   50 Km   100 Km

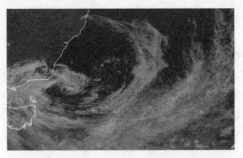

Bass Strait, 2.30 p.m., 27 December 1998
(Bureau of Meteorology from the
Japanese Meteorological Agency)

13. THE EDGE OF HELL: SYDNEY TO HOBART YACHT RACE, 1998

Log on to the Australian Bureau of Meteorology's web site at http://www.bom.gov.au, go to the 'Coastal Waters Forecast' (via 'Weather and Warnings', 'State Forecasts' and 'Forecast Index') and before you get the weather conditions, you'll read the following message: 'PLEASE BE AWARE Wind gusts may be a further 40 per cent stronger than the averages given here, and maximum waves may be up to twice the height.'

However, had you logged on to the same web site in December 1998, you wouldn't have read that warning, because it wasn't there. Back then, it was assumed everyone knew that the wind

speeds and wave heights given were the averages, not the maximums. It was, after all, a convention of meteorological forecasting
around the world. But 'everyone' isn't a trained meteorologist,
and on the afternoon of 27 December 1998, the consequences of
that became abundantly clear for the fleet in Australia's most
famous blue-water sailing event, the Sydney to Hobart Yacht
Race.

By 1998, the understanding and prediction of the weather around
Australia's coasts had advanced beyond recognition from the night
in 1899 when Cyclone Mahina fell on the unsuspecting pearling fleet
at Princess Charlotte Bay (see Chapter 9). Sydney, for that matter,
was unrecognisable from the place it had been when the *Stirling
Castle* (Chapter 4) called there in 1836 and the *Dunbar* (Chapter 6)
was wrecked there in 1857. Still a working port, it had become
a metropolis of 4 000 000 people, with the sails of her most famous
building, the Sydney Opera House, a constant reminder of her close
connections with the sea.

The Sydney to Hobart was another connection. First run in 1945,
the Sydney to Hobart started with the suggestion of a cruise that
soon turned into a race between nine yachts. Since that first storm-
wracked competition, the Sydney to Hobart has become the country's
best known and most closely followed yacht race, as much a battle
with the elements as with other boats. It's not surprising, since the
630-nautical-mile (1167-kilometre) course traverses waters or latitudes that have wrecked ships like the *Sydney Cove* and her longboat
(Chapter 3), *Cataraqui* (Chapter 5) and *Loch Ard* (Chapter 7). It is
perhaps worth repeating that the same area was also indirectly
responsible for the loss of the *Quetta* (Chapter 8) as she was taking
the Torres Strait route rather than face Bass Strait and the roaring
forties. Indeed, considering the litany of death and destruction
attached to the area, and the preference of modern vessels for alternative routes, a student of history might question the wisdom of

running a race there, or appreciate why it is considered the Mount Everest of yachting.

In the week before the 1998 race, the weather forecasters had been struggling to predict what was going to happen when the yachts finally headed south on Saturday, 26 December. Armed with masses of satellite data and powerful computer-modelling tools, they were watching a low-pressure system advance on Bass Strait from the west, expecting it to develop into an east-coast low as it headed into the Tasman Sea.

An east-coast low is an intense low-pressure system characterised by strong winds and high seas (one of the worst being the Great Gale in 1866, mentioned at the end of Chapter 6). As the week advanced it became more certain that it was going to form; the forecasters just didn't know exactly where and when. As they watched, they hoped that it would form far enough into the Tasman that it wouldn't severely affect the Sydney to Hobart fleet.

On the morning of the race, it appeared that the low was going to miss the fleet, which would first get a following breeze before it struck the trailing edge of the low-pressure system, in the form of a southerly buster. It would get rough, but that was nothing out of the ordinary. The weather kits the Bureau of Meteorology distributes on race day said as much until, around 9 a.m., the computer models updated the predictions. Now it appeared the low would develop closer to shore, with stronger winds. The forecast was upgraded to gale force, with winds averaging 34 to 47 knots (63 to 87 kilometres/hour). Nasty, but nothing remarkable.

This was the forecast most boats had received when the race started at 1 p.m., in glorious weather conditions, on Sydney Harbour. As always, enormous crowds lined the headlands to watch the boats sail out to sea, while hundreds of small boats churned the water around the sleek racing yachts. The crews looked fit and skilful, many decked out in matching designer sailing gear. Some were conspicuous in brightly coloured clothing; many showed a preference for stylish navy blues and muted tones – which looked great, but would be difficult to see if they fell overboard.

From the start line the vessels headed down the harbour in a stiff north-easter, then turned south, setting spinnakers in a spectacular display. However, the yachts weren't all examples of the latest high-tech and space-age materials. Among them was the solidly built veteran, *Winston Churchill*, an echo of a bygone era and a competitor in the first Hobart race 54 years earlier.

Meanwhile, over at the Bureau of Meteorology, the weather computers were spitting out another forecast. It was enough to make the forecasters pause. The low wasn't going to form out in the Tasman. It was going to form on the eastern side of Bass Strait, but before it did, it would suck in the hot winds of the north-easter that was blowing the yachts south. As it did, the system would rotate faster, forming a tightly spinning centre of low pressure. From the model, the low looked a lot like a cyclone, with winds to match, but so far south, the forecasters don't use such terminology. Again, not many of the yachts in the fleet knew that.

However, the 'cyclone' was only part of the story. Making matters worse was that the most dangerous quadrant, the leading quadrant where the winds would be strongest, was going to pass right over the Sydney to Hobart course just off the south-east corner of Victoria at Cape Howe. At the corner, conditions are always tricky because it is where the southerly current that flows down the east coast of Australia meets the weaker current flowing east through Bass Strait. The collision creates an effect like a washing machine: confused seas, steep waves, unpredictable countercurrents. Include strong winds in the equation, and it adds up to real trouble.

There is some dispute about exactly what happened after the new prediction. Forecaster Ken Batt maintains that, with his knowledge of the conditions as a competitor in the storm-marred 1993 Sydney to Hobart, he was moved to tears by what he saw. He believed that people were going to die, and with fellow-forecaster Brett Gage, tried to contact the race organisers to warn them of the impending carnage. Either he failed to reach them, or he did not communicate his concerns, based on subsequent evidence given at a New South Wales Coronial Inquiry.

However, he must have spoken to someone. On the official web site for the event, a press release listed as being posted at 12.30 p.m. (on the site) or 1.39 p.m. (on the release) reads:

> The Sydney to Hobart yacht race fleet has been warned to expect atrocious weather conditions later this evening. A southerly change with near gale-force winds will hit the race leaders around midnight. The weather bureau's Ken Batt says when the southerly winds hit the south-flowing current, it will create ugly seas. But Mr Batt says it is the middle and end of the fleet that will get the worst of it.

This may have been based on the earlier prediction. In either case, it was to prove remarkably prescient. There is no doubt, however, that shortly after 2 p.m. on Saturday, December 26, the Bureau of Meteorology issued its highest-level warning for the area:

> Priority Storm Warning Coastal Waters south of Merimbula . . . Issued at 1414 Saturday the 26th of December, 1998 . . . gusty W/SW change 30/40 knots expected South Coast late tonight . . . W wind increasing to 45/55 knots offshore south of Merimbula late Sunday afternoon . . . Seas . . . rising to 3 to 4 metres with the change . . . Swell . . . rising to 2 to 3 metres after the change.

A prudent navigator who knew about average and maximum winds and waves could easily do the maths. An average wind of 55 (102 kilometres/hour) plus the allowance for 40 per cent stronger winds meant gusts might reach 77 knots (142 kilometres/hour). Seas to 4 metres plus swell of 3 metres gave an average wave of 7 metres. Doubling that meant the waves might reach 14 metres. Had the Bureau of Meteorology been using the old Beaufort terminology, and spoken of maximums as well as averages, people might have understood better. Winds of 77 knots are off the scale. Beaufort Force 12 is for winds of 64 knots (120 kilometres/hour) and over. According to the World Meteorological Organisation definitions of 1964, Force 12 is described as 'Hurricane Force.' For the purposes of estimating wind, the sea state is described as 'Air filled with foam; sea completely white with driving spray; visibility greatly reduced.' Incidentally, the definition of a Category 2 cyclone is where the strongest gusts are between 125 and 170 kilometres/hour.

Yet words like 'cyclone' and 'hurricane', and wind speeds in the 70s never entered the language of the race on that Saturday afternoon. The Sydney to Hobart's Race Committee appreciated that conditions were going to get rough, but at least one of its members appears to have been working to the outmoded language of weather forecasting. He believed there were two higher categories after storm: violent storm and hurricane. It also appears that when Batt was trying to reach them, the members of the Race Committee were out on Sydney Harbour officiating at the start. The sailing office was unattended, and in subsequent evidence it appears that at such times the responsibility for taking messages devolved to the yacht club's bar manager. At the time, he may have been too busy pulling beers.

After the start the yachts flew south, almost all of them ahead of the pace set by the previous record-breaking yacht, *Morning Glory*, in 1996 (two days, fourteen hours, seven minutes, ten seconds). No-one considered pulling out. Indeed, during the first evening's sked (a set time when all vessels are required to radio in their positions) there was some levity. At the start of the sked, race control on the sail-training vessel *Young Endeavour* read the storm warming, then it called each yacht in alphabetical order. One was addressed in the following terms: 'From Papua/New Guinea, *Hi Flyer*?' There was no response, due to a radio problem. Race control then commented: 'I think she's heard the weather forecast and gone back.'

By the end of that sked, all yachts had reported in. There were 115 vessels in the fleet heading south. In the course of the evening, the yachts reached the front of the storm, a line of spectacular thunder activity, with almost constant lightning. With the front the wind turned from the north-east to south-west and grew in strength. At 9.30 p.m. that first night came the first report of problems. *ABN Amro* had broken her rudder and was calling for assistance. The Royal Volunteer Coastal Patrol at Bateman's Bay set out to assist. An hour later, *Sledgehammer* broke a steering cable and retired as well. Then, at 11.30 p.m., *Challenge Again* radioed that they'd lost a man overboard. Seven minutes later the yacht *Sydney* called that she'd broken her rudder.

Quick reactions and copybook manoeuvres on *Challenge Again* resulted in their crewman being picked up within minutes of going overboard, a procedure made easier by the fact that the crew had the options of motoring or sailing back to the man in the water. Meanwhile, the yachts that were broken started limping towards the many small ports dotted along the New South Wales coast.

The winds continued to build throughout the night, until most were experiencing 40 knots (74 kilometres/hour) and increasingly rough seas. As dawn broke, there were more retirements. *King Billy* was taking water and couldn't find the source. *Allusive* was having keel problems. *Wild Thing* was the first boat to report mast damage when she retired at 6.15 a.m. on Sunday, 27 December.

At the same time, a weather fax was scrolling out of a machine at the race-control office in Hobart's Royal Yacht Club of Tasmania. It wasn't a prediction; it was a listing of the winds being experienced around the south-east corner of Australia. One in particular stood out. Wilsons Promontory, jutting down into the middle of Bass Strait, had recorded winds of 71 knots (131 kilometres/hour), the strongest wind recorded in December of any year since its equipment was set up in 1988. Compared to the areas around it, the wind speed was a distinct spike. While a nearby oil rig, Kingfish B, had 41 knots (76 kilometres/hour), and Cape Grim, on the western side of Bass Strait, had 50 (93 kilometres/hour), Flinders Island, on the south-east side, had only 11 knots (20 kilometres/hour). Gabo Island, right near the leading boats in the fleet, had just 14 knots (26 kilometres/hour). Nevertheless, it was an ominous warning, especially as winds weren't supposed to get that strong until the afternoon.

At the Coastal Patrol base at the idyllic fishing township of Eden, the Wilsons Promontory windspeed was noted on the radio log and highlighted with three exclamation marks. At Race Control in Hobart, it was copied for the race director's attention when he flew down from Sydney later that morning. Among those also flying to Hobart from Sydney was Sam Hughes (Safety Sam), the race's liaison officer from the Marine Rescue Coordination Centre, Canberra. On the way down the pilot of his commercial flight had dropped down to 12 000 feet to try and spot the leading boats in the fleet. Safety Sam recalled that 'it didn't look good.' When he got to Hobart and was told it was blowing 70 knots (130 kilometres/hour) at Wilsons Promontory, he said, 'We could be in for something here.'

The race committee, however, did nothing. The reasoning was that giving out localised weather information might unfairly advantage some boats. So the yachts sailed on, unaware of what was about to hit them. New South Wales Coroner John Abernethy later found the information 'was of importance to the Race Fleet' and 'should have been conveyed to the Race Fleet as soon as it was known.'

The yachts, meanwhile, were already starting to taste what the storm had in store. Early on Sunday, the yacht *Jubilation*, heading for shelter from a position some 50 kilometres east of Eden, reported winds between 50 and 60 knots (93 to 111 kilometres/hour). At 6.25 a.m., *Maglieri Wines*, which had earlier asked for a weather update and been told to wait until the afternoon sked, retired with mast damage, followed by *Marchioness* at 6.50 a.m. All morning more boats reported that they'd reached their limits. *Assassin* retired, *Tartan* headed to Eden for shelter, *Red Jacket* and *Innkeeper* retired.

Around midday, most of the fleet in the path of the storm had gone into survival mode. At 12.35 p.m. *Doctel Rager* reported severe weather with gusts exceeding 70 knots (130 kilometres/hour). Fifteen minutes later, *Secret Men's Business*, *Wild One* and *She's Apples* reported similar conditions. At 1.07 p.m. *Henry Kendall* reported 40-knot winds (74 kilometres/hour); at 1.18 p.m. *Terra Firma* was in 60 knots (111 kilometres/hour); and at 1.29 p.m. *Secret Men's Business* radioed that she was turning back to Eden with a crewman who had been thrown across the boat so violently his leg was broken.

A minute later another race to Hobart was due to start. However, the Race Committee for the Melbourne to Hobart Yacht Race decided the conditions were so extreme that starting the race was out of the question. A little to the north of Melbourne, in the Southern Alps in the middle of what was supposed to be a scorching Australian summer, it was snowing heavily.

Four minutes later, on the other side of Bass Strait, the yacht *Henry Kendall* radioed that she was heading to Eden for shelter. She was soon followed by *Sea Jay*, *She's Apples* and *Indian Pacific*. The

skipper of the yacht *Siena*, Iain Moray, later reported that in Bass
Strait he experienced winds in the 70-to-80-knot range (130 to 148
kilometres/hour) from 1 p.m. until nightfall. He maintained that they
peaked at 86 knots (160 kilometres/hour). If it had been considered
a cyclone, it was now approaching Category 3. The east-coast low
had finally formed.

At 2.05 p.m. the race organisers began the regular sked. While the
yachts were dutifully reporting their positions, some took the opportunity to state their intentions. *Elusion Blue* was heading for Sydney,
Kickatinalong joined the growing list of retirements, *Polaris*
reported it was heading for shelter behind Gabo Island, *Ruff 'N Tum-
ble* was retiring. No-one mentioned the weather until the sked got to
Sword of Orion: 'I just want to tell you a little bit about the weather
we're experiencing down here. It's a little bit different to the forecast,
over.'

Race control: '*Sword of Orion*, I would appreciate that for ourselves and all of the fleet, over.'

Sword: 'Yes. We are experiencing 50-to-65-knot westerlies (93 to
120 kilometres/hour) with gusts to 78 knots (144 kilometres/hour),
over.'

In fact, the gusts were within one knot of what was predicted, if
you knew how to do the Bureau of Meteorology's maths. Elsewhere,
though, boats were in worse conditions, as later reported by *Siena*.
Making conditions even more dangerous, the wind was coming from
the south-west, building steep waves all the way across the relatively
shallow waters of Bass Strait. Then those waves, with the wind
behind them, hit the south-flowing current at the eastern end of the
strait. The bigger, faster race leaders were already to the south of
the low's centre, but further back in the fleet, even as the sked continued, the real destruction began.

At around 2.30 p.m. the first emergency beacon (EPIRB) was activated. *Team Jaguar Infinity 3*, with a crew of nineteen, had been

dismasted by a severe gust and on trying to start her engine had got the trailing ropes and wires tangled around her propeller. She was adrift and at the mercy of the elements.

Soon after, the yacht *VC Offshore Stand Aside* met a wave over 14-metres high that was almost vertical and breaking at the top. The yacht was caught in the white water and thrown sideways. Then she completely rolled, tearing the mast from the deck. When the boat recovered, the crew below decks suddenly found themselves in the open. A third of the cabin roof had been torn away. If they copped another breaking wave it could fill the boat and send her straight to the bottom. *Stand Aside*'s engine was flooded with sea water, but she did still have a radio. *Stand Aside* started broadcasting a mayday and soon the ABC television helicopter and the yacht *Siena* responded.

At the Marine Rescue Coordination Centre in Canberra, the Search and Rescue Officers had already responded to the earlier EPIRB. A plane was in the air and flying to the location of the *Team Jaguar*. It then searched for and found *Stand Aside*. A problem for the air-craft was that it had no equipment with which to effect a rescue. Down on the water, *Siena* was battling to reach *Stand Aside*.

'It was impossible to see any distance,' recalls *Siena*'s skipper, Moray. 'I mean 100 metres or something; you couldn't see that far simply because there's always walls of water coming at you.'

With the ABC chopper pilot, Gary Ticehurst, guiding her in, *Siena* passed within 50 metres of *Stand Aside*, assessing how they might rescue the twelve aboard (and where they'd put them on a yacht that comfortably carried only six). With the wind slicing the tops off waves and hurling them across the deck, *Siena* manoeuvred under motor to stay close, while the Marine Rescue Coordination Centre tried to get hold of a rescue helicopter to lift the crew off. At one point, sideways to the massive seas, *Siena* got caught. Moray describes what happened:

Keith [Logan] was on the helm, he just screamed out, 'Wave!' Over the conditions he couldn't be heard down below. The guys on deck all [had] safety harnesses on, but we hung on to a winch or whatever we could get our arms around, and this huge amount of water came over the boat. We got rolled, the mast went in the water, and then fortunately, the boat came up. All four heads were still on the boat. A while later, I asked below whether everybody was all right and I was told that Tim [Evans] had been injured and had crashed into the stove. He'd been talking to the ABC helicopter at the time, getting further instructions about the rescue, and didn't hear the call, and was thrown from one side of the cabin to the other, and broke three ribs and punctured his lung.

Elsewhere, the havoc in the fleet continued. *Outlaw* was badly damaged and headed for Eden with *Dixie Chicken* standing by. *Cyclone* (the yacht) retired. *Rapscallion* was headed to Eden along with *Renegade* and *Bobsled*.

At 4.15 p.m. the yacht *Pippin* radioed that she'd just seen a yacht astern of her get rolled. In winds that *Solo Globe Challenger*'s skipper, Tony Mowbray, estimated as constant at 80 knots (148 kilometres/hour), the yacht had been doing up to 5 knots (9 kilometres/hour) under bare poles (no sails, just the mast and boom) when she was hit by a breaking wave. It stopped her forward momentum and slewed her beam on to the seas. Without any boat speed *Challenger* couldn't manoeuvre and was at the mercy of the elements. They showed none. The very next wave capsized the boat and drove it, upside-down and surfing sideways, down its face. The water pressure exploded a perspex skylight on the submerged cabin top, flooding the cabin. The crew below decks hung on as best they could, while those above were dragged through the water at terrifying speed.

After twenty seconds, the boat managed to break free of the wave and recover. She had no mast, radios or navigation systems. She was taking water. The sea-water-affected engine only worked intermittently. The four crew on deck were all badly injured. Two had broken ribs, another had a leg broken below the knee and blood pouring from a gash in his head, a fourth had been slammed up against a winch, severely bruising his back. Race control asked *Pippin* to stand by *Challenger* and she shakily replied that she'd try. As *Siena* had found, just holding position in the wind and huge seas was a huge ask.

Pippin turned back to assist, but Mowbray could only raise his arms as if to say, 'What can you do? Save yourselves.' At least it was easy for him to recover the injured crew who had been washed overboard and were being dragged along in their harnesses. The stern of the flooded *Challenger* was almost level with the sea, and they could practically float back aboard. Mowbray feared that one more wave would sink him. All he could do was turn on his emergency beacons and bail.

Shortly after, *Trust Bank* reported she was heading to Green Cape for shelter; *Canon Maris* retired; *Not Negotiable* and *Sword of Orion* decided to turn back and shelter in the increasingly appropriately named Eden.

Just before 5 p.m., as the Victorian rescue chopper *Helimed 1* was racing far out to sea to reach *Stand Aside*, race control, having considered the information received from *Sword of Orion* and the terrible attrition being experienced, broadcast the following slightly garbled message via the radio-relay vessel *Young Endeavour*:

Firstly, I would like to draw attention to all yachts competing in the Telstra Sydney to Hobart Yacht Race, page 2 of your sailing instructions, paragraph 7. All those taking part in CYCA [Cruising Yacht Club of Australia] races do so at their own risk and responsibility. The CYCA is not responsible . . . [for] a yacht whose entry is accepted or the sufficiency or adequacy of its equipment. The CYCA is not responsible for any damage or injury either ashore or at sea either to persons or yachts which might result from participating in Club races. The decision to race a boat is solely the responsible . . . responsibility . . . is solely responsible for deciding whether or not to start or continue racing. I ask all skippers, before proceeding into Bass Strait or wherever you're proceeding, to give it your utmost consideration as to what you're doing and talk about it with the crew. No problem to call into Eden and perhaps take off again tomorrow.

All of which is well understood by anyone who decides to race and reads the rule book. Coming in the midst of the mounting destruction, though, it was as good as saying, 'You're on your own.' Or as the New South Wales Coroner later put it: 'I find that the Race Management Team was organised in such a fashion that at the time of crisis it was, to all intents and purposes, valueless to the Race Fleet. I find that the Race Management Team had no emergency or crisis plan from which guidance could have been obtained.'

It was a different story at the Marine Rescue Coordination Centre in Canberra. At the same time they were declaring the general area around Bass Strait a mayday area. More helicopters were being diverted to the rescue effort, tows for vessels like *Team Jaguar* were being organised.

The first chopper to try and winch people to safety was *Helimed 1*, over *Stand Aside*. As her crew tried to decide how they'd do so, another chopper, *South Care* from Canberra, was en route. The ABC chopper had remained on station and filmed the start of *Helimed*'s rescue efforts. *Siena* had been stood down, her skipper wishing to head south across Bass Strait, into the waves, until he consulted his seriously injured crewman who gasped: 'Just get me to hospital.' The only pain-killers on board were headache tablets. *Siena* turned north, dangerously exposing her stern to the gigantic waves, trying to reach Eden.

Flying *Helimed 1* was Peter Leigh: 'Five o'clock, 1700 we arrived overhead the *Stand Aside*. Ground speed on the way out was 199 knots [368 kilometres/hour] so it took us about fifteen minutes to get out there and it was 51 nautical miles [94 kilometres]. That's about the fastest I've ever been in level flight.'

Stand Aside had deployed her life raft, and tethered it off her stern. Winching from the yacht was impossible as it tossed in the breaking waves, so Leigh asked them to put two men in the raft and pay out the line so it drifted away. 'We understood there was a leg injury, a head injury and finger amputations, so those people went first. Peter Davidson was winched into the water by Dave Sullivan and we proceeded to pick up these persons.'

The first lift took twenty minutes, during which the chopper had to manoeuvre to avoid the waves advancing towards it. Each lift got easier as the winch crew got the hang of the operation, but it was desperate stuff for all concerned.

In the middle of that rescue, at 5.21 p.m., a chilling message came through: 'Mayday, mayday, mayday. Here is *Winston Churchill*, *Winston Churchill*. At least 20 miles [32 kilometres] south-east of Twofold Bay. We are holed; we are taking water rapidly. We cannot get the motor started to start the pumps. We are getting the life rafts on deck.'

Winston Churchill, a solid timber yacht, had met with yet another steep breaking wave. She hadn't rolled; she'd been picked up and flung sideways through the air. The impact when she landed in the trough below was like hitting a brick wall. The portside gunwale was ripped away. All the windows were smashed. And somewhere below the waterline, the yacht had been holed. The sea was flooding in.

The wave had also taken out the navigation system, which meant that when *Winston Churchill* radioed her position, she'd been forced to make an educated guess. As more aircraft were tasked to the search, the radio relay vessel estimated she was 10 nautical miles

(18 kilometres) away from the position given and was directed to join the rescue effort.

Meanwhile, back at *Stand Aside*, *Helimed 1* winch-man Peter Davidson had picked up four of the crew. The effort had left him exhausted, so his pilot gave him a short break. Pilot Peter Leigh estimated it was 'perhaps two minutes.' Then Davidson went down again. After four more winches there were eight *Stand Aside* crew in the chopper with four to go. The chopper, now with twelve people in it, could take more, but Davidson could not. He was so drained he couldn't so much as lift his arms.

By then another helicopter, *South Care*, was on the scene. Based in Canberra but with a winch and two winch-trained paramedics, it was directed to the rescue. On the way to the scene, though, the storm had flung the machine around so much that both paramedics were violently airsick. Nevertheless, Kristy McAlister and Michelle Blewitt prepared to winch down to the helpless crew below. Their total experience of such rescues was nil, both women having done their training on the placid waters of Canberra's ornamental Lake Burley Griffin – named after an architect, as opposed to the Tasman's namesake: the pioneering Dutch mariner.

Down on the water things were getting worse for *Stand Aside*. Several huge waves broke over the tethered raft, flipping it and throwing one occupant into the sea. Kristy McAlister went down to get him: 'As soon as I hit the water, one of the huge sets of about 20-metre waves actually broke on top of my head, so it seemed like I was under the water for ages. I just lay there looking up, going, "I know I'll get out of here."'

When she finally surfaced, she battled through the water to the floating crewman, put the rescue strop on him and signalled to be lifted out. Back in the chopper, badly shaken, she was asked if she was prepared to go down again, as every rescue is completely voluntary. McAlister gave the winch-man the thumbs up.

Below her, the waves continued flipping the raft, which now had two men clinging to the side. While putting the strop on the second man, another set of breaking waves swept through. McAlister was caught across the neck by the winch cable and flung sideways. Almost throttled, she still managed to get the strop around the crewman. Then, just as they were being winched, another wave flipped the raft, tangling it around the winch cable. The winch-man dropped her and the crewman back into the sea.

McAlister knew that if she didn't free the raft, the winch-man would cut the cable rather than risk the chopper being dragged down. She feared the worst: 'I didn't have a vest on, we're wearing black wet-suits; we didn't have our EPIRBs. No-one would ever have found us.'

However, before she could get to the raft another wave flipped it, and it broke free by itself. Up in the chopper, she asked for a break. The winch-man turned to Michelle Blewitt. She hadn't seen Kristy McAlister's first rescue because she'd been too busy throwing up. She'd then decided that if she was to go down on the wire, she didn't want to watch the second lift. She'd sat in the chopper, con-centrating on her training.

Blewitt explains what happened during her lift: 'I've gone down to get the third guy who was hanging on to the life raft. I've got down to him, tried to put the strop over his head; it wasn't going to work because the strop that we had wasn't long enough to go over the pre-server vest.'

As she'd been trained, she got him to float on his back and threaded the strop up his legs and body. Then she gave the thumbs-up signal to get winched out: 'We've come up out of the water, then I remember something striking me on the head, and going back, dragged back through the water and I'm thinking, "My God, what is going on here."'

A wave had rolled the raft again, smashing the metal cylinder that inflates it into her head, driving her skull over into her shoulder. 'It didn't knock me out. I remember going under the water and seeing black starry things for a minute. I actually had a helmet on, and I've come up but I, I had all my full faculties about me.'

What her faculties revealed was that the life raft was now hopelessly tangled with the winch cable. 'I actually thought that I was going to die . . . there was a high potential that I was going to die, because I actually thought that the winch cable was going to be cut. And I thought, I'm not going to survive out in these seas for very long.'

All she could do was try to cut the raft's tether. She reached for a small plastic 'jay knife' attached to her harness. 'I put the jay knife on the rope and prayed like anything that it would cut the rope, because the rope was quite thick. There was a lot of pressure on the rope when I put the jay-knife on it, and I felt the pressure release and the life raft blew a long distance away very quickly.'

She was winched up with her first rescue, and then South Care's winch-man assessed the cable. It was clearly kinked and might not support the weight of two people being lifted through monster waves. McAlister and Blewitt had both already come close to being cut free in the raging seas, but there was still one man left behind on a sinking yacht, now without so much as a life raft.

The winch-man decided the cable had at least one more rescue in it and Blewitt mustered every ounce of her courage. She agreed to go down again. This time the greatly relieved crewman tied a tether rope to his waist and dived off the yacht into the ocean. He swam clear and Blewitt picked him up easily.

While *South Care* followed *Helimed 1* back to shore with *Stand Aside*'s survivors, the search for *Winston Churchill* continued. So did the storm. In the hour from 5 p.m. to 6 p.m., two more yachts were rolled: *B52* and *Loki*. *Chutzpah* headed to Eden for shelter; *Bin Rouge* turned north; *Impeccable* was heading for Eden, as was *Inner Circle*. *Hawk 5* was retiring with two injured crew. *Hi Flyer*, the Papua New Guinea boat (which, rumours to the contrary, hadn't gone home) headed for Eden with one injured crewman. *Midnight Special* was heading to Gabo Island for shelter in constant 50-to-60-knot winds (93 to 111 kilometres/hour). *Morning Tide* had hove to. Far to the north *Forzado* was heading into Jervis Bay. *Unipro Ocean Road* was making for Eden.

Apart from *Stand Aside*, the Marine Rescue Coordination Centre was trying to organise rescues for *Team Jaguar*, *Winston Churchill*, *Outlaw*, *Secret Men's Business* and *Solo Globe Challenger*. A rescue for the crewman with the punctured lung on *Siena* was considered, but her skipper feared that winching him with a punctured lung would kill him. By then, though, there was only one rescue chopper able to be assigned. The Victorian police chopper *Polair 1* was being tasked, then retasked to different yachts as priorities shifted. Meanwhile the airwaves were becoming increasingly congested as aircraft tried to find out their assignments, pass on messages, communicate with stricken yachts and fight their way through the storm.

Then at 5.49 p.m., another yacht reported a rollover – *Business Post Naiad* was dismasted, her windows were smashed and she was taking water. Five crew had been on deck when she rolled, but were held on the boat by their harnesses. However, not long after the yacht righted, with 15 centimetres of water washing down below, one crew member, Rob Matthews, started showing difficulties moving his limbs – an early sign of hypothermia. He went below and put on his thermal clothing, while a mayday was sent and, shortly after, a chopper requested for three of the crew.

At this stage some twenty staff were at, or making their way to, the Rescue Centre in Canberra where they were handling up to

150 phone calls an hour, plus directing the searches. It was rapidly
becoming clear that the rescuers were running out of aircraft and
radio frequencies. And in the tiny coast airports, aviation fuel was
getting low. The Rescue Centre started calling Royal Australian Navy
bases on the east coast for assistance.

Out at sea, the other problem was yacht identification. Most yachts
were white, with white sails, which made them virtually invisible in
a sea of white spray and breaking waves. And to all but the most
enthusiastic yachtie, they all looked the same. Aircraft talking to
yachts and assessing their situation couldn't be sure that the yacht
they were talking to was the yacht they were circling. Most had their
names written on the side or stern (and small identifying numbers
on their sails, if they were carrying any), but they were unreadable
from the air in the spray and gloom. One aircraft reported passing
over fourteen yachts and not being able to tell who any of them were.
Even to ask 'Can you see me circling you?' didn't help. By now several yachts had aircraft circling them, or trying to home in on the
increasingly confused mass of signals from emergency beacons.

It was this that added to the confusion over the position of the
yacht *Winston Churchill*. At 5.55 p.m. an aircraft reported finding
a yacht in distress, still afloat but dismasted with people aboard,
40 kilometres south of the position reported by *Winston Churchill*'s
crew – but it was the wrong yacht.

At 6.10 p.m. *Adagio* had had enough and announced she was retiring
to Bermagui. At 6.25 p.m. *Relish IV* and *Antipodes* headed for Eden as
well. At the same time *Jack Guy* turned north to avoid the worst of
the storm. Then, at 6.30, yet another mayday came in. With her wind
indicator seemingly nailed at the top of the dial at 68 knots

(126 kilometres/hour) the yacht *Kingurra* had started climbing the face of a wave, only to be caught by 4 or 5 metres of breaking sea. Four crew were on deck when the yacht rolled. When it came back up, two of them were over the side, one having been knocked unconscious.

American John Campbell had been hit hard as the boat rolled over him – sustaining a broken jaw, cheekbone and the bones around one eye socket. He was hanging limply over the side in his safety harness, which was integrated with his waterproof jacket. But as two crewmen tried to drag him aboard, the lifeless man started slipping out of both. As one arm came out, then the other, the crew were reduced to grabbing his hands and trying to pull him aboard. Then a wave hit and he was snatched away, dressed only in dark-blue thermal long johns, floating face down in the water.

Kingurra's storm jib was in shreds, so the crew started the engine. Moments later it died, overwhelmed by the water that had poured below decks. The disabled yacht drifted quickly away from Campbell, but just before they lost sight of him, the crew saw him regain consciousness. He lifted his head above the water. He was alive, but not sufficiently aware even to try to swim towards the boat.

While the crew watched helplessly, *Kingurra*'s skipper, Peter Joubert, was doing everything he could down below. He had broken ribs, a punctured lung and a ruptured spleen, but he still managed to radio that he had a man overboard, yet another in the growing list of emergencies. The only remaining chopper, *Polair 1*, was once again retasked, this time to *Kingurra*, to search for a man in dark blue lost in a dark blue sea. Coincidentally, the day before, *Polair* crewman David Key had watched the start of the yacht race on television. He'd noticed the dark-coloured designer uniforms some crews wore and thought to himself they'd have no hope of being found if they went overboard.

Polair 1 managed to get to the yacht's reported position quickly, but *Kingurra* was nowhere to be seen. So *Polair*'s pilot Daryl Jones started flying in expanding circles, 60 metres above the sea, trying to locate it. Jones couldn't see *Kingurra* but they could see him. Her crew got out their flare pack. They decided the day flares, which put out orange smoke, wouldn't be visible in the high winds. So they used a night flare, which glows red, and it stood out in the darkness of the storm. On *Polair* they caught sight of a faint glimmer. It looked to be 15 to 20 kilometres away, but the storm conditions were so disorienting that it was actually only 2.

Over the radio *Kingurra*'s crew told Jones that Campbell was 300 metres from the yacht, but alerted by the difficulty of judging distance, Jones went further:

> Senior Constable Key was looking out the rear right-hand window and Senior Constable Barclay was searching out the left-hand rear. Senior Constable Key called out that he thought he had our man, he'd spotted one of the orange life rings that boats also carry and he thought that there was someone in that. So I moved – I actually drifted the aircraft sideways rather than turn to fly, it was that sort of head wind.

The lifebuoy was empty. The conditions were so rough that water splashing up inside the ring looked like someone was there. But while the crew were looking down, Barry Barclay thought he saw something. It was just in the corner of his vision, at 'the top of the square.' Slowly panning his vision up so as not to lose sight of the object, he finally spotted what it was. He could just see two hands waving from the darkness of the water. Despite his terrible injuries, Campbell was still afloat. He'd been treading water for forty minutes.

David Key was tasked to go down and get him:

> I noticed that the air speed indicator was between 80 and 85 knots and we were stationary, which meant that I stepped out of that helicopter when it was doing 160 kilometres/hour . . . The first thing was the noise. The wind noise was screaming, howling wind noise. It was

incredible, plus the rain and the sea spray, it was just like being hit by
nails or stabbed in the face with a fork, and I just had to put my hand
up over my face . . .

I hit the water and I just went straight under, how deep I've got no
idea. I forced my way to the surface, and I just looked up at a sheer
side wall of water. I found out later how tall it was, and I just went 'too
old for this, I don't really need to be here.' And I went up the face of
the water, because I was in a wetsuit and rather buoyant. I went up the
face of the wave and it was just near vertical. I've never seen anything
like it, breaking at the top like a surf breaker. At that stage I couldn't
see the helicopter and I couldn't hear it, and that's when I thought I'd
actually been cut off the cable . . . That's not a real good position to be
in. No other rescue helicopters out there, 120 to 140 kilometres off
shore, and it was nearly dark . . . I then fell down the bottom of the
wave and then went through it, held my breath for I don't know how
long, and popped out the back, and fell 30-odd feet [9 metres] till I hit
the bottom, and that winded me.

Up in the chopper, pilot Daryl Jones had problems of his own:

With the conditions the way they were, I selected about 100 feet [30
metres] for a winch . . . It's high – whenever you do a winch rescue,
everything's at the most critical, using maximum power on the aircraft,
you've got no forward airspeed if there are any problems . . . I was
actually using an instrument on the gauge we call the radalt, or radio
altimeter . . . It gives you a readout of your actual height above whatever surface it is. So I picked 100 feet which at times I thought may not
have been enough . . . As the waves passed underneath, that needle
would actually come back up the dial to 10 feet [3 metres]. There's
quite a few of those passed under us. And during the winch I'd actually said to Barry 'Have you got a lot of cable paid out?' And he said,
'Yeah, why?' I said 'Because I think I've got to climb.' I could see

something building, I could half imagine it now that it was like a wall of water was building up and coming towards us. I climbed the aircraft to 160 feet [49 metres] on the radalt. We had this trough of 160 feet and then there was just almost like a vertical wall of water passed underneath us, the radalt needle came back up to 10 feet [3 metres], sat there I'd say for eight to ten seconds. This was like a big plateau of water. It was flat across the top for maybe two, possibly 300 metres and then again just fell away, just as though someone got a knife and cut the back of the wave off and I was back to 160 feet on the radalt.

Jones had climbed to avoid a wave the height of an eleven-storey building.

'When the large wave came through I just thought, "Well that's it, I've had it." I thought I was a goner,' recalls Key. 'I went through that wave, unfortunately I ran out of air and ingested a great amount of salt-water, and somehow I popped out the back of that wave and fell again. I was completely disorientated, I didn't have a clue where I was.'

In fact Key was still attached to the chopper, which was trying to stay over Campbell. Yet the wind had blown Key three waves behind the man he was trying to reach. So the chopper started creeping forward, in the ferocious winds, dragging Key forward through the liquid mountains that were threatening to overwhelm him.

I went through another wave, popped out the back of that, made it to the surface, and I looked around and there was Campbell. And he looked at me, and I looked at him . . . except he was just white, he was completely no blood, bloodless face, virtually. So we swam to each other and I grabbed him and he was just dead weight of 80-odd kilos . . . He couldn't help me very much. I noticed his face was very badly smashed in: nose, jaw, teeth, eye socket was completely crushed in . . . He wasn't making much sense at all. So I put him in the harness.

Key still didn't know where the helicopter was, or if he was attached to it, but he went through the drill anyway. In the rough conditions he wasn't able to fasten the rescue strop around Campbell correctly, so when he was as ready as he'd ever be he got a good grip on Campbell and raised his hand to indicate he wanted to be winched up. It was then that he noticed the cable was wrapped around his leg. He knew that if they started to lift him, the wire would slice off his leg like a guillotine. So he frantically tried to disentangle himself.

And next second we were just jerked out of the water. We got hit by the face of another wave, we sort of went three-quarters of the way through that and popped out, and I looked up and there's the belly of the helicopter, you know, it's the best sight I've ever seen . . . So I thought, 'Beauty, we're out of here.' And just up near the belly of the helicopter towards the top of the winch there was a sudden jerk and I knew what that was. That was a winch freeze . . . That's not a good position to be in because the only thing they can do is, if they can't get you in, they just cut you off, because they can't fly back a distance with people hanging out. We would just have frozen to death anyway . . . So I just hung there, and I looked up at Barry and his eyes were like saucers.

In the chopper Jones and Barclay worked frantically to get the winch working, but it refused to budge. Key, meanwhile, was losing his grip on Campbell, who was starting to slip back down towards the sea. Finally, Barclay gave up on the winch and improvised. Attached to the chopper by a harness and a 'wander lead', a length of wire cable, he leaned out of the door of the chopper, his entire weight supported on the lead. He reached down and grabbed hold of Campbell's long johns. He then dead lifted all 80 kilograms up and into the chopper. It was a manoeuvre they don't teach at rescue school. It probably only works when you're running on pure adrenalin.

Key was too heavy to lift, so he and Barclay considered what to do next. They were discussing heading back to *Kingurra* and dropping him near enough to get picked up when, finally, the winch started working again.

Key got back into the aircraft, they shut the door and started heading for home. Jones radioed an elated *Kingurra* with the good news while his two crewmen huddled around the hypothermic Campbell to keep him warm.

However, while *Polair 1* was saving Campbell, the winds were getting stronger. As he headed into them, Jones calculated he had enough fuel to fly for another eighty minutes and that it would take forty minutes to reach land. After thirty minutes, though, he realised he had a problem. At the rate he was going, it was still going to take forty minutes to get back to land. His safety margin was rapidly shrinking. As he describes it, choppers 'have the glide ratio of a brick and once the power stops you only go one way.' While he tried to nurse the fuel consumption, he mentioned his concerns to the crew, who unknown to him started working out plans for ditching in the sea. Key and Barclay attached themselves to Campbell and a life raft, planning to leap out of the chopper at the top of a wave then pick up Jones if he got out of the aircraft once it ditched. Twenty minutes from land, a wind squall of 110 knots (203 kilometres/hour) came through. For ten minutes the chopper barely made any progress. The safety margin was all but gone.

We got to a point about 8 nautical miles [14 kilometres] from Gabo Island and I had a fuel warning light come on, on number 1 side . . . When the fuel warning light comes on, you've got five minutes left in the fuel tank . . . I didn't say anything to David or Barry, they had enough to do [Key was by this stage vomiting seawater] . . .

When we got to the south-west of Gabo Island, probably 6, 7 to 8 [nautical] miles . . . I thought that what I would do was maybe try and take a bit of advantage of this wind and save us all having to go for a swim if we did run out of fuel. I turned the aircraft and basically let the wind sail us across like a kite. We covered 7 or 8 miles in about seven or eight seconds. It felt like that anyway . . . I then had us within touch of land.

Jones continued stretching the range of the chopper. His confidence in landing on the ground was increasing, but much of the area around the township of Mallacoota is uninhabited and inaccessible. Conscious that setting down just anywhere might cost the rescue effort another chopper to refuel him, he tried to make it to civilisation.

I gave up the option of going for the aerodrome which was about 3 [nautical] miles [6 kilometres] to the west of the township and got the aircraft in on the football oval . . . I'd been flying for the five minutes on number 1 and as I was putting the wheels on the ground I was actually waiting for number 1 to flame out on me. Number 2 fuel light had been on for about three-and-a-half minutes at that time. So I think there was probably just vapours left in number 1 and not much else left in number 2.

Polair 1's crew were more than happy to be back on the ground, as Key recalls:

The three of us got out and we just stood there in silence once we'd shut down . . . I kissed it. I went down and kissed the ground . . . I've done hundreds of rescues and that was the most atrocious conditions we've been in . . . And then just all of a sudden there was this little tap on the window, and inside the helicopter it was Campbell. He was saying, 'Can I hop out now?'

While the *Kingurra* rescue was going on, *Zeus II* was dismasted north of Gabo Island and making for Eden under a jury rig. *Liquid*

Asset was running for shelter at Eden. And the Rescue Centre had spoken to the Navy. Up in Sydney the frigate HMAS *Newcastle* was rapidly preparing for sea. At Nowra, further down the coast, two Sea King helicopters capable of night rescue were being fuelled for immediate deployment.

At 7.06 p.m. an aircraft homed in on the emergency beacon on the dismasted yacht *B52*. The 15 000-tonne merchant vessel *Iron Monarch* was diverted to her location, though there was little she could do in the giant seas.

Of course, retiring from the race didn't mean a yacht was in any less danger than a boat that was still racing. First it had to make it to the safety of a port. *Sword of Orion* had spent the latter part of the afternoon heading north towards Eden. Her skipper later commented that he'd experienced a lull before the wind returned, suggesting he might have passed through the eye of the east-coast low. Had he treated the weather system like a cyclone, he might have kept going south, into the less ferocious south-west quadrant. Instead, he turned north, to run with the wind and waves, back into the most vicious quadrant of the storm.

Crewman and British Olympic yachtsman Glyn Charles was on the helm, trying to head *Sword of Orion* towards Eden. However, as it was for many other yachts trying desperately to escape the storm, the sea was dictating the course. It wasn't safe to head across the wind-whipped masses of water, so Charles had to steer into and over them. And then he got caught. An enormous wave towered beside the yacht before throwing it down its face. When the yacht hit the bottom, the breaking wave swept over the yacht, rolling it completely. The force of the water swept the boom, which had been firmly lashed to the starboard side of the boat, across the deck. It took out the steering wheel and Charles with it. Then it snapped his harness like it wasn't there, washing him overboard.

Somehow the yacht stayed afloat, but it wasn't going anywhere.

The mast was snapped, wires trailing around the prop. Anyway there was no steering. Darren Senogles was also on deck when the wave struck, but had managed to stay on board. He started shouting, 'Man overboard' as the rest of the crew struggled up from the cabin. Charles was conscious but suffering terrible injuries. He tried to swim a few strokes back to the boat, clearly in extreme pain. The crew tried to throw a life ring to him, but the ferocious gale simply threw it back in their faces. Then Senogles, a bowman, tied a rope around his waist, to dive in to get Charles, but his crewmates feared he'd be lost as well. They stopped him just before another wave hit and pushed *Sword of Orion* 100 metres from the floating man. Soon they couldn't see Charles at all.

Sword of Orion's skipper, Rob Kothe, badly battered in the roll and fearing the partially submerged boat was about to sink, tried to call a mayday. He got no reply. So he activated his EPIRB. A fixed-wing aircraft searching for *Winston Churchill* nearby picked it up and homed in. Pilot Neal Boag got close enough to hear on his radio that *Sword* had a man overboard. He called the Rescue Centre, which added yet another desperate situation to the growing list of crises. In Canberra the realisation dawned: they'd run out of choppers. *Helimed 1* and *South Care* were battling back to shore. *Polair 1* was battling to save John Campbell. The Navy Sea Kings were still being prepared to head south.

All the rescuers could do was assign the fixed-wing aircraft on scene to try to locate Charles, but the weather was so bad that the pilot had to abandon his search. The winds were so violent, the clouds so low, that visibility was almost nil and his plane was in danger of being slapped out of the sky. All he could do was drop a couple of beacons to mark the position and Charles's possible drift.

Not long after, the yacht *Margaret Rintoul* passed nearby. The dismasted *Sword* lit flares to attract her attention but the boat, to their dismay, continued on without acknowledging them. The law of the sea requires all vessels to render assistance to vessels in distress. As a court case dating from 1820 says 'none but a freebooter would withhold it.' However, they're not required to do so if it endangers the vessel going to the rescue. Unknown to the crew of the stricken *Sword*, *Margaret Rintoul* had no engine, and her skipper believed that trying to manoeuvre around *Sword* under sail would have added his boat to the list of casualties.

He attempted to signal *Sword* with a torch and instructed his radio operator to alert race control. Race control responded that they had quite a bit going on and would get back to *Margaret Rintoul*. When they didn't, the radio operator turned off his radio and the yacht continued on its way south. No attempt was made to call *Sword*. The radio operator didn't volunteer the information to race control that the decision had been made not to assist. There is no record of race control being told that *Margaret Rintoul* had actually seen a dismasted yacht.

The New South Wales Coroner later concluded that by the time *Margaret Rintoul* passed, Glyn Charles was probably beyond help, and that she would have been justified in a decision not to render assistance. However, he expressed the view that, at least to allay the fears of *Sword*'s crew, the skipper of *Margaret Rintoul* 'should have ordered and controlled the attempt to communicate with *Sword of Orion*, if by no more than an acknowledging flare, and displayed the conduct reasonably expected from Masters of vessels.'

If you're interested in reading more of this in the Coroner's Report, it is on the Net at http://www.equipped.org under 'Survival Stories.'

Darkness was falling early, although in the southern latitudes in December it's normally light after 8.30 p.m. There was no sign of the rafts from *Winston Churchill*. And still the list of broken vessels grew. At 7.42 p.m. *Rapscallion* radioed she was still battling towards Eden, now with injured crew. At 8.06 *Jubilation* was still heading for Eden to shelter. Five minutes later *Adrenalin* headed to Eden for shelter. Five minutes later, *Dixie Chicken* retired. A minute later *Gundy Grey* was thrown over on her side. She'd lost her life raft, injured her crew and started for Eden.

Also in Eden, two police officers had visited the home of Lachlan Marshall, fishing boat manager, to see if there were any trawlers that could tow vessels like *Team Jaguar* back to Eden. Most of Eden's fishing fleet was tucked safely in port. The local crews had read the weather report and decided it was no place for their solidly built vessels of up to 200 tonnes. However, Marshall had two vessels out, one of which, the *Moira Elizabeth*, was on its way to Portland, Victoria, when it was forced to shelter behind Gabo Island. He called the *Moira Elizabeth*'s skipper, Tom Bibby, who told him the seas were extremely dangerous, but that he would do what he could. His estimated time of arrival at *Team Jaguar*'s position was three hours.

As the darkness of night fell, the winds still howled and tore the sea into savage streaks of foam. However, at 8.43 p.m., the yacht *97* reported wind at 12 knots (22 kilometres/hour) from the south. The yacht was practically becalmed. She may have been passing through the eye of the storm, as *Sword* had done earlier in the day. Elsewhere, vessels were still being battered. At 8.55 p.m. *Bright Morning Star* headed for Eden. At 9.06 p.m. *Terra Firma* did the same.

In the darkness, vessels started reporting distress flares from a multitude of positions and directions. In the darkness they only added to the mounting confusion of radio traffic, emergency beacons and maydays. At least the choppers were getting back to the fleet. *Helimed 1* was refuelled and searching for *Winston Churchill*'s crew. The trawler *Moira Elizabeth* had arrived at *Team Jaguar*'s position, but couldn't sight anything. *Team Jaguar* fired flares, which *Moira Elizabeth* couldn't see. At a loss as to what to do, Tom Bibby decided that since he'd come all the way out there he might as well go searching. In the conditions he was experiencing it took courage bigger than the waves that were rolling his vessel and had already washed a quantity of his fishing gear overboard.

At 9.30 p.m. the yachts *Henry Kendall* and *Southerly* reported flares. At 10.18 p.m. the trawler *Moira Elizabeth* fired a flare to attract the attention of *Team Jaguar*. It was seen instead by the relay vessel *Young Endeavour*, which was searching for the crew of *Winston Churchill*. *Team Jaguar* was adrift somewhere nearby. At the same time the yacht *Lady Penrhyn* sighted a flare. Not long after *Hummingbird*, *Adagio* and *Southerly* sighted flares. At 10.45 p.m. *Henry Kendall* again sighted a flare, while *Hummingbird* decided they'd had enough and turned for Eden.

In the darkness, though, unknown to anyone, one yacht was in the grip of a catastrophe. *Business Post Naiad* had already been rolled and dismasted and had requested helicopter evacuation of some of her crew. There were simply not enough choppers to help her, or in the darkness find crew as they tried to limp under motor towards Gabo Island against waves that were pushing them further out to sea. Two of the crew who'd been on deck during the first roll, Rob Matthews and Phil Skeggs, had been forced back on deck to relieve their exhausted crewmates when, around 11 p.m., *Naiad* got hit again. This time, though, when she rolled, she stayed upside down.

As water poured in below decks, mixing with oil and diesel fuel spewing from the inverted engine, the two men on deck fought to free themselves from the harnesses that kept them attached to the boat, but were now threatening to drown them. 'I was under there for a long while; I was under there too long,' said Matthews. 'I was out of air and the boat got thrown up in the air by another wave and a little pocket of air appeared and I just took a last gasp.'

With the little breath left to him, Matthews managed to get free, then grabbed hold of the ropes trailing behind the yacht. Inside, the crew could hear him calling to Phil Skeggs. All they could do was wait in terror, expecting the boat to sink, taking them with it. Matthews, meanwhile, had spotted the keel standing up from the hull, and had a thought that they'd all end up like solo yachtsman Thierry Dubois, rescued the year before in the Southern Ocean after clinging to his keel for more than a day (Chapter 12). Reaching the keel was another matter, but as he swam around the boat he found what he thought was the boom (later found to be the mast) sticking out beside the hull, which gave him a place to sit and rest.

He recalled: 'I just sat there for a few minutes, and then another big rolly wave came through and it got the boat back upright again and because I was sitting on the end of the boom, I actually ended up in the place that I had started off, plonked back in the cockpit.'

It was a simple matter to clip his harness back on. Then he saw Phil Skeggs. He was just near the helm, entangled in a mass of ropes. He'd been trapped beneath the boat the whole time it was inverted, and he wasn't breathing. Matthews started yelling for someone to help resuscitate Skeggs. Down below, however, the crew were waist-deep in water and fearful that the boat was sinking. Skipper Bruce Guy and Steve Walker were struggling up the companionway ladder when Guy suddenly went rigid and fell backwards into the water. Walker caught him and lifted his head above the surface. It was clear he was having a heart attack, but there was little that could be done for him. He died while Walker cradled his head in his lap, then he was placed in one of the bunks.

Up on deck, the crew deployed the life raft while others started CPR on Skeggs. Three of them worked for half an hour, trying to revive him, to no avail. The water having shorted the electrical system, *Naiad*'s crew was without communications. They fired flares, to which there was no response. They bailed as much water as they could and waited – to sink or be rescued, they didn't know.

Solo Globe Challenger was also on her own. The plucky yacht *Pippin* had been unable to stay with her, and rescue hadn't come. Her crew had managed to cut the mast away and, with just over a metre of it protruding above her deck, she was still doing up to 4 knots (7 kilometres/hour), running with the seas. Her skipper, Tony Mowbray, would have preferred to head into them, but without any real steerage, he had little choice.

With his other helmsman injured and his crew helping him as much as they could, Mowbray had been at the wheel for hour after hour, fighting to save their lives.

I and my crew spent that time in constant fear of our life. Every wave we encountered, we felt that there could be one lurking next that would put us under or finish it off. We had one wave that just literally threw us down the face and broke on us. We surfed down the face of the wave at this incredible speed. My boat weighs about eight-and-a-half tonne. It's 43 feet [13 metres] long. And I was standing up steering and it just completely engulfed the boat in white water and only my chest was clear of the water. My crew that were sitting in front of me in the cockpit were completely underwater and the whole boat was submerged under water and all I could see was just the top of the stainless-steel pulpit at the front of the boat as we're hurtling down the face of the wave. And I felt that that was the one that would finish us off.

Elsewhere in the fleet, exhaustion was also taking its toll. The yacht *Miintinta* had been heading to Eden since mid-afternoon with an injured crewman. Then she'd fallen off four big waves. On the last one it felt like she'd hit something, though it may have been the hull below the water-line finally succumbing to the constant pounding.

In any case, soon after it was obvious the yacht was taking water and despite a concerted search, her crew couldn't find where it was coming in. Up to that point the boat had been under a few scraps of sail and motoring, but then the engine overheated and failed. As the water rose, the loss of the engine meant the electric pumps couldn't be used. The crew started operating the manual pump. When that failed, they used buckets and cups. At times they got ahead of the inflow, at others they'd hit a big sea and the boat would fill. For hour after hour they bailed, until they started losing the fight to keep the boat afloat. At which point, they called for help.

Once again, the police visited the Eden fishermen. Lachlan Marshall's other fishing boat, the 20-metre *Josephine Jean*, was fishing close inshore, where it was more sheltered and she could run for port if the storm turned. The *Josephine Jean*'s skipper was Ollie Hreinsson, who had learned to fish in the feared waters of Iceland and the North Sea. Asked later if he would have gone to sea in the conditions the yachts had confronted, he replied: 'No way. There's easier way to die than do that. That is suicide to go out . . . on the big boat, a work, big boat. That sort of weather on the little yacht, that, that is suicide.'

Nevertheless, he agreed to head out to *Miintinta*. She'd at first reported that she could see the lights of Eden, but gave her position as 42 miles (68 kilometres) east. Whatever lights she'd seen weren't Eden. Nearby, trying to home in on her was the container ship *Union Rotomar*. In the wind, spray, and turbulent ocean they may have mistaken the ship's lights for the safety of port. The massive ship eventually located the yacht and with great difficulty held station nearby until, around midnight, the *Josephine Jean* arrived to take *Miintinta* under tow.

As the night wore on, more yachts retired. *Tenacious* was knocked down at 12.03 a.m., *Boomaroo* headed for Eden two minutes later. Noted in the *Young Endeavour*'s radio log with a touch of irony was a message from the yacht *Avanti*: 'Racing to Hobart!!' At the time, *Young Endeavour* had been forced to heave to, having shredded several sails in wind gusts of 65 knots (120 kilometres/hour).

In those conditions, the trawler *Moira Elizabeth* continued to search for *Team Jaguar*. The *Josephine Jean* had *Miintinta* under tow. At the Rescue Centre in Canberra no-one was getting any sleep. The number of incoming calls was already in the thousands. Two officers were drawing up the search patterns and instructions for dozens of aircraft that would take off at first light. Other aircraft were in the air, including the Navy Sea Kings and several fixed-wing aircraft. One of the Sea Kings had managed to locate *Sword of Orion* and fix her position before heading back to shore to refuel. *Naiad*'s EPIRB had also been detected and a fixed-wing aircraft had been dispatched to home in on it.

Considerable thought was also being given to the position of *Winston Churchill*. There was still no sign and it was decided that the yacht spotted during daylight and identified as *Winston Churchill* was most likely *Stand Aside*. The decision was made to shift the search area further north, but still over an enormous area of turbulent ocean.

At around 3 a.m., the officer-on-watch on *Young Endeavour* stuck his head into the radio room where the operators were talking to the trawler *Moira Elizabeth*. Did the operators know there was a large trawler alongside *Young Endeavour* trying to throw them a line? Tom Bibby had thought he'd found *Team Jaguar*, although he'd wondered why it had three masts instead of one. It had been a very long night for the crew of the *Moira Elizabeth*.

Not far away, though, *Team Jaguar* could see *Young Endeavour* and *Moira Elizabeth*. Finally, after nearly twelve hours in seas that had frequently threatened to roll and sink the trawler, *Moira Elizabeth* reached *Team Jaguar* and got her under tow.

Just a few kilometres away, in the rain, spray, wind and waves, the crew of *Winston Churchill* had been enduring hour after hour in the storm-tossed life rafts – four in one, five in the other. The rafts had started out tied together, but the tethers couldn't stand the pressure of the seas, and they'd soon parted. The four-man life raft was rolled twice, once in the afternoon and again at night. Each time, *Winston Churchill*'s skipper, Richard Winning, risked his life to go outside and right the raft. Had he been washed clear by a wave, he'd have been lost forever.

The larger life raft was also rolled, but her occupants decided it was too dangerous to go outside and try to right it. The problem was, the inverted raft had no air vents and the men soon realised they were in danger of suffocation. It was later found that had they done nothing, they'd have drowned within minutes, when they lost consciousness and slumped into the water. Instead they decided to cut a slit in the floor (now their roof) to let in some air.

Minutes later, another wave capsized the raft again, righting it. And then, no matter what they did, the hole in the floor widened until all five were left in little more than a rubber ring, the remains of their raft. The men clung to the edges for hours, until, without warning, they were picked up and thrown headlong by another wave. When it passed, there were only two men, John Stanley and John Gibson, still holding the life raft. Michael Bannister, James Lawler and John Dean were alone somewhere in the darkness.

At 3.20 p.m., the Navy Sea King returned to *Sword of Orion*, lifting three of her most injured crew to safety. The other Sea King was using her night-vision capabilities to search for the men from *Winston Churchill*. At 4 a.m., HMAS *Newcastle* put to sea, racing south to join the search and rescue effort. A fixed-wing aircraft had also located *Naiad,* and was circling until a chopper could reach her. On shore, more aircrews were preparing their planes and helicopters to head back out to sea at first light. The storm was abating, but large waves were still wreaking havoc with the vessels that were disabled or struggling to reach port.

At 5.55 a.m. the crew of *Miintinta* could bail no more. The trawler *Josephine Jean* had been creeping forward at about a knot (1.85 kilometres/hour) into the giant seas, towing *Miintinta*. At that rate it was going to take forty hours to reach safety, and they realised they just couldn't keep bailing for that long.

Yet it was impossible to go any faster. The tow-line had already torn the bollard off the yacht's bow and they were trying to keep the tow attached as best they could. The decision was made to abandon the yacht. *Josephine Jean* manoeuvred skilfully to position herself downwind from the yacht, and the crew took to the life raft. They were blown down to the *Josephine Jean* where they were all recovered successfully.

At about the same time, the remaining crew were lifted from *Sword of Orion*. She was never seen again.

It was now daylight on Monday, 28 December. The length of the New South Wales coast was full of holiday-makers looking at the weather to decide whether they'd be going to the beach or curling up with a good book. Rock fishermen were risking the heavy swell to catch their dinner. Small-boat fishermen were checking the weather forecasts and weighing the risks of heading out to their favourite reefs. Overhead, some thirty-eight aircraft were already en route to their designated search areas for the victims of the Sydney to Hobart Yacht Race.

Down on the water, the rescues continued. Tracking an EPIRB, two fixed-wing aircraft had picked up a dismasted yacht. *Midnight Special* had been rolled at around 8.30 the night before. She'd lost her radios and engine, so her crew activated the emergency beacon and bailed the boat out as best they could. The *South Care* chopper, with fresh crew, was tasked to the scene.

She'd winched two crew when *Midnight Special* was hit by another wave and rolled. This time she stayed upside down for some thirty seconds, with two crew underneath and the boat filling with water below decks. Then she was hit by another wave and righted herself. The cockpit hatch had been torn off and waves were now coming over the top of the boat, and pouring below. *South Care* took off three more men and then headed for shore. *Polair 1*, with the same crew that had saved John Campbell the previous afternoon, raced to the scene to get the remaining crew before *Midnight Special* went down.

Again David Key went down on the winch, and had the first person he was to rescue jump into the water and swim to him.

His head immediately went under the water, so the top of the life jacket was on the water, but because it was around the chest part he'd actually sunk below the height of the life jacket. He was actually under the water while he was swimming towards me and he was battling to stay afloat . . .

We took the first fellow up to the aircraft. I went back down, beckoned the second fellow; that was no great problem either. The only problem I had was probably ingesting a bit of salt water again. And all these people had injuries – bits of fingers missing, skull lacerations – because they'd been thrown around inside or on top of the boat when it rolled.

The first two lifts had been almost routine. By now the rescuers were becoming experienced in winching people in extreme conditions, but it was during the third lift that things began to go wrong. It was obvious that *Midnight Special* was starting to go down, and the third man leapt from the boat in panic. 'He came to me, and we were hit by a wave at the same time,' recalled Key, 'and I actually got kneed in the stomach and areas there below, and as a male that can tend to be a little bit winding. I was pushed under water, took a bit more salt water in.'

Key still managed to get the man up into the chopper. As pilot Daryl Jones recalled:

We did three and at the end of the third one Barry actually said to me over the intercom 'Go for a fly.' And I said, 'What do you mean, go for a fly? There's four, isn't there?' He said, 'Yeah, just go for a fly.' And I had a look back over my shoulder and I could see why. David was totally out of breath, he was vomiting seawater . . . We just had to give him a break for a minute to catch his breath.

He wasn't the only one having problems, as Key realised:

Daryl was starting to cramp up, because this was about twenty minutes this was taking so far. So we went for a fly through the mist. He's locked into a position, he's fighting that machine . . . so it was probably a good time for the lot of us to go for a bit of a fly . . .

We actually flew around in a circle, came back and went straight back out, back down, and when I beckoned for the fellow to jump, he just looked at me, and I'm sort of waving at him to jump. He just looked at me, and then sort of had a stunned look, jumped into the water. I harnessed him up, there was no great problem there, and as we were being winched up, it went under. The boat sank.

We got up to the helicopter and when we were speaking to him he thought we'd left him because he saw us fly off into the mist, and thought, 'Well, he was the skipper and he was going down with the yacht.' And I'm sitting there going, 'Bloody hell, you know. That's a gutsy effort.'

An hour later, the seven surviving crew of *Business Post Naiad* were airlifted by the Careflight chopper. The two crewmen who had died were left aboard and the yacht was later located by HMAS

Newcastle and towed to Eden by the police launch *Nemesis*, which had also put out from Sydney. By now there were thirty-eight fixed-wing aircraft and five helicopters operating in the area off Eden, searching for missing yachts, EPIRBs, *Winston Churchill*'s rafts and the man overboard from *Sword of Orion*, Glyn Charles.

From *Polair 1*'s experience with John Campbell, hopes for his survival were slim. The *Polair* crew were certain that the injured Campbell had been moments from drowning after being in the water for under an hour. Charles, also injured, had been in the water for more than twelve hours. No-one knew, at that stage, that three crew from *Winston Churchill* were also in the water, and two more were partially immersed, clinging to the remains of their raft.

During the night, *Solo Globe Challenger* had been swept far out to sea. They'd originally been about 30 miles (48 kilometres) offshore. By morning they were 120 miles (193 kilometres) offshore. The Careflight chopper went to the furthest extent of its offshore range and homed in on *Solo Globe Challenger*'s EPIRB. When Careflight found her, Mowbray was still at the helm he'd taken at 4.30 p.m. the day before. The Careflight chopper lifted three of the injured crew to safety, but Mowbray and the remaining four were determined to save the boat.

Down below, the two crewmen with broken ribs were working to revive the engine. Later, Mowbray and another crewman used the yacht's spinnaker poles to construct a jury rig.

Back in Eden, the little fishing village looked like a battlefield: its docks littered with smashed boats and people. Ambulances were transporting the seriously injured to hospital.

Early on that Monday morning, an officer at the Rescue Centre in Canberra contemplated the already stretched rescue resources and the massive search being undertaken to find the missing crewmen from *Winston Churchill* and *Sword of Orion*. He suggested to his colleague at race control in Hobart, Sam Hughes, that under the circumstances the race should be abandoned.

However, calling off Australia's premier yachting event wasn't that easy, and it was argued that the damage was already done. As the sun rose, though, the two deaths on *Business Post Naiad* were confirmed. Hopes for Glyn Charles were all but gone. And there was no sign of the nine crew from *Winston Churchill*. Twelve people were either dead or unaccounted for and the largest search and rescue operation in Australia's history was in progress. Yet the race continued. One can only wonder how many lives it would have taken for it to have been called off.

While the rescues continued, the yacht *Siena*, with her injured crewman, finally sighted land. She'd been unable to fight her way west to Eden and had been forced further north, eventually reaching the township of Bermagui at midday. There it was found that the injured crewman had lost 60 per cent of capacity in one lung and pneumonia had set in. He was operated on immediately and eventually recovered.

Meanwhile, the search aircraft flew mission after mission. Many of the aircrews were approaching exhaustion, as were the rescue coordinators in Canberra and along the coast. HMAS *Newcastle* was by then on scene, tasked to search for *Winston Churchill* and assist *Solo Globe Challenger*. Then, at 5.30 p.m., the hours of effort were rewarded. A raft was sighted 60 nautical miles (111 kilometres) east-south-east of Eden. Once again *Helimed 1* found itself winching four survivors from the Tasman Sea.

On board *Helimed 1*, the *Winston Churchill*'s survivors told the aircrew that five others were in a second life raft somewhere nearby. The survivors also found out why it had taken more than a day to find them, even though they had an EPIRB. When it was first activated, aircraft hadn't been able to track it down among the multitude going off at the time. Not long after, the aerial had been broken off as the life raft was tossed in the violent seas. The device had been rendered useless.

As the men were flown back to shore, the search for the second raft intensified in the area where the first had been found. The rescuers didn't know that all that was left of it were two black rings to which two men were clinging. And elsewhere, three crewmen were adrift with the aid of only their life jackets. Still the aircraft searched. In the gathering gloom, the sky was crisscrossed by dozens of aircraft. Thousands of square kilometres were searched and re-searched for any trace of more survivors.

Then, down in the whitecaps and rolling waves, there was the faintest flash of light. It was just a glimmer but one of the aircraft dipped closer to investigate. And there it was again. A tiny light shone upwards from the vast darkness of the ocean below.

John Gibson was holding up a small personal strobe light. John Stanley was shining a torch. As the aircraft approached them, it turned on its wing lights to signal that they'd been seen. At 9.30 p.m., some twenty-eight hours after the *Winston Churchill* sank and about sixteen hours after they'd been left clinging to the remains of their raft, Stanley and Gibson were picked up by a Navy Sea King helicopter.

The following morning, the bodies of Michael Bannister and Jim Lawler were recovered from the sea. The bodies of John Dean and Glyn Charles were never found.

At 9.30 p.m. on Tuesday, 29 December, HMAS *Newcastle* rendez-voused with *Solo Globe Challenger* some 220 kilometres out to sea and sent an inflatable to pick up the remaining crew. By then though, Mowbray and his injured crew had all but stripped and rebuilt their engine. Just as *Newcastle* arrived, they got the thing going, strengthening their resolve to save their vessel. The inflatable informed them that *Challenger*'s insurance company had chartered a fishing vessel to tow the boat back to Eden. By then the conditions were easing, so two of the injured crew were taken to the *Newcastle*, while Mowbray and two others remained aboard to await the arrival of the trawler *Rubicon*.

At the end of the race, a memorial service was held in Hobart for the six men who had lost their lives. Approximately fifty-three people were injured. During the searches and rescues, some forty-five aircraft logged more than 500 hours in the air. A total of fifty-five people were airlifted from yachts. Five yachts sank: *Stand Aside*, *Winston Churchill*, *Miintinta*, *Midnight Special* and *Sword of Orion*. Out of 115 yachts, 71 (three-fifths) didn't complete the race. Three ships were involved in rescues, as were several trawlers. The Rescue Centre in Canberra dealt with 3466 phone calls in coordinating the search and rescue, and handling inquiries from next-of-kin and media. The cost of the rescue effort was estimated at over $1 million. A fund was set up to assist the families of those lost. The father of John Campbell donated $US25 000 to the fund, in honour of the air-crew of *Polair 1*.

In the aftermath, what was supposed to be a sports event came to be regarded as a disaster, the definition used by the New South Wales Coroner being an incident involving the loss of five or more lives. As Tony Mowbray, skipper of the yacht *Solo Globe Challenger*, put it: 'The devil took me by the hand and showed me the edge of hell.'

The Inquiry held into the deaths was substantially more compre-hensive than that for, say, the loss of the *Dunbar* (see Chapter 6). Dozens of sailors, rescuers and expert witnesses were interviewed. The brief of evidence ran to thirty volumes, with hearings extend-ing for over thirty days. The Coroner's report, released two years after the disaster, was 341 pages long, compared to the Dunbar's 142-word paragraph.

Since the race, a raft of changes have been made to the entry requirements for yachts entering Australian ocean races – better life jackets, harnesses, rafts, crew training, yacht identification, weather reporting, weather understanding and communications. Meanwhile, the rules of sailing continue to be unequivocal on the decision to race. Fundamental rule of sailing No. 4, from the International Sailing Federation (ISAF) states: 'The responsibility for a boat's decision to participate in a race or to continue racing is hers alone.'

Yet the 1998 Sydney to Hobart demonstrated how, in the competitive environment of a race, a skipper isn't necessarily in the best position to judge when it is prudent to stop racing. And when the boat does realise its danger, it may be too late to reach safety. Meanwhile, racing provides inducements to participation that have nothing to do with seamanship – trophies, prizes and fame among them. In many instances, boats are actually penalised for retiring, through the scoring system for the event. These are some of the reasons why, in 1998, 115 yachts sailed unflinchingly towards a situation most would normally have sought to avoid.

Yet what is surprising is that the ISAF has long recognised that the decision to race is not the boat's alone. In its *Race Management Manual* several sections deal with the decision to abandon racing and, in its recommendations on race management policy, it offers the opinion that if lives are at risk the event should be stopped immediately.

That makes it a decision for the organisers and it was this manual that the Sydney to Hobart organisers used as a guide to running the 1998 event. Though as their own report puts it:

The responsibilities of this Committee [the race committee] are presented in ISAF *Race Management Manual* Section 2.3. This manual is more specifically targeted at regatta sailing organisations rather than long offshore racing. The Chairman of the Committee was unsure of the precise responsibilities of the Committee as a result.

The New South Wales Coroner was more succinct in describing
the committee as 'practically useless' and 'valueless' at the time of
crisis.

Since 1998, the Sydney to Hobart organisers have put in place
a crisis plan as part of a greatly upgraded and constantly reviewed
Race Management Plan. The Race Management Committee now
includes far greater levels of expertise, including, to date, two former
Australian Navy admirals. While there are no specific guidelines to
cover every contingency, the skills and judgement of the Race Committee, substantially upgraded weather prediction and information
services, and the lessons of 1998 suggest that much higher levels of
safety are in place for the running of future Sydney to Hobarts. The
test will come, though, with the next prediction of say, 50-knot winds
(93 kilometres/hour) and 10-metre waves, a day or two into a race.
And knowing Bass Strait, that test will come. Will the race be abandoned or perhaps modified to Leg 1: Sydney to Eden until the storm
blows over; Leg 2: Eden to Hobart?

In 2001, another yacht race was due to start from Sydney Harbour,
bound for Southport in Queensland. However, a massive east-coast
low was battering the coast with such ferocity that Sydneysiders
flocked to the cliffs and beaches to witness nature's awesome fury,
just as they'd done in 1857 after the wreck of the *Dunbar*.

The onshore gale was tearing so much spray off the sea and hurling it up the cliffs, it was like a fire hose drenching the spectators.
For all their modern navigation aids and propulsion systems, several
ships were forced to stay at sea as the harbour pilots were unable to
board them to bring them into port. When a motor cruiser trying
to head south was sunk and a cruising yacht to the north was rolled

and abandoned, the decision was made to delay the start of the Sydney to Southport Race.

Australia has changed beyond recognition since 1621, when the original skipper chosen to command the ship that became Australia's first shipwreck couldn't convince his wife to let him go (see Chapter 1). Some 380 years later, a modern nation has mapped most of its coastline in meticulous detail and dotted it with lighthouses marking many of the hazards that once struck fear into mariners. Satellites sweep overhead, sensors pricked for every signal of distress, while dedicated rescue services wait on permanent standby.

Yet, as the 1998 Sydney to Hobart Yacht Race showed, there is still much to be learned about the safe navigation of Australian waters. There is still cause to fret when relatives or friends risk the open sea. Every time we sail, our keels pass over a maritime heritage that reaches back to the beginnings of the nation's history. As we log voyages in and out with rescue services, some are based at sites that have been operating since the beginning of European settlement. We're protected by layers of safety that have been built up over the centuries. However, if history teaches us anything, it is to take nothing for granted. Much has changed, but the sea has remained the same. It is still the harshest teacher of all.

EPILOGUE:
AND STILL THEY COME

On 18 October 2001, some 420 men, women and children, most of them fleeing the tyranny of Saddam Hussein's Iraq, but others from troubled countries like Iran, Palestine and Algeria, crowded aboard an unseaworthy 19-metre vessel in the Indonesian port of Lampung, Sumatra. The boat then headed south, probably intending to make for the Australian territory of Christmas Island.

As the vessel left port it was leaking badly, and its two engines were working hard to keep the pumps ahead of the inflowing water. The vessel's condition was so poor that twenty-four passengers soon demanded to be let off, despite having paid $7900 each for the voyage. They were dropped on a small island. The following day, having reached international waters, one of the boat's engines failed while the vessel was in rough seas, and efforts to restart it failed. The vessel immediately began to founder. It took just ten minutes for the Suspected Illegal Entry Vessel (SIEV-X), which was carrying only seventy life jackets, to go down.

Despite surveillance by Australian and Indonesian authorities that had been tracking the vessel from the time it left port, the survivors spent between twenty-two and thirty hours in Indonesia's zone of search and rescue responsibility. By the time rescue vessels (Indonesian fishing boats investigating wreckage that was drifting from the site of the sinking) started picking people up, 353 had died – 146 children, 142 women and 65 men.

The similarities with many of the shipwrecks of the preceding 379 years were many. The ship was unfit for the voyage she'd undertaken,

like the leaky *Sydney Cove*. She was carrying people who were out-
casts from the world, like the thousands aboard the many convict
ships. And the accounts survivors gave were as distressing as any
given by the survivors of the *Cataraqui* or the *Quetta*. Their testi-
monies can be found on the web site http://www.sievx.com

The difference between SIEV-X and almost all the wrecks that pre-
ceded it were that few people in the country the vessel had left, or the
one it was headed for, really cared. The Australian Government in
particular had waged a prolonged campaign to characterise boat
people as 'queue jumpers', 'possible terrorists' and 'illegal immigrants.'
Asylum seekers on an earlier vessel were falsely accused of throwing
their own children overboard to force their rescue. Consequently, the
victims having been portrayed as morally inferior to decent human
beings, there was almost no outcry for the lives of those lost.

There is no doubt the loss of the vessel was primarily the fault of
people smugglers, who put profit before human life, and sent an
unseaworthy vessel into a situation that put everyone aboard at
grave risk. Yet the Australian and Indonesian governments haven't
adequately explained why it was impossible to rescue the survivors,
especially after an Australian navy frigate had demonstrated it could
sail almost to Antarctica to rescue yachtsmen Tony Bullimore and
Thierry Dubois. Even more disturbing, it appears that both governments had been involved in people-smuggling disruption activities,
up to and including sabotage of vessels, according to one of the
Australian government's paid agents in Indonesia. While the Indonesian government cancelled the program in September 2001, it has
been reported that the People Smuggling Taskforce in the Australian
Prime Minister's Department had directed agencies to 'beef up' the
disruption program a week before SIEV-X sank.

As mentioned in the introduction to this volume, many of the tragic
wrecks that have occurred around Australia's coasts have led eventually to some form of positive action to prevent their reoccurrence.

The sinking of SIEV-X has led to improved cooperation between the governments of Australia and Indonesia, in part due to both nations' embarrassment at the ocean and reefs that separate them being strewn with the bodies of drowned refugees and asylum seekers.

These days, the usual method of entry to Australia is by aircraft, and the aviation industry enjoys remarkably high safety standards, especially when compared to the long history of maritime disasters. For that matter, the most common 'queue jumper' or 'illegal immigrant' is a European backpacker overstaying their working-holiday visa. Yet the waves of boat people that have come since the fall of South Vietnam in 1975 indicate that the dispossessed of the world will continue to embark on the perilous voyage to Australia's shores, hoping to find a better life, just as many of our forebears did. In that sense, nothing has changed, except perhaps the attitude towards them when they arrive. What remains to be seen is how in fifty or a hundred years a writer – with only the facts as reported to go on and detached from the vigorous opinion-shaping that surrounds SIEV-X and the issue of asylum seekers – will come to view what happened.

Meanwhile, as asylum seekers embark on their dangerous voyages, yachts of every shape and size, fishing boats, passenger liners, freighters and warships are daily putting to sea from Australian ports. Each year a remarkable number of people are exposed to the perils of Australia's seas, so, inevitably, tragedies will continue to unfold when sea voyages end short of their destinations, and tales of courage will continue to surface. It is to be hoped that each shipwreck will raise the questions 'What were the causes?' and 'Has everything reasonable been done to prevent something similar from happening again?' Standing on the shore, these questions and their answers are the only way to ensure that those the sea has taken didn't die in vain.

SOURCES

Indicates recommended further reading

Chapter 1: Trial
Bronowski, J., *The Ascent of Man*, BBC, 1973, London.
Green, J., 'Australia's Oldest Wreck, The Loss of the *Trial*, 1622,' *British Archaeological Reports*, Supplementary Series 27, 1977.
* Henderson, J., *Phantoms of the* Tryall, St George Books, Perth, 1993.
Jeffreys, Max, *Murder, Mayhem, Fire and Storm: Australian Shipwrecks*, New Holland, Sydney, 1999.
Junger, S., *The Perfect Storm*, Fourth Estate, London, 1997.
Laughlin, G.P., *The Complete Book of Australian Maritime Weather*, W. Gibson Group, Sydney, 1990.
Lee, Ida, *The First Sighting of Australia by the English*, Geographical Journal, London, 1934.
Mahogany Ship Committee, *Proceedings of the First Symposium on the Mahogany Ship*, Mahogany Ship Committee, Warrnambool, 1985.
Playford, P., *Carpet of Silver*, University of WA Press, Nedlands WA, 1996.
Whittaker, M. and Willesee, A., *The Road to Mount Buggery*, Pan Macmillan, Sydney, 2001.

Chapter 2: Batavia
Bronowski, J. *The Ascent of Man*, BBC, 1973, London.
* Dash, M., *Batavia's Graveyard*, Weidenfeld & Nicolson, London, 2002.
* Drake-Brockman, H., *Voyage to Disaster*, University of WA Press, Nedlands WA, 1995.
* Edwards, H., *Islands of Angry Ghosts*, HarperCollins, Sydney, 2000.

* Playford, P., *Carpet of Silver*, University of WA Press, Nedlands WA, 1996.
Siebenhaar, W., *The Abrolhos Tragedy* (translation of *Ongeluckige Voyagie* by Jan Jansz), *The Western Mail*, Perth, Christmas, 1897.

Chapter 3: Sydney Cove
Bateson, C., *Australian Shipwrecks Vol.1: 1622–1850*, A.W. & A.H. Reed, Sydney, 1982.
Government of NSW, *Historical Records of New South Wales*, Government Printer, Sydney, 1893–1901.
http://www.gold.ac.uk/world/endeavour/cook.html
Hughes, Robert, *The Fatal Shore*, Harvill, London, 1996. (Extract from *The Fatal Shore* by Robert Hughes published by Harvill Press. Used by permission of The Random House Group Limited.)
* Nash, M., *Cargo for the Colony*, Braxus, Sydney, 1996.
Sydney Cove web site, http://www.parks.tas.gov.au/historic/shipw/sc.html
Tench, W., *1788*, Text Publishing, Melbourne, 1996.

Chapter 4: Stirling Castle
* Alexander, M., *Mrs Fraser Upon the Fatal Shore*, M. Joseph, London, 1971.
A Mother's Offering to Her Children, (held in Mitchell Library Collection), *Gazette*, Sydney, 1841.
Australians, Events and Places, Fairfax, Syme & Weldon Associates, Sydney, 1987.
Curtis, J., *Shipwreck of the* Stirling Castle, George Virtue, London, 1838.

Lieutenant Otter's Report, State Records
    of New South Wales, *Copy of
    Documents 183*.
Mrs Fraser's Narrative, State Records of
    New South Wales, *Copy of Documents
    183*.
Russell, H.S., *Genesis of Queensland*,
    Turner & Henderson, Sydney, 1888.
'Wreck of the *Stirling Castle*,' *Sydney
    Gazette*, 9 September and 16 October
    1836.

Chapter 5: *Cataraqui*
Explore Australia, Penguin, Melbourne,
    2000.
* Lemmon, A. and Morgan, M., *Poor
    Souls, They Perished – The*
    Cataraqui, Hargreen, North
    Melbourne, 1986.
Press release, 'New buoy takes the
    plunge in the name of safety,'
    Parliamentary Secretary to the
    Minister for the Environment and
    Heritage, 22 March 1998.
Sydney Morning Herald, 10 and 27
    September 1845.

Chapter 6: *Dunbar*
Australians, Events and Places, Fairfax,
    Syme & Weldon Associates, Sydney,
    1987.
*Bradshaw's Narrative of the Wreck of
    the* Dunbar, Bradshaw's Railway
    Printing Office, Sydney, 1857.
http://www.lighthouse.net.au/lights/NSW
    /Macquarie/Macquarie.htm
* Mead, T., *The Fatal Lights*, Dolphin
    Books, Sydney, 1993.
Shipwreck Atlas of New South Wales,
    3rd Edition, NSW Government
    Heritage Office, 1996.
Sydney Morning Herald, 22, 24, 25, 26
    and 27 August and 28 October 1857.
Tench, W., *1788*, Text Publishing,
    Melbourne, 1996.

Chapter 7: *Loch Ard*
Australians, Historical Statistics, Fairfax,
    Syme, Weldon & Associates, Sydney,
    1987.
Bennett, R., *Narrative of the wreck of
    the* Loch Ard, T. Oakley, Sydney,
    1890.

* Charlwood, D., *The Wreck of the* Loch
    Ard, Angus & Robertson, Sydney,
    1971.
Conrad, J., *Nigger of the Narcissus*,
    Heinemann, London, 1897.
Letter from Hugh Gibson to his
    stepmother, 6 July 1878, typescript in
    J. Loney, *The* Loch Ard *Disaster*,
    Marine History Publications, 1993.
Pearce's evidence to the Steam
    Navigation Board, 22 June 1878,
    reported in the *Melbourne Argus*, *Age*
    and subsequent volumes.

Chapter 8: *Quetta*
Brisbane Courier, 3, 4 and 5 March
    1890.
* Foley, Capt. J., *The* Quetta, Nairana
    Publications, Brisbane, 1990.
Internet Microsoft Encarta,
    http://www.encarta.msn.com
Mead, T., *The Fatal Lights*, Dolphin
    Books, Sydney.
Whittaker, M. and Willesee, A., *The Road
    to Mount Buggery*, Pan Macmillan,
    Sydney, 2001.

Chapter 9: Cyclone Mahina
Australians, Events and Places, Fairfax,
    Syme, Weldon & Associates, Sydney,
    1987.
Book of Key Facts, Cassell, Sydney,
    1978.
Brisbane Courier, 10, 11, 14, 15, 20
    March 1899.
Constable Kenny's Report, quoted in
    Cummins and Campbell, May 1956.
*Holthouse, H., *Cyclone*, Rigby, Adelaide,
    1971.
Laughlin, G., *The Complete Book of
    Australian Maritime Weather*,
    W. Gibson Group, Sydney, 1990.
McPhee, E., *Bulletin of Australian
    Maritime Archaeology*, 25, 2001.
Memorial booklet, published 1899,
    quoted in *Cummins and
    Campbell's Monthly Magazine*,
    May 1956.
Nott, J. and Hayne, M., 'How high was
    the storm surge from tropical Cyclone
    Mahina?,' *Australian Journal of
    Emergency Management*, Autumn
    2000.

Chapter 10: HMAS *Sydney*

Frame, T., *HMAS* Sydney, *Loss and
Controversy,* Hodder & Stoughton,
Sydney, 1993.
http://www.aph.gov.au/house/committee/
jfadt/sydney/execsum.htm
http://www.members.iinet.net.au/
~gduncan
* National Archives of Australia
documents, included in R. Summerrell,
The Sinking of HMAS Sydney,
National Archives of Australia,
Canberra, 1999, available in
published form or at
http://www.naa.gov.au/Publications/
research_guides/guides/
sydney/introduction.htm
Sydney Morning Herald, 5 December
1941.

Chapter 11: *Lake Illawarra*

Hobart Mercury, 6 and 7 January, 7 and
20 February, 14 March 1975.

Chapter 12: Bullimore and Dubois

The Australian, 10 January 1997.
Author interview with Mike Jackson-
Calway, 15 November 2002.
Documentary: *Miracle at Sea*, Orana
Films and John Gau Pty Ltd.
http://www-aviso.cls.fr/html/
applications/courses/
vendee_globe_uk.html
http://www.defence.gov.au/yachtsr/
dpr97016.htm
http://www.weather-wise.com/books/
bullimore.htm
Slocum, J., *Sailing Alone around the
World*, Sampson & Low, London, 1900.

Chapter 13: Sydney to Hobart Yacht Race

ABC-TV News, 27 December 1998.
* Abernethy, J., *Coroner's Inquest Into
the Deaths During the 1998 Sydney
to Hobart Yacht Race Report and CD-
ROM of brief of evidence*, New South
Wales State Coroner, Sydney, 2000;
also available at
http://www.equipped.org
   The State Coroner's Findings and
Recommendations and the Brief of
Evidence contain information, data,

documents, pages and images
prepared by the NSW Coroner's
Office and NSW Police Service for
and on behalf of the Crown in right
of the State of New South Wales ('the
Material'). The Material is protected
by Crown Copyright.
   While the information contained in
the Material has been formulated with
all due care, the State of NSW does not
warrant or represent that the material
is free from errors or omission. The
State of NSW further does not warrant
or accept any liability in relation to the
quality or accuracy of the Material
including any material supplied by
third parties. The information
contained in the Material should be
carefully evaluated for its source,
accuracy, currency, completeness and
relevance for your purposes, and you
should obtain any appropriate
professional advice relevant to your
particular circumstances.
   © Copyright – New South Wales
State Coroner's Office 2001.
   This material comprising the
State Coroner's Findings and
Recommendations and some of the
material on the CD-ROM is protected
by copyright which is vested in the
State of New South Wales.
   All rights reserved. You may not
alter, reproduce, re-transmit,
distribute, display or commercialise
the material in any way without the
prior written permission of the New
South Wales State Coroner's Office
and the State of New South Wales,
except as permitted under the
Copyright Act 1968 (as amended).
Beaufort, Admiral Sir F., 'The Beaufort
Scale,' *Oxford Book of the Sea*,
Oxford University Press, Oxford,
1993.
BOM weather forecast, 13 December
1998. Printout in author's 'Sydney to
Hobart' file.
http://www.bom.gov.au/cgi-
bin/wrap_fwo.pl?IDN10023.html on
30 September 2002.
http://www.s2h.tas.gov.au/1998/media/
pre-event/981226_uglyseas.shtml

http://www.unc.edu/~rowlett/units/scales/
    cyclone.html
ISAF Race Management Manual, 1997
    and 2002 editions, International
    Sailing Federation, 2002.
* Mundle, R., *Fatal Storm*,
    HarperCollins, Sydney, 2001.
*Report of the 1998 Sydney Hobart Race
    Review Committee*, 1999.
* Whitmont, D., *An Extreme Event*,
    Random House, Sydney, 2001.
Whittaker, M., 'Mayday', *The Australian
    Magazine*, 6–7 March 1999.

ACKNOWLEDGEMENTS
Every effort has been made to contact the
copyright holders of material reproduced
in this book and the publishers would
welcome any further information.

INDEX